Helping Students Who Struggle with Math and Science

A Collaborative Approach for Elementary and Middle Schools

Dennis Adams and Mary Hamm

ROWMAN & LITTLEFIELD EDUCATION
Lanham • New York • Toronto • Plymouth, UK

Published in the United States of America
by Rowman & Littlefield Education
A Division of Rowman & Littlefield Publishers, Inc.
A wholly owned subsidary of The Rowman & Littlefield Publishing Group, Inc.
4501 Forbes Boulevard, Suite 200, Lanham, Maryland 20706
www.rowmaneducation.com

Estover Road
Plymouth PL6 7PY
United Kingdom

British Library Cataloguing in Publication Information Available

Library of Congress Cataloging-in-Publication Data

Adams, Dennis M.
  Helping students who struggle with math and science : a collaborative
approach for elementary and middle schools / Dennis Adams and Mary Hamm.
    p. cm.
  ISBN-13: 978-1-57886-757-8 (cloth : alk. paper)
  ISBN-10: 1-57886-757-6 (cloth : alk. paper)
  ISBN-13: 978-1-57886-758-5 (pbk. : alk. paper)
  ISBN-10: 1-57886-758-4 (pbk. : alk. paper)
  1. Mathematics—Study and teaching (Elementary)—United States. 2.
Mathematics—Study and teaching (Middle school)—United States. 3.
Science—Study and teaching (Elementary)—United States. 4.
Science—Study and teaching (Middle school)—United States. 5.
Individualized instruction—United States. 6. Mixed ability grouping in
education—United States. 7. Group work in education—United States. 8.
Cognitive styles in children—United States. I. Hamm, Mary. II. Title.
  QA135.6.A33 2008
  372.7—dc22

                                              2007042963

Contents

Preface   v

1 Helping Struggling Students Learn Math and Science   1

2 Student Inquiry in Math and Science   25

3 Collaborative Learning: The Advantages of Small
   Learning Groups   51

4 Differentiated Instruction: Multiple Paths to
   Learning and Assessment   77

5 Reaching Reluctant Math Students: Mathematical Reasoning
   and Collaborative Problem Solving   99

6 Science for All Students: Collaborative Inquiry, Active
   Involvement, and Struggling Students   127

7 Technology and Reluctant Learners: The Motivating and
   Collaborative Possibilities of Powerful Tools   157

8 A Project-Based Approach: Projects, Thematic Units,
   Collaboration, and Struggling Students   203

Preface

Me teach math and science? Those were always my worst subjects.
I stopped taking math and science courses as fast as I could.
I'm definitely NOT a math or science person.

—Anonymous

When prospective teachers in our college classes were asked about teaching mathematics and science, many admitted that their understanding of these subjects was limited. Some said that they "never really understood math or science" and had always had a bad attitude toward the subjects. Others pointed out that they only took the minimum number of math and science courses required for graduation. Experienced teachers had a somewhat more positive response. The majority of practicing teachers in our professional development workshops were comfortable teaching math and science. But they had some of the same concerns as the teacher education students. So, it is little wonder that a certain lack of teacher enthusiasm about math and science instruction has rubbed off on students. Of course, you don't have to like or feel that you can have great success with a subject to gain a reasonable level of competency in it. But it sure helps.

Both new and experienced teachers we surveyed showed a heightened sense of concern when the discussion turned to engaging students who had trouble with math and science. Experienced teachers know that struggling students may or may not have been identified as having learning problems. But with or without learning disabilities, they know that such students need to approach learning math and science in different ways. Like a few teachers, some reluctant learners simply don't like math and science—and others think they couldn't be successful in these subjects. It seems that poor attitude and poor achievement amplify each other.

Most students who struggle with math and science do not sufficiently connect with the content or their successful classmates. In addition, they often don't understand the skills and concepts of mathematics and science as well as students who enjoy these subjects. *Helping Students Who Struggle with Math and Science* builds on the social nature of learning to provide useful suggestions for reaching reluctant learners. It is based on the assumption that instruction that focuses on students' interests and builds on collaborative and differentiated learning will generate more interest in math and science. With teacher assistance, students can move from believing they "can't do mathematics or science" or "don't like these subjects," to a feeling of genuine achievement and confidence. Academically inclined students may even be able to achieve more. Clearly, it helps to make math and science more meaningful to students by connecting them to the questions they ask about their world; questions such as: Why is the sky blue? How far is my house from school? Is there life on other planets? *or* How do I find the information I need to answer my questions?

It is our belief that no one should be sidelined with basic skills and kept away from creative and collaborative engagement—factors that are central to mathematical problem solving and scientific inquiry. So, we suggest ways that a teacher can use to reach those students who tend to be left behind by creating a more instructional differentiated classroom. *Helping Students Who Struggle with Math and Science* helps the differentiation process by presenting research-based methods and standards-influenced organizational approaches for motivating reluctant learners. By opening some unique doors to learning math and science, we hope to help teachers provide opportunities for reluctant learners to construct their own knowledge.

There is general agreement that working with struggling students early on is important. This is made more difficult when elementary and middle school teachers are not well trained in math and science. On top of that, many are a little afraid of these subjects. The good news is that most elementary and middle school teachers are familiar with group work, so there's a relatively easy way for them to approach subjects that they view as difficult. Experienced teachers know that involving students in active, participatory, and connected learning is a proven way to help struggling students come to enjoy the subjects they previously avoided.

To reach underachieving students, this book looks to the possibilities of differentiated instruction. It is a philosophy and a way of thinking that suggests careful consideration of students' learning tendencies. Differentiation requires appropriate levels of teacher support and a combination of teaching strategies that have been shown to have positive effects on student learning. Now, more than ever, teachers are faced with reaching out effectively to students who span the entire spectrum of learning. Student differences include student preparedness, personal interests, and cultural ways of seeing and experiencing the world. Of course, there is no single formula for creating a differentiated classroom. But we suggest combining collaborative learning with differentiated instruction to appeal to students' social interests and various rates of learning.

Helping Students Who Struggle with Math and Science is written in a teacher friendly style. It is organized in a way that is convenient for school districts that are doing inservice work with elementary and middle school teachers. It is also designed as a supplementary text for methods classes in mathematics and science education. The hope is that the teaching ideas presented here will assist teachers as they invite reluctant learners to use technological tools to inquire, discover concepts, and collaboratively explore the interlinking concepts of mathematics, science, and technology. Since the technological products of math and science are so important, this book pays close attention to the instructional possibilities. Technology has forged its link with math and science and has become a powerful force both in and out of school. Including it also makes sense because mathematicians and scientists incorporate it in their work.

Since developing positive attitudes toward math and science goes hand-in-hand with developing competency, *Helping Students Who Struggle with Math and Science* provides interesting math/science methods and connects them to recent pedagogical approaches that reach across the curriculum. It builds on the expanding knowledge of what works in classrooms and suggests how new approaches to teaching and learning can transform math and science instruction. Ideas and activities for standards-based learning, collaborative inquiry, and active problem solving are included. The goal is to deepen the collective conversation, challenge thinking, and provide up-to-date tools for teachers so that they can help reverse the steady erosion of math and science skills in the population.

OVERVIEW OF THE CONTENTS

Chapters one through four address instructional developments in the areas of struggling students, math and science inquiry, and collaborative learning and differentiated instruction. Chapter One is intended as a frame of reference. It describes the world in which teachers teach today, the nature of the struggling learner, and the ways that mathematics and science can effectively meet the needs of disengaged students. Chapter Two focuses on inquiry for students who have difficulties with mathematics and science. It also shows how learning experiences can contribute to the ways students construct new understandings through active thinking and collaborative work. Chapter Three emphasizes practical ideas for providing instruction in collaborative learning so that struggling students can be involved in an effective collaborative classroom. Chapter Four discusses the differentiated classroom and assessment strategies. It includes specific classroom activities aimed at understanding multiple intelligences and ways of adapting to differentiated instruction.

Chapter Five examines reluctant math learners. It tries to help teachers plan standards-based learning experiences that focus on students who feel discouraged with their math performance. It goes beyond the new mathematics curriculum standards and presents math inquiry activities that engage reluctant learners with specific math standards. Chapter Six expands the perception and appreciation of scientific inquiry that allow underachieving students to use their acquired knowledge in a versatile and productive way, while building self-confidence and a sense of shared collaboration. The math and science standards are cited as part of a framework to guide the development and implementation of the mathematics and science program. Chapter Seven takes the reader on a journey through the educational potential of computers, television, and the Internet. The authors offer ideas and activities to help teachers make sense of the new technologies for students who show a lack of enthusiasm for math and science. Chapter Eight addresses project-based learning and inquiry ideas tying together many of the interesting topics of mathematics and science presented in this book. Thematic units and projects are defined, step-by-step procedures are outlined, and several math and science units and projects are presented.

Helping Students Who Struggle with Math and Science builds on what we know about effective instruction to provide experiential learning activities for students. We take a constructivist approach that focuses on observation, everyday examples, and problem-solving activities. The goal is to help teachers develop a community of diverse learners as they facilitate the exploration of education ideas and exercises that are provided. It is our belief that good teachers in the twenty-first century will increasingly teach for understanding. It is also assumed that successful teachers will help struggling students by building instruction around their needs and encouraging them to take an active role in their own learning.

1

Helping Struggling Students Learn Math and Science

Math and science are just about the only subjects where well-educated and intelligent adults freely admit ignorance. Social forces, including family ties, underpin attitudes toward math and science learning. We think of learning as something that happens in school. But what happens in the home environment enables you to learn in school. For many adults, a certain lack of mathematical and scientific interest goes with the territory. So, it's little wonder that many youngsters show a lack of interest. Some simply don't like the subjects; others don't think they can be successful. We identify such students as struggling learners. They may not be identified as having special needs, but they need well-designed alternative learning approaches (Armstrong, 1999; Cathcart, et al., 2005). This chapter is designed to introduce you to

- Problems and possibilities of teaching struggling students.
- The nature of collaborative inquiry and related student activities.
- Processes for making instructional decisions about using differentiated learning.
- Methods for meeting the math and science standards for reluctant learners.
- Teaching strategies that are effective with struggling students.
- Strategies for assessing students' strengths and weaknesses in math and science.

How we teach is as important as *what* we teach. This is especially true when it comes to teaching students who are struggling with math and science (Stigler & Hiebert, 2004). When teaching these subjects, asking disaffected learners to reason, solve problems, and maintain a positive disposition is a tall order. Of course, no one method of teaching math and science has been found to meet the needs of these students all of the time. But various kinds of active and collaborative learning experiences certainly help. The basic idea is to encourage such struggling students, without slowing down those who are already motivated and successful in math and science.

The ideas and activities presented here are all designed to maximize the potential of students who struggle with math and science; they also work for other students in mixed-ability groups. Effective teachers use various interactive learning group strategies and adapt techniques from a wide repertoire of methods. In addition, they design their lessons in a way that connects to students with multiple student needs and learning styles.

In wealthy schools and poor ones, I encountered the same recurring patterns: considerable variation among classrooms in the degree to which students were challenged; an emphasis on procedural knowledge at the expense of analysis, reflection, and understanding; a tendency to focus more on students who were "easy to teach" rather than those who were struggling.

—Richard Elmore

MATH, SCIENCE, AND STRUGGLING STUDENTS

Some students tend to avoid challenge, some don't complete tasks, and some simply are satisfied to just get by. Whether you use the term "struggling students" or "reluctant learners," these youth often have the potential to do well but don't care about achieving in school. Identifying the reasons behind their reluctance to learn is essential if we are going to engage their interest and help them succeed. The challenge is finding something that will spark a struggling student's interest and turn that spark into a flame.

Even the most reluctant learners are naturally curious and able to learn. Most want to get their hands and minds around objects of interest as much as anybody. Struggling students are capable of learning, but have trouble making math and science instruction work for them (Loveless & Coughlan, 2004). It's never too early to get started. The seeds of academic success are planted in early childhood and cultivated through elementary school. Middle school builds on that base and moves children on to deeper mathematical, statistical, and scientific understandings. The students who reach secondary school without enough literacy and numeracy skills to do the work are the ones most likely to drop out. Competency in math and science is important for high school graduation, college entry, the workplace, and thoughtful citizenship (National Research Council, 2001).

Since a learner's mental, emotional, and physical needs have a direct impact on their schoolwork, exploring individual student needs should be near the top of the teaching agenda (Van de Walle & Lovin, 2006). Curriculum reform is often geared more to academically oriented children and young adults, and not to students who have different interests. Fortunately, most kindergarten through ninth grade teachers (our focus) try to teach math and science concepts and skills in a way that helps struggling students (along with everyone else) understand and remember what's being taught. Although we assume that secondary school teachers make the same effort, elementary and middle school teachers often pay special attention to motivating students who aren't too fond of these subjects.

Students often become motivated to learn about math and science as a result of influences outside of school. The better organized and directed these influences, the better the chance of success for the student.

Helen's Student Teaching Log:
At the beginning of the school year my daughter was quite reluctant to ask her peers for help. She feared that other students would tease her because it takes her longer to understand concepts and organize her thoughts. Math and science were scary subjects. What to do? I applied the strategies I learned in my college mathematics and science education classes to the daily homework sessions I have with my daughter. These new strategies worked with the differentiated problem sets and in convincing my daughter to work with her peers. This turned her attitude around. Her performance improved so dramatically that she began tutoring some of the other students!

Students all have different needs and these needs have a tremendous influence on their achievement. What can teachers do to insure academic success? To begin with, they can assess each individual's ability. The next step is choosing teaching strategies that best match students' learning strengths and difficulties. Questions teachers have such as, "How does this child learn best?" or "What kind of learning environment can best bring out a student's natural learning abilities?" are part of this diagnostic process. The focus should be on understanding the child as a learner, and making choices about structuring the learning environment through innovative teaching strategies and methods (Armstrong, 1999).

Effective teachers internalize responsibility for students' learning and examine their practices critically if they aren't reaching some students. They realize that most students want to succeed, but many do not find success when taught from the traditional teaching model. Students who have difficulties with math and science often need alternative approaches and remedial strategies that are designed to promote academic success. The math and science success plan is one technique that we developed to help improve student achievement. It builds on students' strengths and can serve as an assessment tool.

EVERYONE NEEDS TO UNDERSTAND MATH AND SCIENCE

The public's failure to understand chance phenomena, statistics, probability, and the nature of numerical assertions opens the way for all manner of belief in nonsense. Perhaps more important, it leads to distortions in the making of public policy.

—John Poulos

The need to understand and use math and science in everyday life has never been greater. Personal satisfaction and confidence come with making wise quantitative decisions, whether it's buying a house, solving problems on the job, choosing health insurance, or voting intelligently. In many ways, mathematics and science are part of our cultural heritage. Our careers, our workplace, and our community all require a foundation of sound mathematical and scientific knowledge. Although it may not be readily apparent, proficiency in these subjects can open doors to future achievements and sound citizenship.

Everyone needs to understand mathematics and science to make decisions about important societal issues in our democracy. The media doesn't always help. Take the example of global warming. For a long time, the story was reported in a way that suggested some scientists took it seriously and some didn't. And this was after a large number of the scientists had recognized the reality of the problem. Advances in medicine have sometimes been reported in another problematic way. Exciting breakthroughs are reported when only small advancing steps have been taken. Whatever the scientific issue, a better understanding of the mathematical significance of results would help everyone understand the situation, whatever their age.

When we asked struggling learners in a sixth grade class why they weren't interested in math and science, many replied either that it was "not interesting," "too difficult," or "never made much sense." These explanations and other reasons might be classified as students' personal or environmental situations. No matter what gets in the way of learning, teachers have to know what to teach and how to teach it. Four or five years of college and continuous professional development help. So do the suggestions and recommendations that can be found in the math and science standards and state and school district guidelines. Even many textbooks are helpful. But wherever you get them, activities may have to be adapted for struggling students. Like everyone else, they have to be involved in building knowledge by asking relevant questions, reasoning, making connections, and solving problems.

THE CHARACTERISTICS OF STRUGGLING STUDENTS

All students of math and science have individual strengths and weaknesses. However, struggling students often have similar learning problems (Miller & Mercer, 2001). Being able to identify individual problems and knowing some helpful teaching strategies certainly help.

Struggling students may be *passive learners*, who have little motivation or interest in becoming active participants in math and science learning (Levine, 2000). Some students who struggle may think that math and science achievement is a matter of luck. They may think it's too easy, too difficult, or too boring. They may also believe that achievement in these subjects is beyond their control: "I'm just not good at math," "Science is boring." Students with such feelings about these subjects may prefer not to acknowledge that their lack of success may have something to do with personal discipline, hard work, and persistence. They may mistakenly believe that you succeed in math and science through some combination of luck and level of intelligence. The home and school environments also matter a great deal; if poor achievement is expected, then that is the most likely result. Whatever the reason, when students are discouraged or disinterested, their ability to move forward is limited.

Teachers can learn to do a good job with struggling students without simplifying problems or always telling them exactly what to do. It's important to get learners actively involved in interesting and relevant situations. So, the teacher has to encourage reluctant learners to construct ideas and communicate their thoughts. Graphic wall charts can help individual students see how they are doing and track their achievement. Such visual displays give students, teachers, and parents very powerful ways to see the progress of a student's learning (Kame'enui, et. al., 2002).

Some struggling students have difficulty *remembering* basic math and science facts. Let's start with math. Remembering simple math combinations, even basic facts such as addition, subtraction, multiplication, and division are difficult for many. Not to be alarmed, strategies to improve remembering skills can be taught. Repetition games such as having the teacher call out a fact combination problem like "$4 \times 3 =$" and asking students to solve it, and then repeating with a new combination "$2 \times 7 =$" is one example. The game continues as each player calls out a new fact and each student responds with an answer. Students' ability to organize their thinking and use it to recall basic combinations will affect their success (Malone & Lepper, 1987).

Quite often struggling students also have attention problems (Miller & Mercer, 2001). They have trouble sustaining *attention*, avoiding distractions, and controlling their impulses. They may be easily distracted and have difficulty focusing on complex problems. These students are helped by a structured, consistent classroom where clear expectations are spelled out. This does not mean that the teacher must tell students how to do a task; instead, the teacher should give all students opportunities to understand what is expected and ways to monitor their progress. Effective use of visuals, manipulatives, and learning aids could help overcome these problems. Working in pairs also assists the struggling learner. Peer involvement also expands and strengthens language skills and increases students' confidence.

Struggling students with attention difficulties often have trouble with *time management* and changes between subjects and classes. They often benefit from opportunities to be physically engaged in learning. Giving students many chances to move and interact with peers in structured situations is one of the keys to their success (Vaughn, Bos, & Schuum, 2003).

Language problems can result in a bad attitude toward math and science. Even students whose first language is English are often confused by the vocabulary of these subjects. Words that have special meanings such as "equals, divisor, sum, cycle," or "properties," often slow down students' ability to focus and understand the terms being used. When students fail to see the connections among concepts, math and science become a rote exercise and understanding is limited. As experienced teachers will tell you, simply memorizing terms without knowing what they mean is not useful. Comprehension is the goal. Student language understanding is helped by discussing important vocabulary, using creative writing strategies, and asking pertinent questions (White, 2004). Student learning is also assisted by reviewing previous concepts and demonstrating connections in problem-solving situations.

Metacognition is the ability to think about thinking. Students need to reflect on their own thinking in order to be aware of what they need to know (self-knowledge) and how they can go about acquiring information (procedural knowledge). As students become better at figuring out their own reasoning, they can also observe their own learning. The process includes evaluating whether they are learning, using helpful strategies when needed, and making changes when necessary. As children grow and develop, they become better at thinking about their own thinking and how they think. This helps them move beyond their own personal perspective and better understand how others might think about a topic. These are critical skills for a math or science problem-solving situation.

Many struggling students do not understand that being successful in math and science involves employing problem-solving strategies. Teachers have to teach them how to be metacognitive learners and help them recognize the thinking strategies they are using. Along the way, metacognition strategies can amplify self-reliance and creativity for struggling learners. Teachers who model thoughtfulness and encourage students to share problem-solving strategies with each other can go a long way toward fully engaging struggling students (Swanson, 1999).

Students with a vast array of special needs are now found in the regular classroom (inclusion). In addition, the levels of language and cultural differences represented in elementary and middle schools continue to grow. The result is that today's classrooms include students with a very broad range of learning needs (Tucker, Singleton, & Weaver, 2006). A typical classroom today may include struggling students such as José, Maria, Jason, and Carlos. José struggles with a language-based learning problem. Maria has attention difficulties. Jason's inadequate reading skills interfere with his learning in all areas. And although Carlos has excellent cognitive abilities, he still has difficulty with math and science.

Whatever the reason for poor performance, youngsters need opportunities to learn about their individual strengths and weaknesses. The successful teaching of struggling students is most likely when teachers utilize culturally relevant materials, use collaborative instructional activities, and recognize that learning can take many forms through many modalities (Tucker, Singleton, & Weaver, 2006). Of course, there are many ways to go about using collaborative activities in ways that build on the natural learning dispositions of a wide variety of cultural groups. Engaging in problem-solving strategies that are similar to those used in real-life situations certainly helps. And, yes, celebrating individuality and working together to build successful learning communities certainly complement each other.

COLLABORATIVE INQUIRY IN MATH AND SCIENCE

Struggling students can flourish when good teaching is combined with collaborative inquiry and an engaging curriculum (Tomlinson, 2001). Collaborative inquiry is a form of reasoning and peer cooperation that begins with a problem and ends with a solution. It generally involves asking questions, observing, examining information, investigating, arriving at answers, and communicating the results. A collaborative inquiry approach to the teaching of math and science has been found to work well with struggling learners (Brodesky, Gross, & Tierney, 2004). Among other things, it helps these students experience the excitement of mathematics and science activities in learning groups. Knowledge of math and science has always been constructed in association with others. At all levels, mathematical and scientific inquiry is much more than an individual endeavor. So, it's best if elementary and middle school students employ procedures similar to the collaborative procedures that mathematicians and scientists actually use (White, 2004). Structure helps, but too much can stifle the imagination.

Don't tell people how to do something.
Tell them what to do and let them surprise you with their ingenuity.

—Anonymous

The collaborative inquiry approach is a student-centered process of co-operative discovery. The teacher often gives the students directions and materials—but does not tell the small group exactly how to go about doing their work. The teacher encourages conversation and provides activities that help students understand how math and science are applied in the world outside of school. The teacher might also give a brief whole class presentation and then move from small group to small group, encouraging questions and guiding student observations. As students interact with materials and their peers, they can interact with math-science problems and jointly recognize the results of their investigation. The next step is applying what's been learned and recognizing that the knowledge acquired through inquiry is subject to change.

Students certainly have different talents and interests, but they should all have access to high-quality math and science instruction. All students can be motivated with concrete materials, differentiated instruction, and cooperative experiences. But it is especially important for students who are struggling with basic math and science concepts and skills (Stigler & Hiebert, 2004). Since motivation is a major concern, it is important go beyond rote skill building to challenge reluctant learners. This means helping them deal with interesting, difficult, and ambiguous problems where they are expected to discuss, question, and resolve problems themselves.

COLLABORATION, INQUIRY, AND RELUCTANT LEARNERS

Inquiry is sometimes thought of as the way people study the world and propose explanations based on the evidence they've accumulated. It involves actively seeking information, truth, and knowledge. When collaboration is added to the process, it helps build the positive relationships that are at the heart of a learning community. Collaborative inquiry may be thought of as a range of concepts and techniques for enhancing interactive questioning, investigation, and learning. When questions that connect to student experiences are raised collectively, ideas and strengths are shared in a manner that supports the struggling students' search for understanding (Snow, 2005).

Teachers have found that using a collaborative approach to connect math and science instruction is a way to involve disinterested students in active small group learning (Karp & Howell, 2004). When students work together as a team, they tend to motivate each other. Accomplishing shared goals benefits all of the individuals in a group and makes it more likely that collaboration will become a natural part of the fabric of instruction. The teacher provides a high degree of structure in forming groups and defining procedure, but students control the interactions within their groups. Building team-based organizational structures in the classroom makes it easier for teachers to reach out to students who have problems and ensure that all students are successful.

A shift in values and attitudes may be required for a collaborative learning environment to reach its full potential. Some traditional school environments have conditioned students to rely on the teacher to validate their thinking and direct learning. So, getting over years of learned helplessness takes time. As they share and cooperate rather than compete for recognition, many children find more time for reflection and assessment. Although collaborative learning helps teachers achieve a number of motivational and social objectives, it also aims to improve student performance on academic tasks.

By tapping into students' social nature and natural curiosity, collaborative inquiry can go a long way toward helping struggling schools achieve academic and social goals. It's a disciplined and imaginative way of exploring and coming together in community with others. As they work in pairs or in small mixed-ability groups, students can take more responsibility for helping themselves and others learn. As teachers learn when and how to structure group lessons, collaboration can become a regular part of the day-to-day instructional program.

A Sample Collaborative Activity

This science and math example is designed to help students discover the diversity of seeds by using the process skills of predicting, comparing, categorizing, collecting data, organizing, recording, interpreting, and communicating. It's a collaborative inquiry activity that sets out to examine the tremendous diversity of plants and their seeds.

Math and science standards:

- Math and science as inquiry—use appropriate tools to gather, organize, and interpret data.
- Think critically and logically to classify data and make connections between categories.

Materials:
  • Science/math journal, brown paper bag, pencil.

Objectives:
  1. Students will work collaboratively.
  2. Students will make predictions (guesses) about where the seed might be categorized.
  3. Students will describe the categories verbally and in writing and the reasons for putting the seeds in it.
  4. Students will classify seeds and describe the properties of seeds.
  5. Students will compare and order their seeds.

Procedures:
  1. Introduce the concept of the great variety in plant seeds. Tell students that they're going to go on a seeds hunt with a small group of two or three other classmates Their task is to try to find and collect samples of one seed that fits each of these categories: seeds that float, seeds that blow, seeds that hitchhike, helicopter seeds, seeds that twirl, and seeds that are cycled through animals or need animals to grow.
  2. Instruct students to record where the seed was located in their math/science journals. Students may wish to describe, draw, or write their feelings about finding the seeds.
  3. Upon returning, students will be asked to guess where the seed may be categorized. Encourage them to write their predictions in their journals.

Evaluation:
  1. Have student groups bring their seeds back to the class to compare their findings and test their predictions with other groups.
  2. Have students divide and save the seeds in their portfolios.
  3. Have students reflect on this activity.

Reflections:
  1. Allow students time to discuss and write their reflections.
  2. Students may wish to imagine they are the seeds their group collected and compare themselves to their seeds.
  3. Ask students how the group felt about being seeds?
  4. Ask students how this activity relates to their lives?

MAKING INSTRUCTIONAL DECISIONS
WITH DIFFERENTIATED LEARNING

Because we know that students learn in different ways and at different rates, it's important to consider differentiating instruction. The basic idea is to provide individual students with different avenues for learning content. Differentiated learning is an organized approach where teachers and students work together in planning, setting goals, and monitoring progress. In such classrooms, the teacher draws on the cultural knowledge of students by using culturally and personally relevant examples. They show respect for learners by valuing their similarities and differences, not by treating everybody the same. Teachers are the main organizers, but students often help with the design. It is the teacher's job to know what is important and to analyze and offer the best approach to learning. Students can let teachers know when materials or assignments are too hard or too easy and when learning is interesting (or when it's not). As a collaborative effort in shaping all parts of the learning experience, students will assume ownership of their learning.

Understanding how students adapt to learning environments and classroom structure is crucial. When teachers focus on students' strengths, students become more interested and work to achieve. Learners who struggle are frequently rebellious and out of sorts in a learning environment that does not adequately address different teaching strategies and learning styles. This can result in failure for these students, starting with inaccurate diagnosis and remedial, or sometimes, even withdrawal from school.

The most useful teaching approach for the struggling learner is often well-organized differentiated instruction (Tomlinson & Cunningham Edison, 2003). A teacher who is organized examines the conditions surrounding the child, such as curriculum content, the classroom environment, and the students' academic and social behaviors. The ways students react to information and respond to feedback are also important. Planning for manageable units of classroom time and including as many teaching and behavioral approaches as possible certainly help. But teachers know that no approach is effective in every situation, so it's important to be flexible. They also know that when they depend too much on rote memorization (devoid of meaningful applications), many students have trouble recognizing and retaining math/science facts. And they have trouble drawing conclusions.

In general, today's standards-driven curriculum provides many opportunities for students to develop a real understanding of mathematics and science content. As learners become more skillful and experienced, math and science ideas can be built upon and related to previous learning. Disaffected students, too often, are assigned uninteresting drill work each year to help them learn "basic skills." Yet, we know that students who did not understand the concept the first time are not likely to "catch on" the next time. Limiting their chances for math and science reasoning and problem solving puts struggling students at a serious disadvantage (Karp & Howell, 2004). It doesn't take long for youngsters to get the message that teachers have low expectations when it comes to their academic achievement.

Achievement gaps often result when math and science content is not connected to students' ability levels and experiences. What conditions will foster improved achievement? Research has not provided many clear-cut answers. Some suggest student absences or movement between schools may account for some of the problems (Barton, 2004). Other factors include the child's developmental environment and the home and school learning conditions. Gaps exist not only in the curriculum, but also between the student and some of the challenging content of math and science .

What works for reluctant learners? Among other things, working with peers can help disaffected students focus and feel good about themselves. Opportunities to communicate with others, as part of interesting math and science activities, can make also these subjects more motivating. Such a team-based approach is particularly powerful when student efforts are re-warded by peers and the teacher (Garmston & Wellman, 1999).

DISCOVERING WAYS TO DIFFERENTIATE INSTRUCTION

In a differentiated classroom, the teacher accepts students as they are and helps them succeed considering their unique circumstances. Differentiated classrooms are places where the teacher carefully designs instruction around the important concepts, principles, and skills of each subject. The helpful teacher makes sure that struggling learners focus on essential un-derstandings and important skills. The subject is introduced in a way that each student finds meaningful and interesting. Although the teacher in-tends to have all students attain these skills, he or she knows that many won't achieve all there is to know (Tomlinson, 1999).

Recognizing individual learning styles and adapting a differentiated teaching style can make learning easier. With differentiated learning, the teacher provides specific ways for each student to learn deeply, working en-ergetically to ensure that all students work harder than they imagined, and achieve more than they thought possible (Tomlinson, 2001).

What is clear is that struggling students seem to have the hardest time with the traditional classroom setting (straight desks, teacher lectures, text-books, worksheets, lots of listening, waiting, following directions, reading, and writing). In other environments, students who struggle have much less difficulty, for example, in an art classroom, a wood shop, a dance floor, or the outdoors. In these differentiated classroom settings where students have opportunities to engage in movement, hands-on learning, arts education, project-based learning, and other new learning approaches, their interest and desire to learn have been shown to be at or above average (Gardner, 1993).

There are ways that teachers can differentiate or modify instruction to guarantee that each student will learn as much and as competently as possible: Teachers can modify the content of what is taught and the ways they give students information. They can also help students understand the process of how they learn important knowledge and skills. Did they use manipulatives to aid in their understanding? Did they ask others? Teachers want to know what the student understands and is able to do. Did the student show his or her work? The teacher is also interested in discovering students' thoughts and feelings in the classroom. How did students react to the learning environment or the way the class atmosphere worked?

There are several student characteristics that teachers respond to as they design differentiated lessons. They include readiness—what a student knows, understands, and is able to do today; interest—what a student enjoys learning about; and learning profile—a student's preferred learning style.

SEVERAL SAMPLE STRATEGIES FOR DIFFERENTIATING INSTRUCTION

Readiness:
   Provide books at different reading levels.
   Use activities at various levels of difficulty but focused on the same learning goal.

Interest:
   Encourage students to use a variety of media arrangements such as video, music, film, and computers to express their ideas.
   Use collaborative group work to explore topics of interest.

Learning profile:
   Present a project in a visual, auditory, or movement style.
   Develop activities that use many viewpoints on interesting topics and issues.

Today's classrooms are challenging environments for teachers. Designing lessons that are responsive to the individual needs of all students is not an easy task. Teaching math and science in a differentiated classroom can be challenging, especially when teachers are trying to increase the emphasis on math and science inquiry process skills. Skills such as communicating, observing, reasoning, measuring, making connections, experimenting, and problem solving are only a few of the processes of doing mathematics and science.

This chapter introduced the process of instructional differentiation for students with learning problems in mathematics and science and illustrated its application using a sample lesson that emphasized the inquiry process skills described in the *Principles and Standards for School Mathematics* (NCTM, 2000) and the *National Science Education Standards* (NRC, 1996). We hope this introduction on differentiation provided you with some beginning ideas for discussing the *Differentiated Classroom* when you read chapter four.

MEETING THE PRINCIPLES AND STANDARDS FOR STRUGGLING STUDENTS

The six principles discussed below describe important issues of the mathematics and science curriculum standards. Used together, the principles will come alive as teachers develop comprehensive school math and science programs.

- *Equity.* High-quality mathematics and science require raising expectations for students' learning. All students must have opportunities to study and learn mathematics and science. This does not mean that every student should receive identical instruction; instead it demands that appropriate accommodations be made for all students. Resources and classroom support are also a large part of equity.
- *Curriculum.* A curriculum must be coherent, focused on math and science, and articulated across grade levels. Interconnected strands effectively organize and integrate mathematical and scientific ideas so that students can understand how one idea builds on and connects with other ideas. Building deeper understandings provides a map for guiding teachers through the different levels of learning.
- *Technology.* Technology today is an essential part of learning and understanding math and science. Effective mathematics and science teaching are dramatically increased with technological tools. Tools such as calculators and computers provide visual images of math and science ideas. They facilitate learning by organizing and analyzing data, and they compute accurately. Technology resources from the Internet, the World Wide Web, to computer programs like Logo, provide useful tools for mathematics and science learning.
- *Assessment.* Assessment should support the learning of math and science and provide useful information to students and teachers. This enhances students' learning while providing a valuable aid for making instructional teaching decisions.
- *Teaching.* Effective teachers understand mathematics and science, comprehend what underachieving students know and need to learn, and

challenge and support them through learning experiences. Teachers need several kinds of knowledge: knowledge of the subject, pedagogical knowledge, and an understanding of how children learn. Different techniques and instructional materials also affect how well their students learn mathematics and science. Struggling learners are often inundated with only practice materials trying to help them master the "basic skills." They often lack the conceptual foundations of real understanding. Students frequently forget procedures and are referred back to the same uninteresting skill-based drill work. The learner is not the focus, rather the basic skill drill is the center of attention.

- *Learning.* Math and science must be learned with understanding. Students actively build new knowledge from prior experience. Students should have the ability to use knowledge in a flexible manner, applying what is learned, and melding factual knowledge with conceptual understandings—thus, making learning easier. The learning principle is used when all students are involved in authentic and challenging work. Struggling students' interest is sparked and they create a strong understanding of the basic skills whether it's through games, peer involvement, or simple quiz situations.

STRUGGLING LEARNERS AND THE MATH AND SCIENCE STANDARDS

The new millennium has ushered in extraordinary changes. In mathematics and science, new knowledge and new ways of learning, doing, and communicating continue to evolve. Today, inexpensive calculators are everywhere. Powerful media outlets widely disseminate information as mathematics and science continue to filter into our lives.

> *If students can't learn the way we teach, we must teach them the way they learn.*
>
> —Carol Ann Tomlinson

We want all students, particularly struggling learners, to be involved in high-quality engaging mathematics and science instruction. High expectations should be set for all, with accommodations for those who need them. As students become confident about engaging in math and science tasks, they learn to observe, explore evidence, and provide reasoning and proof to support their conclusions. As they become active and resourceful problem solvers, students learn to be flexible as they participate in learning groups (with access to technology).

Students value mathematics and science when they work productively and reflectively—communicating their ideas orally and in writing (NCTM,

2000; NRC, 1996). This is not a just highly ambitious dream, but a successful effort to influence instruction. Here, we reference some of the principles behind the new standards and offer suggestions for effective teaching.

The National Council of Teachers of Mathematics and The National Science Foundation have developed standards that serve as guides for focused and enduring efforts to improve students' school mathematics and science education. These content standards provide a comprehensive set of standards for teaching mathematics and science from kindergarten through grade twelve.

An Overview of The Curriculum and Evaluation Standards for School Mathematics

The principles and standards for school mathematics recommend that all students

- Understand numbers and operations, estimate and use computational tools effectively.
- Understand and use various patterns and relationships.
- Use problem solving to explore and understand mathematical content.
- Analyze geometric characteristics, use visualization and spatial reasoning to solve problems within and outside mathematics.
- Pose questions, collect, organize, represent, and interpret data to evaluate arguments.
- Apply basic notions of chance and probability.
- Understand and use attributes, units, and systems of measurement and apply a variety of techniques and tools for determining measurements.
- Recognize reasoning and proof as essential to mathematics.
- Use mathematical thinking to communicate ideas clearly.
- Create and use representations to model, organize, record, and interpret mathematical ideas.

(These are brief selections. For a full description see National Council of Teachers of Mathematics, 2000).

An Overview of the National Science Education Standards

Principles that guide the standards:

- Science is for all students.
- Learning is an active process.
- School science reflects the intellectual and cultural traditions that characterize the practice of contemporary science.
- Improving science education is part of a systemic educational reform.

The science standards highlight what students should know, understand, and be able to do. Examples include:

- Becoming aware of physical, life, earth, and space sciences through activity-based learning.
- Connecting the concepts and processes in science.
- Using science as inquiry.
- Understanding the relationship between science and technology.
- Using science understandings to design solutions to problems.
- Identifying with the history and nature of science through readings, discussions, observations, and written communications.
- Viewing and practicing science using personal and social perspectives. (National Academy Press, 1996)

GOING BEYOND SKILL MASTERY

Students who complete their math and science lessons with little understanding quickly forget or confuse the procedures (Miller & Mercer, 2001). For example: in doing a long division problem, suppose that students cannot recall if they are supposed to divide the numerator into the denominator, or the reverse, to find the correct decimal. They can do the problem either way, but may not understand what they are doing nor be able to explain their reasoning.

Understanding and skill mastery go together when students build upon ideas they already know in a discovery process (Bruner, 1986). In science, step-by-step directions for an experiment often are quickly given and extra time not provided for explanation. Again, the goal should be to understand what's going on well enough to know how it can be applied in the world outside of school.

Understanding important ideas and accurately completing problems are some of the first steps in becoming mathematically and scientifically skillful. Mathematics and science learning contains five strands of thought:

1. Understanding ideas and being able to comprehend important content.
2. Being flexible and using accurate procedures.
3. Posing and solving problems.
4. Reflecting and evaluating knowledge.
5. Reasoning and making sense and value out of what is learned.

Oftentimes, the struggling student has experienced little success in the five strands. Math and science success can be expected and achieved as adaptations are made to the students' curriculum. This can happen when teachers relate problems to real-life student interests and provide time for collaborative work.

ORGANIZING SUCCESSFUL LESSONS

Students reach higher rates of proficiency when they are involved in organized lessons that pay special attention to their individual learning needs (Karp & Howell, 2004).

Stage 1: Review

Students connect new math and science concepts to old ideas they are familiar with when they are actively engaged at a concrete level of understanding. Math and science manipulatives such as counters, eye droppers, rulers, and blocks are used to answer questions that represent real-life interesting problems. For example, students are asked to show how many more cupcakes need to be made for a class picnic if 7 are already made for the class of 16 students (each student gets one cupcake). Connections are made to former lessons, such as relating subtraction to the mathematical idea of how many more. Questions are asked and students discuss their understanding of the mathematical ideas.

Stage 2: Demonstrate Knowledge or Skill

Next, students show their thinking by drawing a picture of the problem. For example, the set of cupcakes might be shown like this: I have 7 cupcakes. How many more do we need to get 16? Have students draw a basket to show their results.

Stage 3: Guided Practice

Students form a number sentence to match their drawings. $7 + \_\_ = 16$. (Answer: 9). We needed 9 more than 7 to get 16. Students fill in numerals and number sentences.

Stage 4: Check for Understanding

In the last part of the lesson, student practice skills and problems through a range of activities and supporting lessons. The teacher provides ongoing feedback at each step so that procedural errors can be corrected (see table 1.1).

Table 1.1
Organized Strategies to Support
Students with Learning Problems

1. Review important concepts—make connections between familiar and new information.
2. Demonstrate knowledge or skill—increase student engagement and promote independent student activities.
3. Provide guided practice—reinforce language skills, partner, and share. Students do a variety of problems.
4. Check for understanding and provide feedback—summarize strategies and evaluate.
5. Teacher provides continuous reinforcement at each stage so errors can be found and corrected.

ASSESSING STUDENTS' STRENGTHS

Math and science content knowledge, student learning styles, behaviors, and reinforcement that affect learning are all considered in assessment. Assessment data is gathered from teacher observations, performance on daily assignments, math and science quizzes, homework, and in-class work. This information is recorded on a student data sheet. The value of assessment is that it leads to an overall analysis of a student's strengths and weaknesses (see table 1.2).

Table 1.2
Student Data Sheet

Learning setting—indicates the physical environment in which the student works.
Content—includes the subject matter in which the child is engaged.
Process—involves strategies, methods, and tools that students are engaged in (e.g., listening and speaking).
Behavior—refers to academic and social behaviors that students participate in.
Reinforcement—looks at responses from the learning environment that cause behaviors to occur.

Recording Behavior Patterns

Behaviors that are consistent are called likely behaviors. They might include the desire to play video games or use the computer. Unlikely behaviors describe behaviors that usually occur below an average rate or at a very minimal level. For example, a classroom environment that is conducive to student achievement could be rated with a "+" symbol. If a student is having problems in the classroom environment, the teacher would mark this category with a "−" symbol. Collecting and reviewing this information with students allows teachers to focus on recognizing which classroom activities foster positive behaviors.

CREATING MATH AND SCIENCE SUCCESS PLANS

Math and science instruction focuses on student learning while building on students' strengths and identifying error patterns. The teacher judges the students' data sheets, recording the type of learning environment that students were involved in. The content of the lessons is also recorded. The learners' preferred learning style and how they accept and express themselves (including listening, speaking, writing, or drawing) are also recorded information. The teacher notes if the student works well with others or works best alone. The students' academic and social participation are other factors considered when evaluating the students' data sheets. The learners' responses are documented. For example, reinforcement activities such as (likes being with friends, enjoys helping in class, likes being in front of class, doesn't turn in work on time, can't stay focused, or talks out of turn). Based on identifying how students learn, the sample Math & Science Success Plan is designed to recognize and move students toward more positive behaviors and academic success. In this way, the Math & Science Success Plan serves as a guide for an organized and well-planned learning approach for struggling learners.

Table 1.3
Sample Math and Science Success Plan

Time:	30 minutes	15–20 minutes	20–30 minutes
Context:	One on one with teacher	With peers	Working independently
	Small group setting	With teacher	
Content:	Specific activities	Groups objects in 10's	Records quantities
	Counts aloud		
Process:	Oral instructions	Oral activities	Reports answers orally
	Oral answers	Calculator usage	Stays in seat

Behavior:	Completes assignment	Turns in assignment	Monitoring for student use of self-control
	Work is not carefully done	Accepts teacher directions positive response	

Reinforcement:	Oral feedback		Group activities
	Allowed movement in classroom		Peer work

Instruction in math and science now tends to be more research based and standards driven. In addition, it often involves constructing deeper content knowledge through collaborative inquiry. Math and science are more than a collection of isolated rules and procedures to memorize. Understanding and applying these subjects involves certain levels of reasoning, problem solving, and imagination. There are, after all, multiple ways to solve problems and chart the way forward. Creativity and originality are often a matter of perspective. Sometimes, you don't dig up new ground—you just work to see the old ground differently.

BUILDING UNDERSTANDING AND SUCCESS

Recognizing the learning characteristics of struggling students and finding instructional methods that motivate them are important steps in math and science instruction. The basic idea is to use strategies that consider all aspects of the learners' instructional needs so that students can be successful. Of course, the instructional methods mobilized for reluctant learners must not get in the way of the students who are already doing well in math and science. The good news is that differentiated learning doesn't get in the way of providing meaningful opportunities for everyone in the classroom (Elmore, 2005).

Math and science certainly don't attract universal affection. In fact, anything even faintly mathematical or scientific engenders fear in many. Marilyn Burns refers to it as an "American phobia" (Burns, 1998). Still, whether they know it or not, all individuals use math and science in their day-to-day lives. In many respects, these disciplines can't be avoided. To do well, students need to have a fairly positive—or at least disciplined—attitude toward achieving mastery. And sometimes, both students and teachers have to be willing to change to learn something.

Students who struggle with math and science are, by definition, not doing as well as their parents or their teachers think they can. All too many of them view school as boring and irrelevant. Worse, for some, it's a place that they associate with humiliation and failure. It's little wonder that the standards and the dropout rates often go up together. One way or another, everyone is involved in the education of children and young adults, so there is enough blame to go around. Educators need to be aware of social forces (including the family) that so strongly influence what's learned in the classroom. This doesn't mean that someone has to teach you math and science outside of school, although that wouldn't hurt. It's just that the home environment is where you learn to relate to very complicated things.

The self-esteem and spirit of individuals and groups are often expressed through culture. Students who struggle with math and science are helped when community resources, issues, events, and topics connect to what happens in the classroom (Van de Walle & Lovin, 2006). Past and present experiences outside of school can serve as powerful resources for learning. In addition, purposeful classroom linkages with the home environment can be created and sustained by the math/science curricula and by the actions of the teacher.

As teachers use an organized approach to assess their students' math/ science strengths (and error patterns), they can put into practice learning strategies that connect a student's predisposition to a positive classroom learning environment. One of the things that helps is having students explore the practical applications of math and science in their lives. This means connecting math/science rules to student understandings in a way that offers them an authentic invitation to interesting problems. This organized approach may well be the best way to get struggling students to express their reasoning in ways that can lead to academic success (Barton, 2004).

Getting some young people to see math and science instruction as good things can be a challenge, but we know something about making the classroom a positive experience. What seems to matter most for disaffected students is working with others, extracurricular activities, and the particular attention paid by a teacher who takes time to help a struggling student. Whatever the curriculum or methodology, it ultimately comes down to the teacher's energy, knowledge, character, sense of humor, and ability to relate to young people.

Major changes in the productivity of American schools rest on our ability to create and sustain a highly prepared teaching force for all, not just some, of our children.

—Linda Darling-Hammond

QUESTIONS FOR TEACHERS AND PROSPECTIVE TEACHERS

1. Interview four peers. Ask them if they ever had difficulty learning math and science. Have them identify their reasons and explain.
2. How would you identify a struggling learner?

3. What are some teaching ideas for connecting math and science to students' interests?
4. How does learning mathematics and science today differ from how you were taught? Provide examples.

REFERENCES AND RESOURCES

Armstrong, T. (1999). *ADD/ADHD Alternatives in the classroom.* Alexandria, VA: Association for Supervision and Curriculum Development.

Barton, P. (2004). Why does the gap persist? *Educational leadership, 62*(3), 9–13.

Brodesky, A., Gross, A., & Tierney, C. (2004). Planning strategies for students with special needs: A professional development activity. *Teaching Children Mathematics,* 11(3), 146–154.

Bruner, J. (1986). *Actual minds, possible worlds.* Cambridge, MA: Harvard University Press.

Burns, M. (1998). *Math: Facing an American phobia.* White Plains, NY: Math Solutions Publications.

Cathcart, G., Pothier, Y. M., Vance, J. H., & Bezuk, N. S. (2005). *Learning math in elementary and middle school & IMAP.* Upper Saddle, NJ: Pearson Education.

Elmore, R. (September/October 2005). What (so-called) low-performing schools can teach (so-called) high-performing schools. *Harvard Education Letter,* 21(5).

Gardner, H. (1993). *Multiple intelligences: The theory in practice.* New York, NY: Basic Books.

Garmston, R. J. & Wellman, B. M. (1999). *The adaptive school: A source book+0 for developing collaborative groups.* Norwood, MA: Christopher-Gordon Publishers.

Kame'enui, E., Carnine, D., Dixon, R., Simmons, D., & Coyne, M. (2002). *Effective teaching strategies that accommodate diverse learners.* 2nd ed. Upper Saddle River, NJ: Prentice Hall.

Karp, K. & Howell, P. (2004). Building responsibility for learning in students with special needs. *Teaching children mathematics,* 11(3), 118–126.

Levine, M. (2000). *Educational care: A system for understanding and helping children with learning problems at home and in school.* Rev. ed. Cambridge, MA: Educators Publishing Service.

Loveless, T. & Coughlan, J. (2004). The arithmetic gap. *Teaching children mathematics,* 11(3), 55–59.

Malone, T. & Lepper, M. (1987). Making learning fun: A taxonomy of intrinsic motivations for learning. In R. Snow & M. Farr (eds.). *Appitude, learning, and instruction.* vol. 3: *Cognitive and affective process analyses.* (223–253) Hillsdale, NJ: Lawrence Erlbaum.

Miller, S. & Mercer, C. (2001). *Teaching students with learning problems.* 6th ed. Upper Saddle River, NJ: Merrill/Prentice Hall.

Musser, G. L., Burger, W. F., & Peterson, B. E. (2005). *Mathematics for elementary teachers: A contemporary approach.* Hoboken, NJ: John Wiley & Sons.

Musser, G. L., Burger, W. F., & Peterson, B. E. (2005). *Mathematics for elementary teachers, hints and solutions manual for part A problems: A contemporary approach.* Hoboken, NJ: John Wiley & Sons.

National Academy Press. (1996). *National science education standards.* Washington, DC: National Academy Press.

National Council of Teachers of Mathematics (NCTM). (2000). *Principles and standards for school mathematics.* Reston, VA: National Council of Teachers of Mathematics.

National Research Council (NRC). (1996). *National science education standards.* Washington, DC: National Academy Press.

National Research Council. (2001). *Everybody counts: A report to the nation on the future of mathematics education.* Washington, DC: National Academy Press.

Peters, J. M. & Stout, D. L. (2005). *Science in elementary education: Methods, concepts and inquiries.* Upper Saddle, NJ: Prentice Hall.

Polya, G. (2004). *How to solve it: A new aspect of mathematical method.* Princeton, NJ: Princeton University Press.

Possamentier, A. (2004). Marvelous math! *Educational leadership,* 61(5), 44–47.

Safro, J. (2005). *Math word problems made easy: Grade 5.* Scholastic Teaching Resources.

Schwartz, D. L. (1995). The emergence of abstract representations in dyad problem solving. *The Journal of Learning Sciences,* 4(3), 321–354.

Snow, D. (2005). *Classroom strategies for helping at-risk students.* Aurora, CO: Mid-continent Research for Education and Learning.

Solomon, J. (September/October, 1997). Is how we teach science more important than what we teach? *Primary Science Review,* 49, 3–5.

Stigler, J. & Hiebert, J. (2004). Improving mathematics teaching. *Educational Technology,* 61(5), 12–17.

Swanson, H. Lee. (1999). Instructional components that predict treatment outcomes for students with learning disabilities. *Learning Disabilities Research,* 14, 129–140.

Tomlinson, C. (1999). *The differentiated classroom: Responding to the needs of all learners.* Alexandria, VA: Association for Supervision and Curriculum Development.

Tomlinson, C. (2001). *How to differentiate instruction in mixed-ability classrooms.* 2nd ed. Alexandria, VA: Association for Supervision and Curriculum Development.

Tomlinson, C. & Cunningham Edison, C. (2003). *Differentiation in practice: A resource guide for differentiating curriculum.* Alexandria, VA: Association for Supervision and Curriculum Development.

Tucker, B., Singleton, A., & Weaver, T. (2006). *Teaching mathematics to ALL children: Designing and adapting instruction to meet the needs of diverse learners.* 2nd ed. Upper Saddle River, NJ: Prentice Hall (Pearson Education, Inc).

Van de Walle, J. (2004). *Elementary and middle school mathematics:Teaching developmentally.* 5th ed. Boston, MA: Allyn & Bacon.

Van de Walle, J. & Lovin, L., (2006). *Teaching student-centered mathematics.* Boston, MA: Pearson/Allyn & Bacon.

Vaughn, S., Bos, C. & Schuum, J. (2003). *Teaching mainstreamed, diverse, and at-risk students in the general education classroom.* Boston, MA: Allyn & Bacon.

White, D. (2004). Teaching mathematics to special needs students. *Teaching children mathematics,* 11(3), 116–117.

2

Student Inquiry in Math and Science

A pebble drops into a pond. The ripples spread, each ripple complete, compre-
hensive, circular. Ideas within ideas within ideas like ripples spread out to reach
invisible shores. An idea is sparked, questions form, and an inquiry begins.

—Marian L. Martinello & Gillian E. Cook

Inquiry is more than a set of procedures or skills associated with the scientific method. The inquiry skills of mathematics and science are acquired through a process of questioning that engages students in authentic investigation and problem solving. The basic idea is to teach students how to discover information and knowledge. Sometimes the information is new to the individual—and sometimes it's necessary to expand knowledge that has not been fully explored (Peters & Stout, 2005).

This chapter explores how collaborative inquiry can make math and science programs meaningful and exciting for struggling students, without slowing down those who are doing well. We also suggest ways that teachers can

- Help students refine their inquiry skills as they learn math and science.
- Use a variety of instructional strategies to maximize students' potential.
- Introduce all students to planning and leadership roles.
- Involve reluctant learners in active and collaborative learning.
- Arouse student curiosity and interest in math and science.
- Teach for understanding in a way that that makes learning meaningful.

Differentiated instruction easily fits into the process. Teachers in differentiated classrooms begin with a clear understanding of what represents a powerful curriculum and engaging instruction. They, then, modify instruction so that each student comes away with deeper understandings and skills.

When students are engaged in collaborative inquiry, they work together to accomplish shared goals. Although the group sinks or swims together, there is individual accountability. It is up to the teacher to ensure that underachieving students focus on important understandings and skills so they don't get swamped in a mire of disjointed facts. The teacher also supports advanced learners by getting them involved with more complex problems rather than have them go back over what they already know. Personal growth and individual success matter. And every effort is made to introduce subjects in a way that each student finds meaningful and interesting.

Inquiry often raises new questions and new directions for examination, with findings generating ideas and suggesting ways of expressing math and science content more clearly (Llewellyn, 2005). When learners explore topics that are of special interest to them, it is quite motivating, even for those who would rather avoid learning about math and science. Classroom questions: What do mathematicians and scientists actually do? How do they know what they know? The answers will vary greatly, and students may have to go on the Internet to get more complete answers. Whatever the problem, subject, or issue, inquiry is at its best when students use thinking skills that are similar to those used by mathematicians and scientists who are searching for new knowledge in their field (Etheredge & Rudnitsky, 2003).

Teachers and students can explore the kinds of activities that help students who are struggling to build understanding and meaningfully apply the inquiry skills. In this way, teachers can give the students a degree of ownership as they plan and organize some of the class activities together. The teacher shares some of the leadership by inviting students to be part of the planning and teaching process. When learners teach each other, everyone usually learns more. In addition, effective teachers sometimes go one step further and involve students in discussions about class rules, schedules, and teaching procedures. The end result in the collaborative classroom is that inquiry can go beyond math and science to provide struggling students with valuable insights about themselves and the nature of teamwork (Tomlinson, 1999).

INQUIRY SKILLS

Inquiry goes beyond the *what* of math and science to focus on the *how* of these subjects. It is driven by meaningful and authentic questions. In addition, classroom inquiry frequently embeds instruction in a context of social collaboration and encourages students to cooperatively explore and apply a basic body of knowledge. For the teacher, knowing the level of prior understanding is important because the basic idea is to help learners develop the attitudes and skills they need to build a foundation for future discoveries (Karp & Howell, 2004).

Being able to use the knowledge and skills of math and science in meaningful ways is an important objective for struggling students. Meaningful learning means giving students active control over the content they learn as well as being able to use the knowledge in a personal way (Rezba, 2003). The basic idea is to have learners manipulate objects, adapt ideas, and create personal knowledge through interesting small group experiences. Along the way, they have a good chance of developing an appreciation for the rules and principles that guide the inquiry process.

All subjects are built upon important concepts and principles that demand the use of necessary skills. When planning for the class lesson, the teacher should have a specific list of what each student should know, understand, and be able to do. Then, the teacher creates a variety of engaging, exciting activities to help all students accomplish these skills. To be effective, teachers must ensure that lessons are built on the curiosity of children as well as on curriculum content (Carin, Bass & Contant, 2005). As learners construct knowledge (or "process," as Piaget calls it), they make mathematics and science relevant and personal. Teachers should introduce and plan class inquiry discussions and activities that cover each skill.

Inquiry Skills That Address the Needs of Underachieving Students

Observing

The most important tool for young children is observation. Wanting to find out about their world makes students eager to explore and ask questions. Observing involves using all the senses: seeing, hearing, tasting, smelling, and feeling—working together to gather as much information as possible. It is an immediate reaction to the students' environment. Observations are the foundations for all other inquiry process skills. They are the uninterpreted facts of mathematics and science. Students should be directed to describe what they see, hear, smell, touch, and perhaps taste. Encourage passive learners to try and provide some specific measurements to their observations. Most times, even reluctant learners are motivated and excited about what they observe.

Sorting and Classifying

Students learn about objects by grouping and ordering them. Classification relies primarily on observation. As children become more skilled in recognizing characteristics of objects, they learn to recognize likenesses and differences between objects. Classification is an important part of our lives. Shopping at the supermarket, finding a book in the library, or even setting the dinner table would be a tremendous time-consuming chore if things weren't classified. At a young age, children are able to classify or sort objects into groups by color, size, or shape, rearrange the set, and put the groups in some kind of order. Even students who have difficulty remembering are not daunted by sorting and classifying objects.

Comparing

Once students learn to observe and describe objects, they soon begin to compare two or more objects. Young children may say they want more or fewer; they can tell you what is the same or different. Being able to compare individual and sets of objects will help students decide whether four is more or less than six. Comparing is not just a skill for students in the early grades. Struggling students will use this skill in every grade and throughout their work in every discipline. Good math and science involves comparing other studies, experimenting, and reaching conclusions. Teachers should offer a variety of activities that let students use all their senses, group objects in many ways, and encourage students to interact with others and communicate their findings.

Sequencing

Children live with sequences and patterns. They may notice patterns in nature (the symmetry of a leaf, or the wings of an insect) or patterns in the classroom (the tessellations of the floor or ceiling tiles). Sequencing is finding or bringing order to observations. These interesting patterns all around are enlivened when teachers direct even uninterested students' observation and pattern finding. Watch children as they put a variety of objects in order: do their groups have a common attribute? Are their objects arranged in a particular way? Have students explain their groupings and reveal clues about math and science understanding.

Measuring

At the middle elementary level, students are able to master skills of a good inquirer. Many students make measurements using different tools: rulers, thermometers, scales, clocks, and so on. Young children automatically use descriptive language when comparing quantities (one child is taller than another; one backpack is heavier; one ball is larger, etc.). Active measuring experiences in math and science provide many opportunities for struggling learners to describe and compare in terms of quantity. Mathematicians and scientists are constantly measuring. Measuring supplies the hard data necessary to confirm hypotheses and make predictions. It provides firsthand information. Measuring includes gathering data on size, weight, and quantity. Measurement tools and skills have a variety of uses in everyday adult life. Being able to measure connects math and science to the environment. Measurement tools give students opportunities for differentiated learning in subjects such as social studies, technology, art, and music (VanSciver, 2005).

Discovering Relationships

As children compare, classify, and sequence objects, they soon look at relationships among objects. Relationships are rules or agreements used to associate one or more objects or concepts with another. Math and science are collections of relationships among objects or concepts. A concept in nature is that animals have certain needs—air, food, water, and space. A variety of factors affects the ability of animals to maintain their survival over time. The most fundamental of life's necessities are the needs mentioned. Everything in natural systems is interrelated. If one of these needs were eliminated, the animal population would dwindle and die. Remind students with learning problems of the connections among the needs of animals, plants, and themselves to survive sparks interest and motivation.

For teachers of mathematics and science, the fact that math and science concepts involve relationships is very important. It is almost impossible to show children an example of a mathematics or science concept without having them compare it or draw a relationship to something else. Children must create the relationships for themselves. It is critical that we allow students to be active mentally and to reflect on things presented in class. That is the way that the mind of even a reluctant learner can construct a relationship (Van de Walle & Lovin, 2006).

Communicating

Communication stresses the importance of being able to talk about, write about, describe, and explain math and science ideas. Symbolism, along with visual aids such as charts and graphs, should become a way of expressing math and science ideas to others. This means that students should learn not only to interpret the language of math and science, but also to use that language both in and beyond the classroom. Middle school students often find math and science curriculum most appealing when it helps them to focus on themselves. Young people are in the process of discovering who and what they are. It is necessary for adolescents to form some positive impressions of themselves based on sound observations and evidence. Struggling learners benefit as they come to realize that they are not alone in having problems with math and science. All students gain by regularly talking, writing, drawing, graphing, using symbols, numbers, and tables to help them think and communicate their ideas. By making sense to others, they indirectly convey the concept in a meaningful way for themselves. Learning to communicate effectively makes the world of mathematics and science outside of school more successful. It also promotes interaction and the investigation of ideas within the classroom, as students learn in an active, verbal environment (Campbell & Fulton, 2003).

Valuing Mathematics and Science

"Why do I need to know this stuff?" This retort is heard way too frequently by teachers of math and science. Valuing emphasizes children's feelings, emotions, and attitudes as they learn math and science. After decades of research, we have learned that a student's success in a curricular area is often determined by how well his or her personal needs are met in that area. While computation for the sake of computation is definitely open to criticism, the mathematics and science of reasoning, problem solving, and finding patterns are intimately connected with the very fabric of our society. Essentially every role in today's society requires mathematics and science and, more important, math and science thinking. Children need to see themselves not just learning skills, but learning to reason and solve problems. Connecting realistic life situations will reinforce the conclusion that this is "important stuff."

> *Every day, somewhere, teachers look out over the classroom and see a void, a space made vacant by the crossfire of street violence. Every day, somewhere, a teacher makes yet another change on the class roster, which by the end of the year will reflect a 40 percent turnover in student population due to transience and homelessness. Every day, somewhere, a teacher reaches out to comfort the deep hurt and suffering of an abused or hungry child. Every day, somewhere, a child's self-image is shattered, as she or he silently withdraws from active participation in learning.*
>
> —Eldon Katter

Using Data

The disciplines of mathematics and science identify statistics and probability as important links to many content areas. The skills of data gathering, analyzing, recording, using tables, and reading graphs provide many opportunities for representing, interpreting, and recording that apply many math and science concepts and skills.

Many decisions are based on market research and sales projections. If these data are to be understood and used, all people should be able to process such information efficiently. For example, consider the math/science concepts involved in the following:

Weather reports (decimals, percents, probability, observing weather patterns, classifying climate zones, identifying weather fronts).
Public opinion polls (sampling techniques and errors of measurement).
Advertising claims (hypothesis testing, product research, polls, sales records, projections, and so on).
Monthly government reports (involving unemployment, inflation, and energy supplies percentages, prediction, and extrapolation).

All media depend on techniques for summarizing information. Radio, television, the Internet, and newspapers bombard us with statistical information. The current demand for information-processing skills continues to grow. Teachers can provide a tape or CD that struggling students can listen to several times as they try to complete difficult statistical tasks.

Graphing

Graphing skills include constructing and reading graphs as well as interpreting graphical information. They should be introduced in early grades. The data should depend on children's interest and maturity. Here are a few kinds of survey data that could be collected in the classroom:

Physical characteristics—height, eye color, shoe sizes
Sociological characteristics—birthdays, number in family
Personal preferences—favorite television shows, favorite books, favorite sports, favorite food

Each of these concepts gives struggling students the opportunity to collect data themselves (Karp & Howell, 2004). Graphic messages can provide a large amount of information at a glance. In creating a graph, it is important to make the graph large enough for disabled students to manipulate and make interpretations, predictions, or analyses.

Using Language

Language is a window into students' thinking and understanding. For most individuals, oral language is the primary means of communication. One of the overriding objectives in the collaborative classroom is to facilitate the use of oral language and listening as different means of communication and learning. Language also reveals the quality of the students' math and science communication. Listening to students' language is a valuable way to get feedback from their efforts. There are many ways to give students opportunities to practice and use language effectively (Strickland, Ganske, & Monroe, 2002). Effective communication will, of course, depend on topical knowledge, but also on students being aware of how to go about communicating orally. Self-awareness also fits in—how well are underachieving students applying their oral communication skills. There are many different ways to involve students actively in this differentiated process. A few are mentioned here: storytelling, directed reading activities, art (clay modeling, drawing, sculpture), music (playing, singing, listening), oral presentations, small group discussions, and creative dramatics.

Sharing

The process of sharing helps students feel more comfortable and less inhibited in speaking before an audience. Sharing allows students to develop independence, to share their work and ideas. Again, self-confidence is very important. Whole class discussions are held after the children have had time to explore a particular activity or idea. Teachers use these group sharing times to summarize and interpret data from explorations. Group sharing is a time for students to discuss their ideas, focus on math and science relationships, and help learners make connections among activities.

Exploring

Exploring as the dictionary defines it means "to examine carefully, to travel in little known region for discovery." Exploring means allowing students to reach their own conclusions and decisions. Not only do children have the ability to reach out into their world through self-initiated processes, but they must also be given the opportunity to do so. For teachers, the goal of exploring suggests that struggling students should be provided with many opportunities to direct their own learning. Some of the inquiry processes used in the goal of exploring include predicting, estimating, experimenting, and investigating.

Predicting

Will it snow tomorrow? Now, this question can be answered, but it can only be answered by a guess—not a prediction. It requires speculation. How can we turn speculation (guesses) into predictions? For example, the answer to the question about whether it will snow tomorrow can be highly speculative. But observers can turn that speculation into a prediction. First, students must know something about current weather conditions. How fast are weather systems moving? From what direction are they moving? What is the temperature, relative humidity, dew point? What kinds of clouds are there? Last year at this time I remember it snowed. Are there any low pressure systems nearby? What about cold or warm fronts? With this data readily available, students can check past weather conditions. In the past when conditions were similar, it snowed fifty percent of the time; there is a 50/50 chance that it will snow tomorrow, too. Tomorrow might turn out to be the brightest day of the winter, or it might snow. Predictions tell us that, given these conditions, it has snowed every time, sometimes, or perhaps never.

Students learn that not all predictions are accurate. Often, there is a high degree of uncertainty in predicting. The ability to make predictions is based on skillful observation, inference, quantification, and communication. Students who understand predicting are aware that unforeseen events can change the conditions of a prediction and that one hundred percent accuracy is not likely.

Estimating

The curriculum should include estimation so students can explore estimation strategies, recognize when estimation is appropriate, determine the reasonableness of results, and apply estimation when working with quantities, measurement, computation, and problem solving (NCTM, 2002).

Inferring

The basic process skill of inference involves making conclusions based on reasoning. Children often make inferences about their observations. Observations and inferences are directly related. Inferences are based on observations and experiences. Students are often very creative in making inferences based on what they have observed. Inferences extend observation by allowing learners to explain their findings and predict what they think will happen. Are these inferences correct? All anyone can say is that inferences either relate to the observations in a logical way, and are therefore reasonable, or they don't. The interesting and challenging thing about making inferences is the language that takes place among the students. Discussing important terms and writing about them help struggling students often confused by the vocabulary. Language is a powerful tool for gathering and sharing information. Students are encouraged to talk with their teachers, other adults, and with each other while they are engaged in observing and making inferences based on their senses and experiences.

The basic inquiry processes just discussed are global in their application— not limited to math and science investigation. For example, students might use the process of inferring to try to understand why their teacher was angry with them in class yesterday. A student might sort and classify his or her supplies for the field trip tomorrow.

Experimenting

Inquiry processes such as forming a hypothesis, identifying variables, or analyzing data are skills used in an experiment. Skills such as predicting, estimating, and inferring are part of experimenting. The ability to make predictions is based on skillful observation, inference, quantification, and communication. Experimenting is one of the most exciting skills for all students, particularly those who have difficulties with math and science. Encourage students to work together when they are experimenting.

Forming Planning Groups: Helping Students Assume a Leadership Role

Whether they're first graders or middle school students, all students want to help the teacher with classroom chores. We designed a planning group project to assist the teacher and help students assume a leadership role. At the beginning of the year, the teacher announces that he or she would like some help in planning for the math or science class. He or she excitedly explains that all students will be involved. The teacher makes a chart with nine months and spaces for the name of each student.

The teacher gives students a chance to decide which month they will choose and explains the planning group directions to the class. She is careful to explain that when students sign up for the task, they are responsible for coming to the planning group session at that time. He or she also emphasizes that each student signed up becomes a leader of their group.

The teacher and students spend time discussing what a group leader is. Students are asked their views about a team leader. Can anyone do it? Of course, there will be different ideas, but the task of the teacher is to describe that all students are leaders—there are many examples of leaders: sports leaders, music leaders, art leaders, building leaders, race car leaders, government leaders, the list goes on. The teacher's job is to get students excited about their leadership role (Rhoton & Bowers, 2001).

Planning Group Directions for Students

You will sign up for a planning group session that meets for two weeks. In that session, you will meet with the teacher and help plan the class session. You will be the *leader of your group* for two weeks. The planning group sessions might take place during recess or free time when the rest of the class is not present.

Planning Group Jobs

1. Organize materials for the class.
   - Get materials from classroom cupboards/shelves.
   - Organize the tables and chairs for the class.
2. Get directions from the teacher for the activities to be done in class.
3. Try out the activities you will be doing with other planning group members.
4. Discuss ideas, questions, or changes you feel would be useful.
5. Discuss the following with planning group members:
   - Any question you feel students in the class may have.
   - Any items that need to be clarified.
   - Decide how you will divide up the class into groups.
6. Prepare learning materials:
   - Write notes on large paper.
   - Tack up posters with tape.
   - Arrange books around the room.
   - Arrange manipulatives for activities.

Sample Planning Group Chart

(Please sign up for two weeks)

March 1   to   March 14

_____   _____

_____   _____

March 15   to   March 28

_____   _____

_____   _____

The teacher explains the directions to the class.

Math and Science Inquiry Activities

The activities presented here, unless otherwise specified, are designed for elementary and middle school students who struggle with math and science. The following activity was planned with primary children in mind, but with creativity, the techniques can be adapted for elementary levels and middle school learners.

To Observe and Describe Using the Five Senses

Description: Grades K–2. This primary activity uses the five senses. The process skills of observing, inferring, communicating (sharing), and hypothesizing are introduced.

Objectives:
1. Children will observe and make inferences with their senses.
2. Children will talk and share their ideas with others.
3. Children will ask questions and make hypotheses based on their senses.
4. Children will verify their thinking through personal experiences.

Planning Group: Members should arrange the classroom and materials.

Procedures:
1. Select several objects that are safe to touch, smell, and taste (cookies, orange, apple, popcorn are good choices).
2. Put one object in a clean paper bag and ask students to feel the object without looking inside.
3. Have children describe what they feel.
4. Have children smell the object without peeking.
5. Encourage students to describe what they smell.
6. Shake the bag and invite students to describe what they hear.
7. Next, you may wish to have students taste the object and describe it.
8. Finally, allow students to look at the object and verify their guesses.

It's important to discuss with students the strategies they used in making their guesses. Point out the invaluable role of others. Ask what they learned from other classmates about making inferences. Experiences such as these in inferring and describing give children an opportunity to develop and refine many math and science concepts. Children may use vague or emotional terms rather than specific descriptive words. It's important to discuss the communication process: which words are most effective in describing what they did. Let children discuss which words give better descriptions. Have children relate their everyday language to math and science language and symbols. The following activity gives students a chance to refine their skills.

Evaluation: Have students share their experiences through language and cultural anecdotes. Language materials designed to teach non-English-speaking students are valuable when helping the struggling student.

What Do You See?

Description: Grades 3–4. This group center activity involves the process skills of observing, inferring, measuring, comparing, and recording.

Process Skills: Measuring, comparing, inferring, ordering by distance, formulating conclusions.

Objectives:
1. Students will be able to observe and record data accurately.
2. Students will use simple scientific equipment.
3. Students will demonstrate ability to work in groups in an organized and productive manner.

Planning Group: Members should arrange the classroom and materials.

Materials:
1. Five samples: a house fly, a computer disk, a flower, a piece of fabric, and a sample of paper. (Other samples may be substituted for those listed.)
2. Twelve magnifying glasses.
3. Six rulers.
4. An observation sheet for each student.

Procedures:
1. Six stations, each including two magnifying glasses, one of the samples listed above, and a ruler are set up around the room.
2. Each student receives an observation sheet.
3. Students are divided into six groups of four students each.
4. Each group is assigned a station. At this station, the group has ten minutes to record as many observations about the sample as possible.
5. Each student in the group, while using the magnifying glass and the ruler, makes an observation for the group to record. Students take turns as time allows.
6. As a class, students compare and discuss their observations.
7. Struggling students are actively involved whether they're the group leader or part of the team. If students have difficulty, encourage them to work together as a partnership.

Evaluation: Data sheets are evaluated on organization, observation skills, and accuracy.

Math/Science Nature Search

Description: Mathematics and science applications are all around us. Mathematical patterns in nature abound. Architecture, art, and everyday objects rely heavily on mathematical principles, patterns, and symmetrical geometric forms. Students need to see and apply real world connections to concepts in science and mathematics. This activity is designed to get students involved and become more aware of the mathematical/scientific relationships all around them, and to use technology to help report their findings. This activity requires students to use the process skills of observation, classification, comparison, sequence, measurement, and communication.

Objectives:
1. Students will participate in observing, communicating, and collecting samples.
2. Students will exhibit their understanding by recording their observations in their notebooks.
3. Students will show their ability to work in groups in a responsible, interactive, and productive manner.
4. Students will reflect their thinking orally and in writing.

Planning Group: Members should arrange the classroom and materials.

Procedures: Divide the class into four groups. Each group is directed to find and bring back as many objects as they can that meet the requirements on their list. Some objects may need to be sketched out on paper if they are too difficult to bring back to the classroom, but encourage them to try to bring back as many as possible

Group One: Measurement Search

Process Skills: Measuring, comparing, inferring, ordering by distance, formulating conclusions.

Procedure: Find and bring back objects that are
-as wide as your hand   -a foot long
-further away than you can throw   -waist high
-half the size of a baseball   -as long as your arm
-smaller than your little finger   -wider than four people
-thinner than a shoelace   -as wide as your nose
If an item is too big, just report about it.

Group Two: Shape Search

Process skills: Comparing shapes, recognizing patterns, recording data.

Procedure: Find and bring back as many objects as you can that have the following shapes. Record them in your notebook.
-triangle   -rectangle
-circle   -hexagon

-square	-oval
-diamond	-other geometric shapes

Group Three: Number Pattern Search

Process skills: Comparing number, shape, and patterns; recording data.

Procedure: Find objects that show number patterns. For example, a three-leaf clover matches the number pattern three.

Group Four: Texture Search

Process skills: Observing, collecting, classifying, recording data, comparing, labeling.

Procedures: Find as many objects as you can that have the following characteristics:

-smooth	-bumpy
-furry	-rough
-sharp	-soft
-wet	-grooved/ridges
-grainy	-hard

Evaluation: When students return, have them arrange their objects in some type of order or classification. Using a graphing program on the computer or colored paper, scissors, and markers, have them visually represent their results in some way (bar graph, for example).

Boxes Revealing Identity (Middle School)

Description: Just what do we mean when we talk about identity? This activity tries to answer that question. Identity is your personality, friends, family, talents and abilities, the place you live now, and the place from which you came. It's the thing that makes you proud: your clothes, music, works of art, writings, photos, books, memories, and hopes for the future. This activity is designed to awaken students to the value of themselves, and to share and communicate who and what they are.

Process Skills: Communicating, analyzing, discovering relationships, solving problems, collecting data, testing predictions, constructing, valuing, and reflecting.

Objectives:
1. Students will define and discover what identity means for them.
2. Students will create autobiographies in small rectangular boxes with hinged lids (a shoe box is a good example).

3. Through writing exercises, timelines, and visual webs of important things in their lives, students will gather artifacts to put in their boxes.
4. Students will display their boxes in a class gallery exhibit and share their feelings.
5. Through drawings and writing, the students will not only respond to their own boxes, but also reflect upon what they learned about others.

Planning Group: Members should arrange the classroom and materials.

Procedures:
1. Collect as many objects as you can that reveal your identity.
2. Construct a timeline or visual map of important things in your life.
3. Gather artifacts (pictures, maps of important places, toys, hobbies, sports memorabilia, baby teeth, lucky rocks, etc.) to put in your box.
4. Use brightly colored paper, "glitz" from silver and gold contact paper, small mirrors, colored pencils, and markers to add excitement.
5. Create your autobiographies and express your ideas/feelings in writing.
6. Construct your project.

Evaluation: Through drawing and writing, have students respond to their own boxes and reflect upon what they learned from others. Students display and present their projects.

Measuring Sticks (Middle School)

Process Skills: Observing, inferring, communicating [sharing], and comparing.

Description: Oftentimes, elementary and middle school students are quick to compare and criticize others. This activity stresses similarities and attempts to play down differences. The method used in this activity is creative drama. Creative dramatics involves children in group interaction. It is especially useful for reaching out to ESL (English as a second language) learners, allowing them to work with other students while developing oral language. Creative dramatics is a drama for the actors themselves—connecting their feelings and attitudes with reading, literature, and other language skills.

In recent years, teachers have become interested in finding ways to bring students' values and moral decisions into their classrooms. Activities drawn from these areas involve and motivate youth partly because they focus on issues that students really care about. Students are particularly stimulated by questions that deal with their own values, such as: Who am I? What do I care about? How am I perceived by others? How might I change? What kinds of things do other people think important?

Values and morality activities can be taken from newspapers, personal experiences, or books. The skills of using language, valuing, recording, gathering data, and sharing ideas are all part of the foundation of the communication goal explored here.

Moral Development Activity: Laura's Dilemma

Laura and her best friend, Vicki, walked into a department store to shop around. As they looked around, Vicki saw a bathing suit she really liked and told Laura she wanted to try it on. While Vicki went to the dressing room, Laura continued to shop.

After a short time, Vicki came out of the dressing room fully dressed. She caught Laura's attention and, without a word, turned and walked out of the store. Moments later, the store security officer, the store manager, and the store clerk approached Laura. "That's her, that's one of the girls. I know her friend walked off with a new bathing suit under her clothes," the clerk said. "I think they planned this together."

The security officer asked the manager if he wanted to follow through on the case. "Absolutely," he insisted. "Shoplifting is costing us a lot." The security officer turned to Laura. "What's the name of the girl you were with?" he asked. Laura looked at him silently. "Come on now, tell the truth," said the security officer. "If you don't tell us, you'll be aiding the person who committed the crime, and that's a crime, too." Should Laura tell? Why or why not?

Objectives:
1. Students will describe and become familiar with the issues.
2. Students will take a position on the dilemma issue.
3. Students will present an argument based on their position.
4. Students will plan their debate strategies with their group.
5. Students will demonstrate ability to work in groups in an organized and productive manner.
6. Students will actively participate in the debate.

Process Skills: Communicating, analyzing, solving problems, collecting data, and reflecting.

Procedures:
1. Introduce students to moral reasoning by asking them to think about times when they weren't sure what would be the right thing to do.
2. Students will show their understanding of the issue (dilemma) by discussing, reading it aloud, or acting it out.
3. Students will divide into small groups, making sure that each group has roughly equal numbers on both sides of the issue.

4. Students will discuss the issue within their small group and plan their debate strategies for the group.

5. In small groups, students will prepare a list of reasons that support their group position. For example, students who say "turn Laura in" in *Laura's Dilemma* would form a group and come up with the best reasons for turning Laura in, and the students who say "keep quiet" would meet to come up with reasons to support their position. (In a 30-student class, the teacher might have five groups of six students—two groups figuring out the best reasons to tell and three groups coming up with the best reasons for not telling.)

6. Students will conduct their debates for the class based on their position.

7. A class discussion of the reasons would come at the end. When the discussion is completed, the teacher may wish to share his/her opinion.

Evaluation: Encourage students to reflect on this activity by putting their ideas in writing.

Some suggestions follow. Working in groups, choose one evaluation activity:

Write an article for your class newspaper.

Write a letter to students in other classes, suggesting issues for debate.

Make a video of the outstanding debate in your class.

Leaf Exchange

The falling motions of a leaf are very complex.
Sometimes the leaf may drift randomly to the right or left as it falls.
At other times it may tumble erratically while maintaining a downward
course . . . suggesting its motion is chaotic.

—(Petersen, 1994)

With the dramatically colorful fall season, it seems like an ideal time to set up a leaf exchange with students in other regions of the country. If it's not fall—or everything stays green all year—the shapes of leaves can also be quite interesting. Students are naturally captivated with gathering, comparing, and preserving leaves. This activity gets students involved in collecting and gathering many different types of leaves; they examine, sort, classify, investigate, and discover patterns.

Leaf exchange is a class-to-class leaf exchange similar to pen pals. Leaf exchanges get everyone interested and active—from collecting and classifying leaves into a range of sizes, shapes, and textures, to observing similarities and differences in leaves. Students learn to appreciate the value of exchanging data and gain experience in communicating with students in another region of the country. Student awareness is heightened to the wide variety of plants and trees in their own environment. A class map is, then, set up to track the journeys of their leaves.

Description: Communicating at a personal level for elementary and middle school students can be very rewarding and exciting.

Process Skills: Gathering, identifying data, communicating, exploring preserving methods, comparing, graphing, and sharing.

Objectives:
1. Students will collect and gather leaves.
2. Students will choose a leaf exchange partner.
3. Students will sort, classify, and discover patterns.
4. Students will participate in preserving the leaves they gathered.
5. Students will improve their observation skills and increase their awareness of the plants in their environment.
6. Students as leaf pals will learn how their environment compares with others.
7. Students will learn to appreciate the value of exchanging data.

Planning Group: Members should arrange the classroom and materials.

Procedures:
1. Introduce students to leaf exchange, a class-to-class leaf exchange similar to pen pals. Explain that they are going to take part as a class exchanging preserved leaves with students in another area of the country.
2. The first step in this project is to gather leaves for the exchange. Have students bring in leaves from their neighborhoods. Or, take students on a nature walk.
3. Students are to collect at least ten different leaves.
4. When returning to the classroom, focus students' attention on the leaves' colors, shapes, and sizes.
5. Most students will want to identify the leaves. Using reference materials (slides, computer disks, prints, etc.) have students label each leaf.
6. Preserve the leaves. There are several methods for preserving leaves:
   - Press/dry method. Place the leaves in an old telephone book, newspaper or magazines. Apply bricks or weights on top (to permanently preserve use a laminating process).
   - Quick iron method. Preheat iron to permanent press setting. Place a thin sheet of cardboard on the ironing board.
     Cut two pieces of wax paper that are larger than the leaf to be pressed. Lay one piece of wax paper on top of the cardboard,

place the leaf on top of the wax paper, and put the second piece of wax paper on top of the leaf.

Cover the wax paper with a cotton rag, and then press each part of the leaf with the iron for at least twenty seconds.

Remove the rag, cool the leaf for about two minutes, and carefully peel the wax paper from the leaf.

- Using glycerin. Materials: 1.5 L water, 750 mL glycerin (available at drug store), a 500 mL measuring cup, newspaper, a shallow pan. (You will have enough room in the pan to preserve about 70 leaves. The remaining solution can be saved.)

Mix the glycerin and water in the pan.

Place the leaves in the solution, making sure that each leaf is completely coated, and that the students are wearing aprons and goggles.

Soak the leaves in the solution for twenty-four hours.

The next day, remove the leaves and press each one between newspapers for three days or until completely dry.

These pressed leaves will be flattened making them easier to mail.

7. Lamination. If teachers have access to laminating equipment, they can preserve leaves for many years:

Dry and press leaves using one of the drying methods, make sure leaves are dry.

Follow laminating machine directions.

Insert the leaves like a flat piece of paper.

Trim the lamination film around the leaf.

8. Before packaging the leaves, have students compose a letter to their leaf partner describing the leaves and why they chose to send them.

Evaluation: Have students make a wall map charting where their leaves were sent. Research the vegetation of the areas, and do a comparison analysis. Put the data into the computer. (This activity was adapted from M. Shelton's article in *Science and Children,* 1994.)

Exploring Supports (Preschool, Primary Students)

Description: There are many kinds of structures that can be described in the natural world. This beginning activity attempts to show how different kinds of structures are related. In this activity, children will find out about supports. The skills introduced include experimenting, testing strength and durability, comparing size and weight, recording data, and communicating. Introduce the activity by talking about structures, the classroom, and tables in the room. Generate questions, such as: What makes the ceiling stay where it is? What keeps the table from falling? Children will soon come up with the idea of structural support. The walls of the classroom and the ceiling supports hold the ceiling up and the legs on the table keep it from falling. Discuss these ideas with the class. Explain that the name we give to these items is structural support.

Process Skills: Measuring, comparing, inferring, ordering by distance, formulating conclusions.

Planning Group: Members should arrange the classroom and materials.

Materials: Give each of the children some items to form a tower (a cardboard box, a tall block of wood, a paper towel roll, for example). Provide them with the following support materials: styrofoam, wood, cartons, slitted cardboard boxes, and so on; supply some clay, sand, and white glue. Include the following art materials: paints, brushes, construction paper, scissors, paste, and felt pens.

Objectives:
1. When presented with a problem of how to support their tower, children will explore with materials.
2. Children will discuss and share their discoveries with other class members after experimenting and trying many different support structures.
3. Children will compare their tower supports with other children.
4. Students will test the strength of their tower.
5. Students will modify their support structure by adding a balcony.
6. Children will decorate their towers.
7. Children will present their investigation by answering these questions:
   Describe how your tower and balcony are supported.
   Show how much weight your balcony holds.
   Explain how you made your supports.

Procedures:
1. Challenge the students to find a way to make their tower stand up so that it cannot be blown over by a strong wind.
2. Helpful ideas for getting started:
   Glue supports around the base of the tower.
   Fill a box with sand.
   Attach the base to a larger surface.
   Set the tower in sand or clay.
3. After children have determined a way to support their towers, have them share what they found out.
4. Children can compare their solutions and test their towers to see how strong they really are. For example, children may decide to test their tower by having six or more students blow on it at once. Or, they could place a fan near their tower to see if it continues to stand up.

5. Encourage students to experiment further with different supports to make their towers as sturdy as they can be.
6. Have children decorate their towers with the art supplies provided.

Evaluation: To find out how much they learned about supports, present students with another challenge. Using any of the materials, can you construct a balcony? Then, test it by adding weights. How many weights (if any) will your balcony hold? Add more and more weights until it begins to show signs of collapsing.

(This activity was adapted from Joan Westley's *Constructions*, 1988.)

Magnets Attraction (Elementary Students)

Description: Given a group of materials and a magnet, groups of students will predict and then test whether the objects will be/are attracted to the magnet. Students will record their findings and hypothesize (or "guess") why some objects are attracted while others are not.

Process Skills: Describing, predicting, experimenting, forming hypotheses, testing predictions, recording data, inferring, and recognizing cause and effect relationships.

Planning Group: Members should arrange the classroom and materials.

Background Information: Before conducting this activity, students should vaguely know what a magnet is, that it attracts (or sticks to) certain objects. Magnets only attract certain objects. Not all objects made of metal are attracted to the magnet. Objects made of iron or steel are attracted to the magnet.

Materials: Sack or brown bag (to hold objects to test), magnet (large enough for students to handle with ease), paper or notebook.

Approximately 20 objects (about half of which will be attracted to the magnet). Examples of objects:

-tacks	-nails	-rubber bands	-pieces of sponge
-paper clips	-pins	-pebbles	-chalk
-needles	-coins	-wood	-paper
-pencils	-copper	-glass	-plastic
-screws	-aluminum	-cloth	-leather

Objectives:
1. Students will predict which objects are magnetic.
2. Student will test the objects they have identified as magnetic.
3. Students will record their findings in their journals.
4. Groups will then review and discuss their findings with the class, sharing their discoveries and comparing with other groups.

5. Students will actively participate in their groups. Each student will learn that magnets attract only certain metal objects—iron and steel.

Procedures:
  1. Divide students into groups of three, four, or five.
  2. Present this problem to the class: Which of these objects are magnetic?
  3. Assign jobs or have students determine jobs themselves: supply getter, record keeper, object displayer (from bag), and clean up person.
  4. Before letting students get their supplies, explain to students that each group will be given a magnet and a bag of objects.
  5. Students will view their objects one at a time, make a prediction as to whether it will be attracted to the magnet, and then test the object. Both predictions and results should be recorded in their notebooks.
  6. After the objects have been tested, students should review and discuss their findings, and answer the following questions:
     What do the objects that were attracted to the magnet have in common?
     What do the objects that were not attracted have in common?
     What can you conclude from your investigation?
  7. Groups of students will see how many objects they can find in the classroom that are attracted to their magnets.
  8. Students will keep a list of all the things that are attracted to their group's magnet.
  9. Students will share their group's findings with the class.
  10. Students will compare and discuss what other groups found out.

Evaluation: Group written work along with oral discussion will provide feedback as to whether students are understanding the concept of magnetism. Direct students to write what they learned about magnetism. Have them reflect on their group's process, expressing their knowledge as well as their impressions about this "magical" thing called magnetism. (Contributed by Kerry Twohy.)

SUMMARY AND CONCLUSION

Math and science inquiry processes are considered tools for helping students gather and discover data for themselves and use that data to solve problems. Such experiences can encourage students who struggle with math and science to feel the power of creating their own knowledge. Here, we have outlined observing, classifying, inferring, measuring, comparing, sequencing, communicating, predicting, recording, investigating, and experimenting. To learn these processes, students investigate a variety of subject-matter contexts with concrete materials. Teachers can cultivate the quality of their students' mathematical and scientific thinking. They can also guide student thinking with questions throughout each process.

In *observing*, students learn to use all of their senses, note similarities and differences in objects, and become aware of changes. In *classifying*, students group things by properties or functions; they may also arrange them in some sense of order. *Sequencing* is part of this ordering system. *Measuring* teaches students to find or estimate quantity. Measurement is often applied in combination with skills in an integrated math and science program. *Communicating* involves students in organizing information in some clear form that other people can understand. *Recording, graphing,* and *using maps, tables,* and *charts* contribute to the communication process. The skill of *inferring* requires students to interpret or explain their observations. When students infer from data what they think will happen, often the term *predicting* is used.

Math and science processes are often called inquiry skills because they are the searching questions designed to find out about the world. The most challenging process, one that usually takes place with students in fourth grade and up, is *experimentation*. It is divided into the following subskills: forming hypotheses, identifying variables, collecting data, analyzing data, and explaining outcomes. Math and science experiences become meaningful for struggling elementary and middle school students when they understand the inquiry processes and are able to apply them.

The national standards for mathematics and science make a strong case for teaching content through inquiry (National Research Council, 1996). The standards make it clear that inquiry is more than hands-on investigations and problem solving. It involves developing abilities (skills) and understandings (meaningful ideas). Although they don't recommend a single method of teaching, the standards do emphasize inquiry and suggest using various collaborative strategies.

It is important that teachers individually and collectively value struggling students and challenge them to reach their full potential. Faced with students who are not interested in school, it sometimes too easy to blame the home environment, the students themselves, or last year's teachers. But whatever the reason for disaffection or learning difficulties, it is the teachers' responsibility to do everything they can to motivate their students.

By taking a collaborative approach to inquiry, teachers can provide reluctant learners with opportunities for directly examining and applying the process skills of math and science. Students, especially those who are struggling, profit from working in small groups to learn how math and science applications relate to problems and situations found in daily life. Better yet, the level of skill and the depth of understanding increase as struggling students repeatedly engage in inquiry (Campbell & Fulton, 2003).

In the future, students studying math and science will spend more time involved with collaborative inquiry. Teachers will guide explorations, help students become active learners, and spend less time lecturing the entire class. This approach stems from the notion that education at its best is personal, purposeful, collaborative, and intrinsically motivating. As students form active learning teams and communicate more freely, they will teach one another and extend their inquiry (discoveries) to the real world. For teachers today, a major task is creating classrooms that recognize students as thinkers, doers, active investigators, and cooperative problem solvers.

> . . . *the student is not a bench-bound listener, but should be actively involved in the learning process.*
>
> —Jerome Bruner

QUESTIONS FOR TEACHERS AND PROSPECTIVE TEACHERS

1. Have a struggling student formulate four or five questions about a topic they would like to investigate.
2. For each question, select resources the struggling student could consult, such as books and other media, places, people, and additional sources of information.
3. Pair a slow learner with a regular learner, and have both students begin their search collaboratively. Record the processes of their inquiry. What difficulties did they encounter? How did you assist?
4. Encourage students to reflect on their participation in the planning group.

REFERENCES AND RESOURCES

Adams, D. & Hamm, M. (1995). *New designs for teaching and learning: promoting active learning in tomorrow's schools.* San Francisco, CA: Jossey-Bass.

Bruner, J. (1986). *Actual minds, possible worlds.* Cambridge, MA: Harvard University Press.

Campbell, B. & Fulton, L. (2003). *Science notebooks: Writing about inquiry.* Arlington, VA: National Science Teachers Association.

Carin, A., Bass, J., & Contant, T. (2005). *Methods for teaching science as inquiry.* Upper Saddle River, NJ: Pearson Education Ltd.

Etheredge, S. & Rudnitsky, A. (2003). *Introducing students to scientific inquiry: How do we know what we know.* Boston, MA: Allyn & Bacon.

Hammerman, E. (2005). *Eight essentials of inquiry-based science, K-8.* Thousand Oaks, CA: Corwin Press.

Karp, K. & Howell, P. (2004). Building responsibility for learning in students with special needs. *Teaching Children Mathematics, 11*(3), 118–125.

Katter, E. (1994). Art and identity: in search of self and connections with others. *School Arts,* Sept. 1994 (1), 8.

Llewellyn, D. (2005). *Making inquiry second nature to students: Teaching high school science through inquiry.* Arlington, VA: National Science Teachers Association.

Martin, R., Sexton, C., Franklin, T., & Gerlovich, J. (2004). *Teaching science for all children: Inquiry methods for constructing understanding (with "video explorations" video workshop CD-ROM).* Boston, MA: Allyn Bacon.

Martinello, M. & Cook, G. (1994). *Interdisciplinary inquiry in teaching and learning.* New York: Macmillan.

National Council of Teachers of Mathematics (NCTM). (2001). *Principles and standards for school mathematics.* Reston, VA: NCTM.

Peters, J. M. & Stout, D. L. (2005). *Concepts and inquiries for teaching elementary school science.* 5th ed. Upper Saddle River, NJ: Prentice Hall.

Peterson, I. (1994). Catching the flutter of a falling leaf. *Science News.* J. Miller, B. Potter (eds.) Washington, DC: Science Service Publication.

Rezba, R., Sprague, C., & Fiel, R. (2003). *Learning and assessing science process skills. Grades 5–8.* 4th ed. Arlington, VA: National Science Teachers Association.

Rhoton, J. & Bowers, P. (2001). *Professional development leadership and the diverse learner.* Arlington, VA: National Science Teachers Association.

Shelton, M. (1994). Leaf Pals. *Science and children, 32*(1), 37–39.

Strickland, D., Ganske, K., & Monroe, J. (2002). *Supporting struggling readers and writers: Strategies for classroom intervention 3-6.* Portland, ME: Stenhouse.

Thorp, L. (2005). *The pull of the earth: Participatory ethnography in the school garden (Crossroads in qualitative inquiry).* Lanham, MD: Alta Mira Press.

Tomlinson, C. (1999). *The differentiated classroom: Responding to the needs of all learners.* Alexandria, VA: Association for Supervision and Curriculum Development.

Van de Walle, J. & Lovin, L. (2006). *Teaching student-centered mathematics.* Boston, MA: Allyn & Bacon.

VanSciver, J. (2005). Motherhood, apple pie, and differentiated instruction. *Phi Delta Kappan, 86*(7), 534–535.

Westley, J. (1988). *Constructions,* Sunnyvale, CA: Creative Publications.

3

Collaborative Learning

The Advantages of Small Learning Groups

There is much we can do alone.
But together we can do so much more.

—Lev S. Vygotsky

Collaborative learning builds on what we know about how students construct knowledge. It does this by promoting active learning in a way not possible with competitive or individualized learning models. When it comes to collaborative math and science instruction, the teacher organizes major parts of the curriculum around tasks, problems, and projects so that students can work together in mixed-ability groups. Lessons are designed with learning teams in mind so that students can combine their energies as they work toward a common goal (Lapp et al., 2004).

In one form or another, collaborative learning is one of the more important instructional tools to come along in the last twenty years. It rests on a solid data base of research and practical experience (Langer, Colton, & Goff, 2003). This chapter will

- Introduce you to collaborative learning and the power of teamwork.
- Explore the benefits of collaborative learning for struggling students.
- Help teachers design math and science lessons that foster teamwork.
- Offer collaborative strategies designed to help struggling learners succeed.

Like the standards, we purposely avoid the debate surrounding comparisons with cooperative learning. Both the math and the science standards recommend certain elements of collaborative learning for reaching a diverse group of students. And that is the focus here.

Collaborative learning is an educational approach that encourages students at various skill levels to work together, in small groups, to reach common goals. The basic idea is to move students from working alone to working in learning groups where they take responsibility for themselves and other group members. Although the group "sinks or swims" together, individuals are held accountable because students receive information and feedback from peers and from their teacher. As they cooperate on math and science tasks, it is our view that students move toward becoming a community of learners as they work together to enhance everyone's knowledge, proficiency, and enjoyment (Thousand, Villa, & Nevin, 2002).

COLLABORATION AS AN APPROACH TO LEARNING

Collaborative learning is both a personal teaching philosophy and a classroom technique. In the collaborative classroom, there is for respect individual group members' abilities and contributions. There is also a sharing of authority and acceptance of responsibility among group members for the group actions. The underlying message is based upon consensus building through cooperation by group members. Practitioners apply this philosophy in the classroom, with community groups, and generally, as a way of living with and communicating with other people. The collaborative learning model allows students some say in forming friendships and interest groups (Johnson et al., 2005). We often have the students turn in a confidential list of the four people that they would most like to work with. And we make the final choices.

The content standards in mathematics and science recommend having students collaborate as they go about doing some of their schoolwork. In addition, student talk is stressed as a way of working things out among group members (NCTM, 2000; National Research Council, 1996). What's missing from the standards are specific activities and organizational techniques for making collaborative groups work in the classroom. Here we try to correct the imbalance between theory and practice by giving you a selection of easy-to-use collaborative group activities for teaching struggling students in math and science. Along the way, suggestions are made for arranging your classroom in a way that most effectively puts collaborative learning to work for you and your students.

Collaborative learning builds on what teachers know about how students construct knowledge, promoting active learning in a way not possible with competitive or with individualized learning. In a cooperative classroom, the teacher organizes major parts of the curriculum around tasks, problems, and projects that students can work through in small mixed-ability groups.

Lessons are designed around active learning teams so that students can combine energies as they reach toward a common goal. If someone else does well, you do well. Social skills, like interpersonal communication, group interaction, and conflict resolution are developed as the collaborative learning process goes along. After each lesson, the learning group examines what they did well and what they might be able to do better (social processing). Many new math and science programs are using collaborative learning without making an issue of it; it is simply a part of a well-planned curriculum.

The following points are standards-driven and supported by the research. Collaborative learning

- Motivates students who are having difficulties with math and science. Students talk and work together on a project or problem and experience the fun of sharing ideas and information.
- Increases academic performance of students who are falling behind. Classroom interaction with others causes students to make significant learning gains compared to students in traditional settings.
- Encourages active listening for disinterested students. Students learn more when they are actively engaged in discovery and problem solving. Collaboration sparks an alertness of mind not achieved in passive listening.
- Promotes literacy and language skills. Group work offers students many opportunities to use and improve speaking skills. This is particularly important for second-language learners.
- Provides greater psychological health for frustrated learners. Collaborative learning gives students a sense of self-esteem, builds self-identity, and aids in their ability to cope with stress and adversity. It links individuals to group success, so that students are supported, encouraged, and held responsible individually and collectively.
- Helps prepare students for today's society. Team approaches to solving problems, combining energies with others, and working to get along are valued skills in the world of work, community, and leisure.
- Increases respect for diversity. Students who work together in mixed-ability groups are more likely to select mixed racial and ethnic friendships. When students cooperate to reach a common goal, they learn to appreciate and respect each other, from those who are physically handicapped to those who are mentally and physically gifted.
- Improves teacher effectiveness with struggling learners. Through actively engaging students in the learning process, teachers also make important discoveries about their students' learning. As students take

some of the teaching responsibilities, the power of the teacher can be multiplied (Slavin, 1990; Bess, 2000; Thousand, Villa, & Nevin, 2002).

SOME SUGGESTIONS FOR ARRANGING THE COLLABORATIVE CLASSROOM

In schools across the country, teachers are spending less time in front of the class and more time encouraging students to work together in small groups. Straight rows are giving way to pods of three, four, or five desks. Of course, collaborative learning is more than rearranging desks. It involves changing how students interact with one another and designing lessons so that teamwork is required to complete assigned tasks. In the collaborative classroom, group learning tasks are based on shared goals and outcomes. Teachers structure lessons so that to complete a project or activity, individuals have to work together to accomplish group goals. At the same time, they help students learn teamwork skills like staying with the group, encouraging participation, elaborating on ideas, and providing critical analysis.

One of the keys to success is building a sense of cooperation in the classroom. Teachers often start by providing the class with a collaborative activity. The second step is to have groups of three or four students work together on an initial exploration of ideas and information. To encourage group interdependence, teachers can use a small group version of a strategy like K-W-H-L-S.

- What do we know?
- What do we want to learn?
- How I will work with others to learn it?
- What have I learned?
- How have I shared what I learned from others?

We suggest that teachers give time for individual and group reflection in the last phase of any collaborative learning activity. This way, struggling learners can analyze what they have learned and identify strengths and weaknesses in the group learning process. Questions like "what would help us work better together next time" and "how did you contribute to the quality of the group work" also help in this social processing stage. Teachers might go on to have student groups engage in activities to reshape their knowledge or information by organizing, clarifying, and elaborating on what has been learned. It's often a good idea to ask student groups to present their findings before an interested and critical audience.

Besides encouraging a sense of group purpose, teachers need to help each student feel that he or she can contribute actively and effectively to class activities. The group may sink or swim together, but individuals are still held accountable for the understanding the material. In the collaborative classroom, teachers do more than set standards for group work. They use various assessment tools to evaluate group projects, assignments, and teamwork skills. To get at individual accountability, consider randomly quizzing group members after group work is completed. Whether or not you decide on interrupting the group is one thing, but providing for some form of individual assessment is a basic requirement.

COLLABORATIVE LEARNING IN THE INTEGRATED EDUCATION CLASSROOM

Collaborative learning has been cited as an instructional strategy that can connect a wide range of struggling students to the regular classroom routines (Slavin, 1990; Correia & McHenry, 2002). It has become popular because of its potential for motivating and academically engaging all students within a social setting.

Inclusion used to refer to educating students with special problems and their peers in the regular classroom. A new vision is replacing inclusion called "integrated education" where specific adaptations and strategies are used to improve the learning of all students (Sailor & Blair, 2005). These students can be those with mild to severe emotional or physical problems, general education students, non-English-speaking students, gifted learners, and so forth. Three decades of inclusive education have produced a great number of teaching adaptations and approaches to enhance learning.

Today, "no child left behind" encourages us to teach all students to the highest possible standards and offers an opportunity to achieve the path to integration. Of course, it is difficult to arrange educational policy around a single policy—especially one that may change with the political winds. We suggest that a variety of approaches and a wide range of educational research are needed to determine what works best in certain situations.

Mounting evidence suggests that integrated applications can provide positive outcomes for all students (Sailor & Blair, 2005). It requires the combined talents of the regular classroom teacher and those of the special educator as well as the related service providers (Giangreco & Doyle, 2002).

An integrated educational model called the schoolwide applications model (SAM) is being implemented is some schools today. It is intended to engage schools in a collaborative team decision that is focused on improving academic and social outcomes for all students (Sailor & Blair, 2004). This approach is a work in progress. It represents an effort to join all aspects of school reform with a new and innovative approach to the delivery of education support and services and has established a solid foundation for the adoption of this approach attending to the diverse learning needs of students. It is hoped that the integrated education program will receive additional manpower and funding for its implementation in the years ahead (Education and Manpower Bureau, 2005).

THE ADVANTAGES OF COLLABORATIVE LEARNING

Understanding the important role that collaboration plays in the process of integrated education provides a way to look at the benefits of collaboration.

1. Each person brings experiences to the collaborative process that are shared with others.
2. Support is provided for the classroom teacher.
3. Realistic expectations are determined.
4. Classroom teachers are given support for making modifications.
5. Students can be successful when appropriate modifications are made.
6. Teachers become part of a team in dealing with learning and behavior problems (Murphy, 2003).

It is frequently the case that when a student with disabilities is included in the regular classroom, the assumption is made that he or she is there for academic reasons. The reality is that he or she is there to learn. The regular classroom provides a wealth of opportunities for learning.

APPLYING THE POWER OF COLLABORATIVE LEARNING

By engaging students in the process of making sense of what they are studying, children have more power to explore freely and meaningfully connect to the subject. In a collaborative environment, the teacher assists children in the construction of meaning and acts more like a facilitator and less like a transmitter of knowledge. When questions that connect to student experience are raised collectively, ideas and strengths can be shared in a manner that supports the cooperative search for understanding.

A supportive team structure leads to greater productivity for all students. To be successful, each child needs to be held responsible for doing a fair share of the group work. At their best, cooperative groups go beyond individual learning to promote an informal style of question asking, critical thinking, and action plans for all students. Critical analysis and creative problem solving are a natural part of this active learning process.

Some common characteristics of collaborative groups are that the small group of students share learning tasks and outcomes and positive group collaboration is developed by setting mutual goals by the teacher and the students. When this is achieved, there is a group task commitment and individual accountability. Group learning thrives in an atmosphere of mutual helpfulness where students know what's happening—and why. Part of creating the right environment means having the teacher define objectives, talk about the benefits of collaborative learning, and explain expectations and behaviors such as brainstorming, peer teaching, and confidence building.

PROMOTING ACTIVE LEARNING

Whether finding out about new concepts, solving problems, or questioning factual information, a collaborative approach has shown that it helps develop academic skills. At the same time, it taps students' self-esteem and builds students' understanding and attitudes about the subject. Working together to accomplish shared goals is the key to collaborative learning. Academic success, future employment, and even everyday life demand the ability to sort through information, educate others, make sound judgments, and work as a team. Learning to work with others, persevering, solving problems, and dealing collectively with a rapidly changing world are all part of the challenges facing today's students.

Struggling learners often face a difficult challenge in trying to keep up with today's classroom activities. The key to assisting students is to identify who is going to have trouble early on and provide a number of ways for students who are at risk to receive support. For example, early intervention programs can provide intensive support at the onset of a child's school career. There is growing evidence that such programs can also prevent problems from occurring in later years (Illinois State Board of Education, 2000).

TEAMWORK SKILLS

No matter how you view collaborative student teamwork, there are many common principles. Instruction is not viewed as something that isolated students should have done to them; learning is something done best in association with others (Bess, 2000). The social context matters. And the way different communications are authored or coauthored affect the understanding, reception, and production of information and knowledge.

Teamwork skills do not develop automatically. They must be taught. As group members work together to produce joint work projects, teachers need to quietly help students having problems promote each other's success through sharing, explaining, and encouraging. Teachers may not be on center stage all the time, but with collaborative learning they constantly guide, challenge, and encourage students. They can also help build supportive group environments by explaining collaborative procedures to students, monitoring small group questions, and helping students assess group effectiveness at the end of an activity (Newbridge Educational Publishing, 2000).

Crafting group work that supports learning for all students requires content and activities that supports cohesive small groups and meets the needs of individuals. Some teachers use some form of collaborative learning in pairs or groups of three or four students about half of the time. Others may set aside less time for cooperative group work. However you set it up, collaborative learning can help your students move beyond competitive and individualistic goal structures.

As individuals within a group come to care about one another, they become more inclined to provide each other with academic assistance and personal support (Lapp et al., 2004). They are also more likely to make suggestions for what might be done to improve group efforts in the future. As each person adds their unique spirit, the cooperative group takes on enough power to illuminate the consequences of alternative courses of action. It sometimes takes a little time to get cooperative groups up to speed, but it's worth the effort.

MAKING COLLABORATIVE LEARNING WORK

Like anything else, the ability of the teacher is the key to successfully using collaborative learning. By arousing interest and broadening horizons, teachers can amplify the joy and curiosity that are natural parts of the teaching and learning process. For these things to happen, teachers must be masters of content and equally familiar with the characteristics of effective interactive instruction (NCTM, 2000; National Research Council, 1996).

Getting collaborative learning to work for you requires more than giving well-meaning instructions to "work together" and "be a team." Not all groups are collaborative. To structure lessons so that students do work collaboratively with each other requires an understanding of what makes collaboration work.

An important part of collaboration is structuring an environment where group members understand they are connected with each other in a way that one student cannot succeed unless everyone succeeds (your success benefits me and my success benefits you). Group goals and tasks must be designed and carefully communicated so that students believe they share a common fate (we all sink or swim together in this class). When the team is solidly structured, it tells students that each member has a unique contribution to make to the joint effort (we cannot do it without you). This creates a commitment to the success of the group as well as the individual student. No group member has all the information or all the skills. Even the least able student can recognize this (Garmston & Wellman, 2000).

Teaching Suggestions for Using Collaborative Learning

The following suggestions can be used to facilitate collaborative learning:

- Use your existing lessons, content, and curricula and structure them in cooperative groups. Take any lesson in any subject area with a student of any age and structure it collaboratively.
- Tailor collaborative learning lessons to your unique instructional needs. This may mean that you may need to provide additional time for planning.
- Diagnose the problems some students may have in working together and intervene to increase the effectiveness of the group process.
- Teach students the skills they need to work in groups. Social skills do not magically appear when collaborative lessons are employed. Skills such as "use quiet voices," "stay with your group," "take turns," and "use each other's names" are the beginning collaborative skills.
- It is important to have students discuss how well their group is doing. Groups should describe what worked well and what was harmful in their team efforts. Continuous improvement of the collaborative learning process results from careful analysis of how members are working together (Damian, 2005).

Arranging the Classroom for Collaborative Learning

Effective teachers know that an important step in changing student interaction is changing the seating arrangement. Architecture and the organization of our public and private spaces strongly influence our lives at every level. The same principle applies to schools and individual classrooms. The way teachers arrange classroom space and furniture has a strong impact on how students learn. When desks are grouped in a small circle or square, or when students sit side-by-side in pairs, collaborative possibilities occur naturally. Straight rows send a very different message.

A classroom designed for student interaction makes just about anything more interesting. The way you design the interior space of your classroom helps focus visual attention. It also sets up acoustical expectations and can help control noise levels. Natural lighting, carpets, comfortable corners, occasional music, and computers that are arranged for face-to-face interaction can all help set the general feelings of well-being, enjoyment, and morale. Classroom management is actually easier if students know that they can't shout across the classroom but they can speak quietly to one, two, or three others depending on the size of the small group. Even many questions that students are used to asking the teacher can come after asking one or two peers. All students benefit from this kind of group learning situation, even the most reluctant student.

As students engage in collaborative learning, they should sit in a face-to-face learning group that is as close together as possible. The more space you can put between groups, the better. Occasionally you will want to remix the groups so that everybody gets the chance to work with a variety of class members. The physical arrangement should allow you to speak to the whole class without too much student movement. Struggling students benefit from this grouping arrangement. Teachers can give students more of their attention and better differentiate instruction. When the whole class is together, you should be able to make eye contact with every student in every group without anyone getting bent out of shape or moving desks (Joiner, Miell, Faulker, & Littleton, 2000).

Ways Teachers Can Organize for Collaborative Learning

1. Formulate objectives. Decide on the size of groups, arrange the room, and distribute the materials students need.
2. Explain the activity and the collaborative group structure.
3. Describe the behaviors you expect to see during the lesson. Group behaviors might include:
   - share ideas
   - respect others
   - ask questions
   - stay in your group
   - give encouragement
   - stay on task
   - use quiet voices
4. Assign roles. Classes new to the collaborative approach sometimes assign each member of the group a specific function that will help the group complete the assigned task. For example, the reader reads the problem, the checker makes sure that it is understood, the animator keeps it interesting and on task, and the recorder keeps track of the group work and tells the whole class about it. If you have groups of three, then everyone can share the animator's role. Struggling learners need to be included in these roles. No matter how you set up collaborative learning, group achievement depends on how well the group does and how well individuals within the group learn (Lee & Smagorinsky, 2000).
5. Monitor or intervene when needed. While you conduct the lesson, check on each learning group when needed to improve the task and teamwork. Bring closure to the lesson.

6. Evaluate the quality of student work. Ensure students that they themselves will evaluate the effectiveness of their learning groups. Have students construct a plan for improvement. Be sure that all students are on task. Groups may be evaluated based on how well members performed as a group. The group can also give individuals specific information about their contribution. Groups can keep track of who explains concepts, encourages participation, checks for understanding, and who helps organize the work.

Learning with a small circle of friends can help students navigate around the untidy clutter of doubt and strive for things that had previously exceeded their grasp. Working in community with others is the best way for struggling students to gain the confidence and the power to see what can be, but that isn't yet.

PROBLEM SOLVING IN A SOCIAL SETTING

Problem solving and collaboration are common themes that cut across the content standards and the curriculum. But learning to solve problems in school is often different than the way it happens outside of school. When they get out in the real world, students may feel lost because nobody's telling them what to solve. In real life, we are usually not confronted with a clearly stated problem with a simple solution. Often, we have to work with others to just figure out what the problem is. The same thing is true when it comes to asking and answering questions. When teachers and students can relate to other people, it can bring out the best in themselves and in others.

Knowledge is constructed over time by learners within a meaningful social setting. Students talking and working together on a project or problem experience the fun and the joy of sharing ideas and information (Thousand, Villa, & Nevin, 2001). When students construct knowledge together, they have opportunities to compare knowledge, talk it over with peers, ask questions, justify their position, confer, and arrive at a consensus. Even students who usually struggle with a project will feel a sense of belonging to the group.

Collaboration will not occur in a classroom that requires students to always raise their hands to speak. Active listening is not sitting quietly as a teacher or another student drones on. It requires spontaneous and polite interruptions where everyone has an equal chance to speak and interact. Just let others complete a thought and don't break into the conversation in midsentence. Try to get everyone to ask a question or make a comment. It may be best not to make students put their hand up first. Encourage the more talkative class members to let everyone make a contribution before they make another point. The inattentive listener may need to assume a leadership role and help monitor the discussion.

Collaborative learning will involve some change in the noise level of the classroom. Sharing and working together even in controlled environments will be louder than an environment where students work silently from textbooks. With experience, teachers learn to keep the noise constructive. Whether you are a parent or a teacher, you know that a little reasoning (regarding rules) won't hurt children. Responsible behavior needs to be developed and encouraged with consistent classroom patterns.

When collaborative problem solving is over, students need to spend time reflecting on the group work. A basic question to ask at the end: "What worked well and how might the process be improved?" Students and teachers need to be involved in evaluating learning products and the collaborative group environment.

Effective interpersonal skills are not just for a collaborative learning activity; they also benefit students in later educational pursuits and when they enter the workforce. Social interactions are fundamental to negotiating meaning and building a personal rendition of knowledge. Mixed-ability learning groups have proven effective across the curriculum. It is important to involve students in establishing rules for active group work.

Class Rules for Collaborative Learning

Rules should be kept simple and might include the following:

- Everyone is responsible for his or her own work.
- Productive talk is desired.
- Each person is responsible for his or her own behavior.
- Try to learn from others within your small group.
- Everyone must be willing to help anyone who asks.
- Ask the teacher for help if no one in the group can answer the question.

Group roles and individual responsibilities also need to be clearly defined and arranged so that each group member's contribution is unique and essential. If the learning activities require materials, students may be required to take responsibility for assembling and storing them. Avoid getting too many materials too fast. Three or four problems with materials are enough for the struggling learner. All students want to be using materials. Unlike competitive learning situations, the operative pronoun in collaborative learning is "we," not "me."

Teaching the Collaborative Group Lesson

During the initial introduction of a lesson, you can help your students understand what it is they're supposed to do by establishing guidelines on how the group work needs to be conducted. Present and review the necessary concepts or skills with the whole class and pose a part of the problem or an example of a problem for the whole class to try. Provide a lot of opportunities for your students to discuss a wide range of issues meaningful to them. Present the actual group problem after you finish the conceptual overview. Then, encourage them to discuss and clarify the problem task.

When they're ready, students start to work collaboratively to solve problems. You'll need to listen to the ideas of the different teams and offer assistance when you detect that some of them are getting stuck. You're also responsible for designing extension activities just in case the faster teams finish early. There are different ways of handling teams that are stuck. One way would be for you to help them discover what they know, so far, and then, pose a simple example, or perhaps, point out a misconception or erroneous idea that may be getting in their way.

For example, team members may have trouble getting along with each other or focusing on the one very specific task they're supposed to be doing. Pull their energies together by asking them simple questions like, "What are you supposed to be doing now?" "What is your team's task?" "How will you get organized from where you are now?" "What materials do you need?" "Do you think you have enough time to cover everything you set out to do?" "Do you know who will do what?" This is very helpful for disengaged students.

After students complete the problem task and group exploration stages, they will need to meet again as a whole class to summarize and present their findings. Each team needs to present their solutions and tell their classmates how they worked toward their resolution as a group. You or the other students in class could very well ask questions like "How did you organize the task?" "What problems did your team have?" "What method did you use?" "Was your group method effective? Why or why not?" "Did anyone have a different method or strategy for solving the same or similar problem?" "Did your team think that your solution made sense?"

Encourage your students to listen and respond to their classmates' comments. You may, in fact, point out to them that they could earn participation points in this exercise by responding precisely to their classmates' remarks and building upon them. Ask the recorder in the group to make notes on the chalkboard and write down students' responses to help summarize class data at the end of the lesson.

HELPING STRUGGLING LEARNERS SUCCEED

This section introduces classroom strategies for helping struggling students succeed in a regular classroom setting. Ten suggestions are offered from a variety of research studies from "Strategies for Helping At-Risk Students" (Snow, 2005) to "Alternative Approaches in Planning for Academic Content"(Yard & Vatterott, 1995).

A collaborative group structure allows for high levels of flexibility and creativity. One approach that has promise is the use of flexible grouping strategies essential in collaborative learning, which according to a number of studies, improves everything from achievement to self-esteem (Johnson & Johnson, 1991). Here we describe a flexible grouping strategy that can be used with students of all ability levels.

1. Assign students to flexible groups.

   Organize the class into four-student groups. One way to accomplish this is to use partner groups. Rank the class from the "most prepared" to the "least prepared" for the subject (e.g., number the students from 1 to 30). Next, divide them into subgroups (1 to 10, 11 to 20, 21 to 30) so that the groups are similar to the traditional high, middle, and low ability groups. Finally, achieve mixed grouping by assigning the top student in each of the three groups to one group, the second-highest student in each to another, the third-highest to another, and so on. You will, then, have students 1, 11, students 10, 20, and 30. In this way, the mixed groups should comprise students who are sufficiently different in ability that they can benefit from each other's help, but not so different that they find one another intimidating.

   Inform students of their group assignments, and tell them that they are partners and must help each other as needed, whether by reading each other's work before it is turned in, by answering questions regarding assignments, by showing a partner how to do something, or by discussing a story and sharing their ideas. Let them know that this is only one of many grouping arrangements that you will be using. Grouping procedures may be based on skills, levels, or interests. Collaborative groups can be based on tasks or goal achievement.

2. Focus on the needs of students.

   Students learn best when they satisfy their own motives for learning the material. Some of these motivations include the need to learn something in order to complete a particular task or activity, the need for new experiences, and the need to be involved and to interact with other people (Yard & Vatterott, 1995).

3. Make students active participants in learning.

   Students learn by doing, making things, writing, designing, creating, and solving problems. The first step is to honor the different ways that students learn (Checkley, 2005).

4. Help students set achievable goals for themselves.

   Often students fail to meet unrealistic goals. Encourage students who are struggling to focus on their continued improvement. Help students evaluate their progress by having them critically look at their work and the work of their peers.

5. Work from students' strengths and interests.

   Teachers may give students interest inventories to help them find areas where they have a special talent or interest, such as sports, art, or car mechanics. Ultimately, each student selects an area of special interest or curiosity and discusses the topic with the teacher and their peers. Then, they begin a search for more information, which may lead to a group project or a team presentation (Tomlinson & Cunningham Edison, 2003).

6. Be aware of the problems students are having.

   Meet with your students individually for a brief conference. It's helpful to tape the conversation so you have an oral explanation of their understandings. Play the tape for your student and ask questions if the student is confused.

7. Organize a conducive team-meeting environment.

   Oftentimes, students are easily distracted by the sights and sounds in the room. Choose an area of the classroom that presents the fewest distractions and keep visual displays purposeful (Snow, 2005).

8. Incorporate more time and practice for students.

   Students who are having difficulties remembering skills need small doses of increased practice throughout the day. This increases performance.

9. Provide clarity.

   Clarity is achieved by modeling and using open-ended questions so that you can adjust your approach to different students.

10. Intervene early and often.

    The key to intervention strategies are identifying students who need extra help and provide ways for struggling students to receive support (Johnson & Rudolph, 2001).

COLLABORATIVE LEARNING ACTIVITIES

A carefully balanced combination of integrated education, subject matter knowledge, knowledge of the students, instruction, self monitoring, and active group work help meet diverse needs of all students. The activities suggested here are designed to provide a collaborative vehicle for active learning in math and science.

Activity 1. Build a Square

This can be used with just about any elementary or middle school class. It relates to the geometry standard in math and the communication standard in both math and science.

Materials: An envelope containing five puzzle pieces. Either the teacher or the students can make the puzzle pieces from 3-inch squares of index cards. Cut the index cards into three pieces. Place the puzzle pieces in an envelope.

Procedures:
1. Five people around your table will all make an individual square. Each square has three pieces.
2. Each group leader opens the envelope and passes out the puzzle pieces like a deck of cards so that each person has three pieces. No one is allowed to talk or gesture during this activity.
3. Group members can pick up a piece and offer it to someone in their group. They can take it or refuse it. No reaching over and taking pieces!
4. Students raise their hands when all the exchanges have been made and all the five squares are completed. Students work together silently. They are eagerly trying to get their squares done. It is almost impossible for a struggling student to fail when the whole group is focused.

Evaluation: Next, try the activity again, only this time everyone is allowed to talk.

Take time to have a class discussion concerning the problems your group had. Suggest ideas that would make this activity work better.

Activity 2. Back-to-Back Communication

This can be used from third grade on up through middle school. It relates to the geometry and measurement standards in math and the communication standard in both math and science.

Materials: Cut out shapes that can be easily moved on a desk. Make many geometric shapes and make each shape a different color. Colored paper is the simplest material, but attribute blocks or pattern blocks can also be used.

Procedures:

1. Give each group of two people two envelopes with matching sets of shapes. Students at a beginning level should get five or six shapes. More advanced students might use a dozen or more.
2. Have children get into groups of two, seated back to back, with their envelopes in front of them.
3. Tell students one of them is the teller and the other listens and tries to follow directions exactly.
4. The teller arranges one shape at a time in a pattern. As the teller does this, he or she gives the listener exact directions—what the shape is and where to place it.
5. When the pattern is finished, have students check how well they have done.
6. Switch roles and do it again.

Evaluation: Have students explain the activity to a partner and describe what was difficult and how they did it.

Activity 3. Investigate Your Time Line

This works from third grade on up through middle school. Among other things, it relates to the measurement standard in mathematics.

Objectives:

1. Working in groups of four or five, each group makes a time line of the ages of the people in their groups and the events in their lives.
2. Students will compare the events in their lives with those of other students. (For example: "the most important event for me when I was five years old was _____.")
3. Students record and report the results.

Background Information:

A time line can show different cultural and ethnic patterns.
Students are able to see how maturity affects decisions.
A time line exercise is designed to find out how time changes students' math and science perceptions.

Materials: A 13-foot long piece of butcher paper for each group, rulers, fine point markers, and a time line prepared by the teacher to post on the board for the students to use as a model.

Procedures:

1. The teacher will explain that the students will be working in collaborative groups to make time lines of the ages and lives of the people in their groups.

2. The teacher will divide students into groups of four or five students.
3. The teacher and students will pass out the materials to each group.
4. The teacher will explain his or her model time line and give students directions for making their own time lines:

    Students will find out the ages of the people in their group: who is the oldest, next oldest, youngest, and so on.

    Students will start the time line on January first of the year that the oldest person in the group was born.

    Students will end the time line on the last day of the current year.

    Each student will use a different color marker to mark off each year.

    Each year equals one foot and an inch equals a month.

    At the bottom of each year, the students will write the important events in their lives.

    A color key with the colors of markers and each student's name will identify the student. Students can put a dot or star by the important events in their lives such as birthdays, birth of siblings, and other important events in their lives.

Evaluation: A volunteer from each group will present their group's time line and post it on the classroom bulletin board.

Activity 4. Bridge Building

This is intended for grades three through nine. It supports the measurement, geometry, and communication standards in math and the physical science and the investigation and experiment standards in science. Bridge Building is an interdisciplinary math and science activity that reinforces skills related to communication, group process, social studies, language arts, technology, and the arts.

Materials: Lots of newspaper, masking tape, one large heavy rock, and one cardboard box. Have students bring in stacks of newspaper. You will need approximately a one-foot pile of newspapers per small group.

Procedures:
- For the first part of this activity, divide students into groups of about four. Each group will be responsible for investigating one aspect of bridge building.

    Group One: Research. This group is responsible for going to the library and looking up facts about bridges, collecting pictures of all kinds of bridges, and bringing back information to be shared with the class.

    Group Two: Aesthetics, Art, Literature. This group must discover songs, books about bridges, paintings, artwork, and other items that deal with bridges.

Group Three: Measurement, Engineering. This group must discover design techniques, blueprints, angles, and measurements of actual bridge designs. If possible, visit a local bridge to look at the structural design and other features.

- Have the group representatives get together to present their findings to the class. Allow time for questions and discussion. The second part of this activity involves actual bridge construction with newspapers and masking tape.

  1. Assemble the collected stacks of newspaper, tape, the rock, and the box at the front of the room. Divide the class into groups. Each group is instructed to take a newspaper pile and several rolls of masking tape to their group. Explain that the group will be responsible for building a stand-alone bridge using only the newspapers and tape. The bridge is to be constructed so that it can support the large rock and so that the box can pass underneath.

  2. Planning is crucial. Each group is given ten minutes of planning time in which they are allowed to talk and plan together. During the planning time, they are not allowed to touch the newspapers and tape, but they are encouraged to pick up the rock and make estimates of how high the box is, make a sketch of the bridge, or assign group roles of responsibility.

  3. At the end of the planning time, students are given about fifteen minutes to build their bridge. During this time, there is no talking among the group members. They may not handle the rock or the box—only the newspapers and tape. (A few more minutes may be necessary to ensure that all groups have a chance to get their constructions to meet at least one of the two "tests"—rock or box). If a group finishes early, its members can add some artistic flourishes to their bridge or watch the building process in other groups. (With children, you may not want to stop the process until each group can pass at least one "test.")

Evaluation: Stop all groups after the allotted time. Survey the bridges with the class and allow each group to try to pass the two tests for their bridge. They get to pick which test goes first. Does the bridge support the rock? Does the box fit underneath? Discuss the design of each bridge and how they compare to the bridges researched earlier. Try taking some pictures of the completed work before you break them down and put them in a recycling bin. Awards could be given for the most creative bridge design; the sturdiest, the tallest, and the widest bridge; the best group collaboration; and so on. Remember, each group is proud of their bridge.

PROBLEM SOLVING IN COLLABORATIVE CLASSROOMS

In a classroom that values teamwork, teachers provide time for students to grapple with problems, try out strategies, discuss issues, experiment, explore, and evaluate. A key element in collaborative classrooms is group interdependence. This means that the success of each individual depends on the success of each of the other group members. Student investigations, team discussions, and group projects go hand-in-hand with preparing students for the new information, knowledge, and work arrangements that they will encounter throughout life (Langer, Colton, & Goff, 2003).

Whatever variation of collaborative inquiry a teacher chooses, students can be given opportunities to integrate their learning through interactive discovery experiences and applying their problem solving skills. Whatever the subject, it is more important to emphasize the reasoning involved in working on a problem than it is getting "the answer." Near the end of a group project, the teacher can develop more class unity by pointing out how each small group's research effort contributes to the class goal of understanding and exploring a topic.

Teachers need to model attitudes and present themselves as collaborative problem solvers and models of learning. They do this by letting students know that learning is a lifelong process for teachers and other adults. A suggestion: let them in on some of your more positive professional development experiences.

ATTITUDES CHANGE AS CHILDREN COLLABORATE

Some students may require a shift in values and attitudes if a collaborative learning environment is to succeed. The traditional school experience has taught many students that the teacher is there to validate their thinking and direct learning. Getting over years of learned helplessness may take time.

Attitudes change as students learn to work cooperatively. As they share rather than compete for recognition, struggling students find time for reflection and assessment. Small groups can write collective stories, edit each other's writing, solve problems, correct homework, prepare for tests, investigate questions, examine artifacts, work on a computer simulation, brainstorm an invention, create a sculpture, or arrange music. Working together is also a good way for students to synthesize what they have learned, collaboratively present to a small group, coauthor a written summary, or communicate concepts.

It is important that students understand that simply "telling an answer" or "doing someone's work" is not helping a classmate learn. Helping involves learning to ask the right question to help someone grasp the meaning or explaining with an example. These understandings need to be actively and clearly explained, demonstrated, and developed by the teacher.

A major benefit of collaborative inquiry is that students are provided with group stimulation and support. The small group provides safe opportunities for trial and error as well as a safe environment for asking questions or expressing opinions. More students get chances to respond, raise ideas, or ask questions. As each student brings unique strengths and experiences to the group and contributes to the group process, respect for individual differences is enhanced.

The group also acts as a motivator. We all feel a little nudge when we participate in group activities. Many times, ideas are pushed beyond what an individual would attempt or suggest on their own. Group interaction enhances idea development and students have many leadership skills when they become teachers as well as learners. In addition, the small group structure extends children's resources as they are encouraged to pool strategies and share information. If the group is small enough, it's hard for the more withdrawn students not to participate. Students soon learn that they are capable of validating their own values and ideas. This frees teachers to move about, work with small groups, and interact in a more personal manner with students.

SKILLFUL COLLABORATION AMPLIFIES LEARNING

Collaborative learning has proven itself to be an effective way to bring about change in a traditional school environment. Collaborative group problem solving, reciprocal teaching, and cross-age tutoring are now generally accepted as useful tools for helping students get the most out of any subject. By collaboratively exploring new concepts in different contexts, students can internalize mental images, perform actions, and discover underlying concepts.

To gain and share expertise, team members challenge each other's thinking in a way that doesn't breed conformity or hostility. Work teams can also be used to provide struggling students with a support network that can gradually be withdrawn as children move to higher levels of confidence. In collaborative learning, mutual achievement and caring for one another can result in learning actually becoming more personalized. Students and teachers can come to view each other as a learning community of collaborators who help group members with cognitive, emotional, physical, and social change.

LEARNING IN COMMUNITY WITH OTHERS

Knowledge is rarely constructed in isolation. At just about any age, individuals do better at building understanding when they have the help of others.

In a learning community, individuals collaborate in meaning-making activities. Community members are recognized for what they know (as well as what they need to learn). To be successful, each member of the group must learn how to contribute to the overall outcome. When the class is divided into collaborative groups, helping other team members isn't cheating: it is a highly regarded approach to learning subject matter. Such collaborative group work provides the keystone for building broader learning communities.

Increasingly, educational systems set out to develop individuals who can understand the world and are capable of working with others to alter it for the better. Teamwork skills are at (or near) the top of the job skills ladder. As teachers, it is our responsibility to prepare students to enter an increasingly international world with openness, confidence, and intelligence. Much of what we do is more implicit than explicit. So, it is as important for the classroom teacher to embody and to exhibit what we value in students.

To reach group goals, each individual must contribute in some way to the outcome. The result is the development of a kind of social cohesion that stems from students learning how to be contributing members of a learning team. Students who are struggling to learn math and science need to go beyond the lower-level basics that are often designed only to improve test scores, to experience the same high quality education that many in affluent areas take for granted. In addition to teamwork skills, a collaborative structure can help by providing group support for self-discovery, problem solving, and higher-level reasoning for all students. One of the side benefits for teachers is that positive instructional changes are most likely to occur when there is a cooperative school climate and a peer support system in place (MacGregor, et al., 2000).

In many ways, collaborative team learning becomes a useful instructional partner because it supports the kind of deep learning that shines toward the future. It is little wonder that in one form or another, cooperative group work has become one of the most widely used instructional innovations. In skillful hands, it can build on social interaction to unleash the full potential of our children's minds. As students learn to accomplish shared goals, they also learn how to get the most out of learning and life. In addition, as teachers who have experienced or implemented collaborative group learning will tell you, the habits of the mind and the emotions of the heart associated with successful peer collaboration can be like a breeze of fresh air in the classroom.

SUMMARY AND CONCLUSION

Yesterday, today, and tomorrow. Successful schools have (and will) come in many colors. But there are a few common features that cut across time and space. One of the constants is the need to create a close-knit learning community where all students care for each other. By tapping into students' natural curiosity and creating a caring learning community, teachers can help their students learn how to use collaboration to achieve academic goals. Consistent with this, we would argue, is including struggling students in daily classroom routines and teams where group accomplishment matters. Within collaborative groups, all students can build on one another's strengths to develop a sense of group solidarity and accomplishment. As they work together, learners can share alternative viewpoints, support each other's inquiry, develop critical thinking skills, and improve on their academic performance.

There are many important findings on the benefits of collaborative learning including improved motivation, increased academic performance, enhanced active listening skills, improved language and literacy skills, and a greater sense of self-esteem (Correia & McHenry, 2002). Another major benefit of collaborative learning is that individuals are provided with group stimulation and support. The learning group provides safe opportunities for trial and error—as well as a safe environment for asking questions or expressing opinions. Students also get more chances to respond, raise ideas, or ask questions. Each participant brings unique strengths and experiences to the group process. Along the collaborative way, respect for individual differences is enhanced and it becomes relatively easy to draw everyone into the group work.

When teachers build on the social nature of learning, disaffected students usually become more motivated to explore meaningful inquiry and problem solving (Arends, 2004). As students learn to cooperate and work in small mixed-ability groups, they can also take on more responsibility for themselves and helping others to learn. The dynamism of frequent and in-depth collaboration can serve as an engine of educational transformation. The process includes gradually internalizing instructional concepts through interactions with peers and adults—with individual and group reflection encouraged along the way. By building on group energy and idealism, the thinking, learning, and doing processes can be pushed forward in math, science, and just about everything else.

The age of cooperation is approaching.
Teachers and administrators are discovering an untapped resource for accelerating students' achievement: the students themselves.

—Robert Slavin

QUESTIONS FOR TEACHERS AND PROSPECTIVE TEACHERS

1. What is a real-world experience you could use to engage students in a collaborative discussion?

2. As you look over the information on underachieving students, which points do you most agree with? Provide examples.
3. This chapter offered many practical suggestions for organizing collaborative learning. With a partner, pick two and describe how you would use them to help struggling students.

REFERENCES AND RESOURCES

Arends, R. (2004). *Learning to teach.* 6th ed. New York, NY: McGraw-Hill.

Bess, J. L. (2000). *Teaching alone, teaching together: Transforming the structure of teams for teaching.* San Francisco, CA: Jossey-Bass.

Checkley, K. (2005). Resiliency and achievement: Meeting the needs of at-risk kids. *Education Update, 47*(10), October, 6–8.

Correia, M. & McHenry, J. (2002). *The mentor's handbook: Practical suggestions for collaborative reflection and analysis.* Norwood, MA: Christopher-Gordon Publishers.

Damian, C. (2005). Teaching in the standards-based classroom. Student learning groups that really work. *ENC Online.* Retrieved January 5, 2006, from http://permanent.access.gpo.gov/lps52706/Vol_8_No_2_2001.pdf

Education and Manpower Bureau. (2005). *Whole-school approach to integrated education.* Hong Kong: The Government of Hong Kong Special Administrative Region.

Garmston, R. & Wellman, B. (2000). *The adaptive school: Developing and facilitating collaborative groups.* El Dorado Hills, CA: Four Hats Seminar.

Giangreco, M. & Doyle, M. B. (2002). Students with disabilities and paraprofessional supports, benefits, balance and band-aids. *Exceptional Children, 68,* 1–12.

Hamm, M. & Adams, D. (2002). Collaborative inquiry: Working toward shared goals. *Kappa Delta Pi Record, 38*(3), Spring, 115–118.

Illinois State Board of Education. (2000). *Critical Issue: Beyond social promotion and retention—Five strategies to help students succeed.* Springfield, IL: Illinois Board of Education.

Johnson, D. W. & Johnson, R. (1989). *Cooperation and completion: Theory and research.* Edina, MN: Interaction Book Co.

Johnson, D. W. & Johnson, R. (1991). *Teaching students to be peacemakers.* Edina, MN: Interaction Book Co.

Johnson, D. W. & Johnson, R. (1992). *Creative controversy: Intellectual challenge in the classroom.* Edina, MN: Interaction Book Co.

Johnson, D. W. & Johnson, R. *Cooperative learning.* Retrieved on January 6, 2006, from the University of Minnesota website: http://www.co-operation.org/pages/cl.html

Johnson, D. & Rudolph, A. (2001). *Critical issue: Beyond social promotion and retention—Five strategies to help students succeed.* Retrieved January 8, 2006, from the website of the North Central Regional Education Laboratory: http://www.ncrel.org/sdrs/areas/issues/students/atrisk/at800.htm

Johnson, L., Finn, M. E., & Lewis, R. (eds.) (2005). *Urban education with an attitude.* Albany, NY: SUNY Press.

Joiner, R., Miell, D., Faulkner, D., & Littleton, K. (eds.) (2000). *Rethinking collaborative learning.* London, UK: Free Association Books.

Kagan, D. (1986). Cooperative learning and sociocultural diversity: Implications for practice. *Beyond language minorities*, 98–110, Los Angeles: Evaluation, Dissemination and Assessment Center, California State University.

Langer, G., Colton, A., & Goff, L. (2003).*Collaborative analysis of student work: Improving teaching and learning*. Alexandria, VA: Association for Supervision and Curriculum Development.

Lapp, D., Block, C. C., Cooper, E. J., Flood, J., Roser, N. L., & Tinajero, J. V. (eds.) (2004). *Teaching all the children strategies for developing literacy in an urban setting*. New York, NY: Guilford Press.

Lee, C. D. & Smagorinsky, P. (2000). *Vygotskian perspectives on literacy research: Constructing meaning through collaborative inquiry*. New York, NY: Cambridge University Press.

MacGregor, J., Cooper, J. L., Smith, K. A., & Robinson, P. (eds.) (2000). *Strategies for energizing large classes: From small groups to learning communities*. San Francisco, CA: Jossey-Bass.

Murphy, F. (2003). *Making inclusion work: A practical guide for teachers*. Norwood, MA: Christopher-Gordon Publishers.

National Council of Teachers of Mathematics (NCTM). (2000). *Principles and standards for school mathematics*. Reston, VA: National Council of Teachers of Mathematics.

National Research Council. (1996). *National science education standards*. Washington, DC: National Academy Press.

Newbridge Educational Publishing. (2000). *Cooperative learning*. Littleton, MA: Newbridge Educational Publishing.

Sailor, W. & Blair, R. (2005). Rethinking inclusion: Schoolwide applications. *Phi Delta Kappan*, 86(7), March, 503–509.

Sailor, W. & Blair, R. (2004). School wide applications model. Web version. Kansas City, Kansas:(wsailor@ku.edu).

Sharon, S. (1990). *Cooperative learning: Theory and research*. Westport, CT: Bergin & Garvy/Praeger.

Slavin, R. (1990). *Cooperative learning: Theory, research, and practice*. Englewood Cliffs, NJ: Prentice Hall.

Snow, D. (2005). *Classroom strategies for helping at-risk students*. Aurora, CO: Mid-continent Research for Education and Learning.

Thousand, J. S., Villa, R. A., & Nevin, A. (2002). *Creativity and collaborative learning: A practical guide to empowering students and teachers*. 2nd ed. Baltimore, MD: Paul H. Brookes Publishing Company.

Tomlinson, C. & Cunningham Edison, C. (2003). *Differentiation in practice: A resource guide for differentiating curriculum*. Alexandria, VA: Association for Supervision and Curriculum Development.

Vygotsky, L. S. (1962). *Thought and language*. Cambridge, MA: MIT Press.

Yard, G. & Vatterott, C. (1995). Accommodating individuals through instructional adaptations. *Middle School Journal*, 24, 23–28.

4

Differentiated Instruction

Multiple Paths to Learning and Assessment

> *A differentiated classroom provides different avenues to acquiring content, processing or making sense of ideas, collaboratively developing products, and assessing.*
>
> —Linda Starr

Differentiated instruction is not a totally new concept for teaching struggling students. Teachers have always been faced with the challenge of dealing with the fact that individual students learn things in different ways. Yet tracking didn't seem to do anybody much good. Differentiated learning involves building mixed-ability group instruction around the idea that individual students learn in unique ways and at varying levels of difficulty. Assessment follows a similar path (Tomlinson, 2003).

In a classroom that differentiates instruction you will find students doing more thinking for themselves and more work with peers. Self-evaluation and a gentle kind of peer assessment is part of the process. In addition, small collaborative groups within the class are often working at different levels of complexity and at different rates.

This chapter introduces differentiated learning, examines changing assessment practices, and explores multiple entry points to knowledge about math and science. It also:

- Examines the principles that guide differentiated learning.
- Suggests classroom activities that build on multiple intelligence theory.
- Assists teachers in lesson planning and using adaptive teaching strategies.
- Introduces ways for teachers and students to do their work collaboratively.

- Makes suggestions for evaluation, performance assessment, and portfolios.

When it comes to math and science, our experience suggests that differentiated instruction is most effective when concepts are taught in context and relate to relevant prior knowledge. Differentiated instruction (DI) gives students multiple paths to understanding and expressing what has been learned. The process involves having reluctant learners construct meaning by working with peers to explore issues, problems, and solutions. In this way, it is different from individualized instruction because it moves beyond the specific needs and skills of each student to address the needs of student clusters, including struggling students. Whatever your philosophy of teaching, you can be sure that it will take a varied arsenal of techniques and activities to meet the diverse needs of today's students.

THE EVOLUTION OF IDEAS ABOUT
THINKING AND LEARNING

A number of new ideas have come from psychology, cognitive science, and related research about how the brain functions. We now understand many things about teaching, learning, and how the mind works that we didn't know about even a few decades ago. For the last decade or so, researchers have been trying to understand the mind's capabilities and figure out how the results might be applied to learning (Bransford, 1999). Although connecting the research to actual classroom practice remains a problem, the gap is being closed. Differentiated learning, for example, builds on some of the new ideas gleaned from brain research and goes on to suggest using a balance of visual, auditory, oral, and written materials to match the preferences of different kinds of learners (Tomlinson, 2003).

Like cognitive science, the field of education is constantly growing and changing. We now have a better understanding of both the problems and the possibilities associated with teaching struggling students. The math and science standards have helped by building on the research to inform practice. Several libraries could be filled with books, journals, research papers, and projects that relate to the expanding educational knowledge base. Here we narrow the focus to some of the concepts and developments that relate to helping students who struggle with math and science. Although we mention a few theoretical milestones, special attention is given to suggesting practical approaches that teachers can use to help underachieving students.

Until well past the midpoint of the twentieth century, the theoretical ideas about learning were dominated by a behaviorist view of rewards and punishment. Over the last few decades, the cognitive perspective has largely taken its place. Cognitive science provides ways for thinking about how the mind works and how knowledge is acquired and represented in the memory system. Developments in neuroscience have further extended the field. Brain research suggests that students learn best in different ways. For many, collaborative group work inspires their best efforts. Other students learn best when pursuing learning projects on their own—or with a partner for some of the work.

Cognitive science, multiple intelligence theory, differentiated learning, and constructivism are at least indirectly related. Constructivist educators emphasize teaching students to classify, analyze, predict, create, and problem solve. Student ability to learn new ideas is viewed as having a lot to do with the information an individual has prior to instruction. Facts can be important building blocks, but constructivist teachers emphasize actively building new structures on prior knowledge. In the differentiated classroom, carefully designed student-centered learning and self-reflective teaching can ensure that we are serving students of diverse abilities and interests. This goes beyond helping struggling students to making sure that all students perform as well as they can.

Opinions about the usefulness of brain research, cognitive science, and educational research may vary, but you can be certain that a more thorough understanding of the human brain will be part of our expanding educational knowledge base in the twenty-first century. Clearly, the differentiated instruction notion of helping each child succeed in numerous and varied ways will be part of the formula for keeping struggling students involved and successful. It is also clear that students from different cultural and economic backgrounds will need extra inspiration and multiple approaches for learning math and science.

MULTIPLE ENTRY POINTS TO KNOWLEDGE

Learning has a lot to do with finding your own gifts. Many questions remain, but no one doubts that today's students are a complex lot, with varying needs, abilities, and interests. To make learning more accessible to such a wide range of students means respecting multiple ways of making meaning. The brain has a multiplicity of functions and voices that speak independently and distinctly for different individuals (Tomlinson & Kalbfleisch, 1998). No two children are alike. An enriched environment for one is not necessarily enriched for another.

The basic idea is to maximize each student's learning capacity. We use the term *differentiated instruction* to refer to a systematic approach to teaching academically diverse learners. It is a way of thinking about students' learning needs and enhancing each student's learning capacity. This approach suggests that teachers become aware of who their students are and how student differences relate to what is being taught. The hope is that by having the flexibility to differentiate or adapt student assignments, teachers can increase the possibility that each student will learn (Tomlinson & Cunningham Edison, 2003).

ELEMENTS THAT GUIDE DIFFERENTIATED LEARNING

Teachers can differentiate or modify instruction in four ways.

The *content* that teachers teach and how students have access to information is an important way for teachers to differentiate instruction. Student readiness is the current knowledge understanding and skill level of a student. Readiness does not mean student ability, rather it reflects what a student knows, understands and is able to do.

Interest is another way to differentiate learning. Topics students enjoy learning about, thinking about, and doing provide a motivating link. Successful teachers incorporate required content to students' interests to engage the learner. This helps students connect with new information by making it appealing, relevant, and worthwhile.

A student's *learning profile* is influenced by an individual's learning style and intelligence preference (Gardner, 1997; Sternberg, 1988), gender, and culture. In tapping into a student's learning profile, teachers can extend the ways students learn best.

A *differentiated learning environment* enables teachers and students to work in ways that benefit each student and the class as a whole. A flexible environment allows students to make decisions about how to make the classroom surroundings work. This gives students a feeling of ownership and a sense of responsibility. Students of any age can work successfully as long as they know what's expected and are held to high standards of performance.

> *To differentiate instruction, you need to clarify the content (what you want students to know and be able to do), the process (how students are going to go about learning the content), and the product (how they will show what they know).*

> —Amy Benjamin

IMPORTANT PRINCIPLES OF DIFFERENTIATION

There are several key principles that describe a differentiated classroom. A few of them are defined here:

1. A *high quality engaging curriculum* is the primary principle. The teacher's first job is to guarantee the curriculum is consistent, inviting, important, and thoughtful.
2. Students' work should be appealing, inviting, thought provoking, and stimulating. *Every student should find his or her work interesting and powerful.*
3. Teachers should try to *assign challenging tasks* that are a little too difficult for the student. Be sure there is a support system to assist students' success at a level they never thought possible.
4. *Use adjustable grouping.* It is important to plan times for groups of students to work together—and times for students to work independently. Provide teacher-choice and student-choice groups.
5. *Assess, assess and assess!* Assessment is an ongoing process. Pre-assessment determines students' knowledge and skills based on students' needs. Then, teachers can differentiate instruction to match the needs of each student. When it's time for final assessments, it's helpful to plan several assessment strategies, for example, a quiz and a project.
6. *Grades should be based on growth.* A struggling student who persists and doesn't see progress will likely become frustrated if grade-level benchmarks remain out of reach and growth doesn't seem to count. It is the teacher's job to support the student.

Over the last few decades, researchers have suggested that since the human brain is "wired" in different ways, it is important for teachers to realize that students learn and create in different ways. Although it is often best to teach to a student's strength, we know that providing young people with deep learning experiences in different domains can enrich their "intelligence" in specific areas (Sprenger, 1999). Howard Gardner and Robert Sternberg have contributed to the awareness that students exhibit different intelligence preferences. Sternberg (1988, 1997) suggests three intelligence preferences: analytic (schoolhouse intelligence), creative (imaginative intelligence), and practical (contextual, street-smart intelligence). Gardner suggests eight.

TOWARD A NEW VISION OF INTELLIGENCE (MULTIPLE INTELLIGENCES)

The biggest mistake of past centuries in teaching has been to treat all children as if they are variants of the same individual, and thus to feel justified in teaching them the same subjects in the same ways.

—Howard Gardner

Howard Gardner's framework for multiple entry points to knowledge has had a powerful influence on differentiated learning and the content standards. Both the math and the science standards recognize alternate paths for learning. There are many differences, but each set of content standards is built on a belief in the uniqueness of each child and the view that this can be fused with a commitment achieving worthwhile goals. Being able to base at least some math and science instruction on a student's preferred way of learning has proven to be especially helpful in teaching struggling students (Sprenger, 1999).

When *Frames of Mind* was published in 1983, Gardner was critical of how the field of psychology had traditionally viewed of intelligence. So, he set out to stir up some controversy. He succeeded. An unexpected result of his writing about multiple intelligences (MI) was the enthusiastic response within the educational community. Teachers showed unexpected enthusiasm for exploring MI theory and putting some activities based on that theory into practice (Armstrong, 2000). Lessons built around Gardner's concept of multiple intelligences proved to be particularly helpful in meeting some of the challenges of heterogeneous grouping and an increasingly diverse student body.

Multiple Intelligences

1. Linguistic intelligence: the capacity to use language to express ideas, excite, convince, and convey information—includes speaking, writing, and reading.
2. Logical/mathematical intelligence: the ability to explore patterns and relationships by manipulating objects or symbols in an orderly manner.
3. Musical intelligence: the capacity to think in music, the ability to perform, compose, or enjoy a musical piece—includes rhythm, beat, tune, melody, and singing.
4. Spatial intelligence: the ability to understand and mentally manipulate a form or object in a visual or spatial display—includes maps, drawings, and media.
5. Bodily/kinesthetic intelligence: the ability to use motor skills in sports, performing arts, or art productions (particularly dance or acting).
6. Interpersonal intelligence: the ability to work in groups—includes interacting, sharing, leading, following, and reaching out to others.
7. Intrapersonal intelligence: the ability to understand one's inner feelings, dreams and ideas—involves introspection, meditation, reflection, and self-assessment.

8. Naturalist intelligence: the ability to discriminate among living things (plants, animals) as well as demonstrate a sensitivity to the natural world (Gardner, 1997).

Within this framework, intelligence might be defined as the ability to solve problems, generate new problems, and do things that are valued within one's own culture. MI theory suggests that these eight "intelligences" work together in complex ways. Most people can develop an adequate level of competency in all of them. And there are many ways to be "intelligent" within each category. But will the intelligences listed above be as central to the twenty-first century as they were to the twentieth? It is possible to take issue with MI theory on other points, like not fully addressing spiritual and artistic modes of thought, but there is general agreement on a central point: *intelligence is not a single capacity that every human being posseses to a greater or lesser extent.*

No matter how you explain it, there are multiple paths to competency in math and science. And, it makes instructional sense to differentiate instruction in a way that builds on different ways of knowing and understanding.

Activities that Reflect Multiple Intelligence Theory

1. Upper elementary and middle school students can comprehend MI theory. Why not explain it to them and have them do some activities to remember it? We like having students work with a partner. Here are some possibilities:

linguistic intelligence
write an article
develop a newscast
make a plan, describe a procedure
write a letter
conduct an interview
write a play
interpret a text or piece of
    writing

musical intelligence
sing a rap song
give a musical presentation
explain music similarities
make and demonstrate a musical
    instrument
demonstrate rhythmic patterns

logical/mathematical intelligence
design and conduct an experiment
describe patterns
make up analogies to explain
solve a problem

spatial intelligence
illustrate, draw, paint, sketch
create a slide show, videotape
chart, map or graph
create a piece of art

bodily/kinesthetic intelligence
use creative movement
design task or puzzle cards
build or construct something

interpersonal intelligence
conduct a meeting
participate in a service project
teach someone

bring hands-on materials to demonstrate

use the body to persuade, console, or support others

use technology to explain

advise a friend or fictional character

naturalist intelligence

prepare an observation notebook

describe changes in the environment

care for pets, wildlife, gardens or parks

use binoculars, telescopes, or microscopes

photograph natural objects

intrapersonal intelligence

write a journal entry

describe one of your values

assess your work

set and pursue a goal

reflect on or act out emotions

2. Encourage various learning styles:

Mastery style learner—concrete learner, step-by-step process, learns sequentially.

Understanding style learner—focuses on ideas and abstractions, learns through a process of questioning.

Self-expressive style learner—looks for images, uses feelings and emotions

Interpersonal style learner—focuses on the concrete, prefers to learn socially, judges learning in terms of its potential use in helping others.

3. Build on students' interests. When students do research either individually or with a group, allow them to choose a project that appeals to them. Students should also choose the best way for communicating their understanding of the topic. In this way, students discover more about their interests and concerns, their learning styles and intelligences.

4. Plan interesting lessons. There are many ways to plan interesting lessons.

(Lesson plan suggestions presented here are influenced by ideas as diverse as those from John Goodlad, Madeline Hunter, and Howard Gardner.)

Lesson Planning

1. Set the tone of the lesson. Focus student attention, relate the lesson to what students have done before, and stimulate interest.

2. Present the objectives and purpose of the lesson. What are students supposed to learn? Why is it important?

3. Provide background information: what information is available? Resources such as books, journals, videos, pictures, maps, charts, teacher lecture, class discussion, or seatwork should be listed.

4. Define procedures: what are students supposed to do? This includes examples and demonstrations as well as working directions.
5. Monitor students' understanding. During the lesson, the teacher should check students' understanding and adjust the lesson if necessary. Teachers should invite questions and ask for clarification. A continuous feedback process should be in place.
6. Provide guided practice experiences. Students should have a chance to use the new knowledge presented under direct teacher supervision.
7. Offer students opportunities for independent practice where students can use their new knowledge and skills. This is equally as important as working under teacher supervision.
8. Evaluate and assess students' work. It is necessary to show that students have demonstrated an understanding of significant concepts.

A Sample Multiple Intelligence Lesson Plan

The following is a sample of a multiple intelligence lesson.

Differentiated Brain Lesson: How Neurons Work

The basic idea is to develop understandings of personal health, changes in environments, and local challenges in science and technology. The human body and the brain are fascinating areas of study. The brain, like the rest of the body, is composed of cells, but brain cells are different from other cells (Sprenger, 1999). Neurons grow and develop when they are used actively and they diminish when they are not used. All students must be involved in vigorous new learning or they risk losing brain power. High interest/low vocabulary materials such as colorful charts are desirable when teaching new concepts to struggling learners. A chart of a neuron of the brain including cell body, dendrite, and axon is a helpful teaching tool when introducing this concept.

This lesson focuses on the math standards of problem solving, estimation, data analysis, logic, reasoning, communication, and math computations. The science standards of inquiry, life science, science and technology, and personal and social perspectives are included.

Lesson Goals: The basic goal is to provide a dynamic experience with each of the eight intelligences and map out a chart on construction paper.

Procedures:
1. Divide the class into groups. Assign each group an intelligence.
2. Allow students time to prepare an activity that addresses their intelligence. Each small group will give a three minute presentation (with large map) to the entire class. Let reluctant students see, hear, touch,

and write about new or difficult concepts. Utilize materials that assess present learner needs. Allow the class to develop their own problems.

Objective: To introduce students to the terminology of the brain and how the brain functions, specifically the function of neurons.

Grade level: With modifications, K–8.

Materials: Paper, pens, markers, copy of the picture of the brain, the neuron, songs about the brain, model of the brain (recipe follows):

Brain "Recipe"
> Pour 5 cups of instant potato flakes, 5 cups of hot water, and 2 cups sand into a 1 gallon ziplock bag.
> Combine all ingredients, mix thoroughly. It should weigh about 3 pounds and have the consistency of a real brain.

Background Information: No one understands exactly how the brain works. But scientists know the answer lies within the billions of tiny cells, called *neurons* or nerve cells, which make up the brain. All the body's feelings and thoughts are caused by the electrical and chemical signals passing from one neuron to the next. A neuron looks like a tiny octopus, but with many more tentacles (some have several thousand). Neurons carry signals throughout the brain that allow the brain to move, hear, see, taste, smell, remember, feel, and think.

Procedures:
1. Make a model of the brain to show to the class. The teacher displays the brain and says: "The smell of a flower, the memory of a walk in the park, the pain of stepping on a nail—these experiences are made possible by the 3 pounds of tissue in our heads—'the brain!'
2. Show a picture of the neuron and mention its various parts.
3. Have students label the parts of the neuron and color if desired.

Activity 1. Message Transmission: Explaining How Brain Cells (neurons) Work

A message traveling in the nervous system of the brain can go 200 mph. These signals are transmitted from neuron to neuron across synapses. To understand this system, have students act out the neuron process.

1. Instruct students to get into groups of five. Each group should choose a group leader. Include all students, even those who seem not interested.
2. Direct students stand up and form a circle. Each person is going to be a neuron. Students should be an arms' length away from the next person.

3. When the group leader says "Go" have one person from the group start the signal transmission by slapping the hand of the adjacent person. The second person then slaps the hand of the next, and so on until the signal goes all the way around the circle and the transmission is complete. Utilize materials that address learner's needs. Allow the entire class to become involved in this learning exercise. This helps underachieving learners realize they can work successfully and have fun with peers.

Explanation: The hand that receives the slap is the "dendrite." The middle part of the student's body is the "cell body." The arm that gives the slap to the next person is the "axon" and the hand that gives the slap is the "nerve terminal." The space in between the hands of two people is the "synapse."

Inquiry Questions: As the activity progresses, questions will arise. What are parts of a neuron? A neuron is a tiny nerve cell, one of billions that make up the brain. A neuron has three basic parts: the cell body, the dendrites, and the axon. Have students make a simple model by using their hand and spreading their fingers wide. The hand represents the cell body, the fingers represent the dendrites, which bring information to the cell body, and the arm represents the axon, which takes information away from the cell body. Just as students wiggles their fingers, the dendrites are constantly moving as they seek information.

If the neuron needs to send a message to another neuron, the message is sent out through the axon. The wrist and forearm represent the axon. When a neuron sends information down its axon to communicate with another neuron, it never actually touches the other neuron. The message goes from the axon of the sending neuron to the dendrite of the receiving neuron by "swimming" through the space called the synapse. Neuroscientists define *learning* as "two neurons communicating with each other." They say that neurons have "learned" when one neuron sends a message to another neuron (Hannaford, 1995).

Activity 2. Connect the Dots

This exercise is to illustrate the complexity of the connections of the brain.

1. Have students draw ten dots on one side of a sheet of paper and ten dots on the other side of the paper.
2. Tell students to imagine these dots represent neurons, assume each neuron makes connections with the ten dots on the other side.
3. Then connect each dot on side one with the dots on the other side. This is quite a simplification. Each neuron (dot) may actually make thousands of connections with other neurons.

Another part of this activity is teaching brain songs to students. Teach a small group of students the words and the melody of the songs. Include struggling students in this song process. They will become the brain song "experts."

"I've Been Working on My Neurons"
(sung to the tune of "I've Been Working on the Railroad")

I've been working on my neurons, All the live long day.
I've been working on my neurons, Just to make my dendrites play.
Can't you hear the synapse snapping? Impulses bouncing to and fro,
Can't you tell that I've been learning? See how much I know!

"Because I Have a Brain" (sung to the tune, "If I Only Had a Brain")
I can flex a muscle tightly, or tap my finger lightly,
It's because I have a brain,
I can swim in the river, though it's cold and makes me shiver,
Just because I have a brain.
I am really fascinated, to be coordinated,
It's because I have a brain.
I can see lots of faces, feel the pain of wearing braces
Just because I have a brain.
Oh, I appreciate the many things that I can do,
I can taste a chicken stew, or smell perfume, or touch the dew.
I am heavy with emotion, and often have the notion,
That life is never plain.
I have lots of personality, a sense of true reality,
Because I have a brain.

Activity 3. Introduce Graphic Organizers

Graphic organizers help students retain semantic information. Mind mapping or webbing illustrates a main idea and supporting details.

1. To make a mind map write an idea or concept in the middle of a sheet of paper
2. Draw a circle around it. Then, draw a line from the circle. Write a word or phrase to describe the idea or concept.
3. Draw other lines coming from the circle in similar manner.
4. Have students draw pictures or symbols to represent their descriptions.

Multiple Intelligences Learning Activities

Linguistic: writing a reflection about the activity, researching how a neuron works, keeping a study journal about how neurons work.
Bodily/kinesthetic: move like a neuron group drama, signal transmission.
Spatial: mapping the connections of the brain (connect the dots).

Musical: singing songs about neurons, tapping out rhythms to the song "Because I Have a Brain."

Naturalist: describing changes in your brain environment, illustrating a dendrite connection.

Interpersonal: participate in (act out) a group signal neuron transmission, observing and recording.

Intrapersonal: reflecting on being a neuron, keeping a journal of how the brain works.

Mathematical/logical: calculating neuron connections.

Evaluation: Each group will write a reflection on the activity. Journal reflections should tell what they learned about neurons and how that helps them understand how the brain works. Encourage students to organize their work and put it in a portfolio.

If either you or your students want to find or publish information about math or science topics, like the human brain (or anything else), we suggest trying *Digital Universe* (digitaluniverse.net). It combines some of the wide-reaching strengths of *Wikipedia* with the trustworthiness of *Britannica*. Anyone can contribute to the *Digital Universe* online encyclopedia, but experts will check and edit the information that is submitted.

BRAIN RESEARCH AND LEARNING

The unique aspects of the brain cells are arranged in such a way that it's malleable or plastic enough for learning to occur and stable enough for the learning to solidify into wisdom. Recently, a report was issued that promises to upset what has been one of the long-held certainties about the brain: the adult brain cannot form new neurons (people are born with a fixed amount of neuron cells, they die off one by one, and they're lost forever). A shocking experiment found that thousands of new neurons a day were being formed in the brains of monkeys, migrating into areas of the brain in charge of intelligence and decision making. If a steady stream of new brain cells is continually arriving to be integrated into new circuitry, then the brain is more malleable than anyone had realized.

This contradicts the idea that the most important neurological action occurs in the first three years of human development. "Our brains remain remarkably plastic and we retain the ability to learn throughout our lives" (Jensen, 2005). Another study finds a small well-connected region of the brain in charge of organizing and coordinating information, acting like a global workspace for solving problems. Neuroscientists also emphasize that the brain is extremely plastic and dynamic, very responsive to experience, "it's an ever-changing place." More active research for evidence of successful learning applications in the classroom is still needed.

THE IMPORTANCE OF ASSESSMENT IN
THE DIFFERENTIATED CLASSROOM

Since teachers have to perform many types of assessment, they are in the best position to put the data to good use. Official assessment, instructional assessment, and social (sizing-up) assessment are the most common types. *Official (administrative) assessment* includes formal grading, interpreting standardized test results, and testing for special needs placement. *Instructional assessment* is used to plan how and when instruction will be delivered. What materials will you use? How is the lesson progressing? What changes have to be made in the planned activities? *Social (sizing-up) assessment* involves figuring out how to set up groups and enhance communication within the classroom community.

There is general agreement that the methods for assessing educational growth have not kept up with new subject matter standards and the way the curriculum has changed. Multiple choice testing just doesn't do a very good job of capturing the reality of today's students. Such tests convey to students that bits and pieces of information count more than deep knowledge. On the other hand, assessing performance conveys the notion that reasoning, in-depth understanding, taking responsibility, and the ability to apply knowledge in new situations is what counts (Hales & Marshall, 2004). Here, we concentrate on how performance portfolios can help you energize small group instruction in the basic skills.

Howard Gardner (1997) argues for assessment practices that "look directly at the performance that we value, whether it's a linguistic, logical, aesthetic, or social performance." We suggest including diagnostic assessment for prior knowledge, teacher observations, interviews, response to prompts, self-assessment, peer reviews, products, projects, and even the occasional quiz. This chapter focuses on how certain elements of performance assessment, like portfolios, can be helpful in teaching the basics. We view performance portfolios as a good way to link assessment directly to instruction. Within this context, the teacher and the students jointly develop some important criteria for assessment; they go on to use these criteria to determine the quality of the product or performance.

Portfolios are different things to different people. How you define the term has a lot to do with how you are planning to use them. In our view, the portfolio is a purposeful collection of student work that can be used to describe a student's effort, progress, and performance in a subject. There is no harm in using portfolios to showcase the best of what a student has achieved. But most elementary and middle school teachers get more useful information when portfolios reflect student growth over a period of time. Before you get started, it's best to figure out whose interests are going to be served and what processes you want the portfolios to measure.

Assessment can be used to motivate students in several ways. To begin with, students can be assigned to collaborative teams for interdisciplinary inquiry and peer assessment. When students are brought into designing assessment procedures as responsible partners, the whole process is enhanced. Students can then use portfolios to keep their own records and reflect on how well they are doing. By viewing the evidence of their increasing proficiency, they become reflectors of their own progress. Finally, learning to communicate with peers, teachers, and parents about their achievement means struggling learners take more responsibility for academic success (Costantino, De Lorenzo, & Kobrinski, 2006).

USING GROWTH PORTFOLIOS

Many teachers share a vision of what they think should be happening in their classes. It goes something like this: students work in small groups doing investigations or accomplishing tasks using tools such as manipulative materials, blocks, beakers, clay, rulers, chemicals, musical instruments, calculators, assorted textbooks, computers, the Internet, and other materials. They consult with each other and with the teacher—keeping journals and other written reports of their work. Occasionally, the entire class gathers for a discussion or for a presentation. Teachers want students to be motivated and responsible. Unfortunately, traditional testing methods do not support this vision (Tucker & Stronge, 2005).

As students and teachers use product criteria (the performance or work samples) and progress criteria (effort or class participation), they conduct experiments, collaborate in interdisciplinary projects, and construct portfolios. Portfolios represent a more authentic and meaningful assessment process. They are a major performance assessment tool for having students select, collect, reflect, and communicate what they are doing. Having students think about the evidence that they have collected—and deciding what it means—is clearly a good way to increase student engagement.

Portfolios have long been associated with artists and photographers as a means of displaying collected samples of representative work. They have also been used for over ten years by various reading and writing projects (Hebert, 2001). In the 1990s, the National Assessment of Educational Progress suggested using portfolios to assess students' writing and reading abilities. In addition, portfolios have been helping some teachers monitor student performance in the language arts for the better part of a decade. They usually begin by specifying the essential concepts to be covered, figuring out how to link what is taught to the assessment process, and finding ways to display an understanding of the results. What is new is the interest in using these performance assessment techniques now stretches across the curriculum.

Teachers have found that collecting, organizing, and reflecting on work samples tie in nicely with active interdisciplinary inquiry. Portfolios not only capture a more authentic portrait of a student's thinking but can serve as an excellent conferencing tool for meetings with students, parents, and supervisors. In addition to portfolios, teachers often create other performance assessment tasks: projects, exhibitions, performances, and experiments. By creating opportunities for students to reveal their growth, we help them understand *what* they are doing and *why* they are doing it.

DRAWING MEANING FROM WHAT IS OBSERVED OR MEASURED

Assessment and evaluation are so intertwined it's hard to separate them. Assessment is collecting data to gain an understanding or make a judgment. Evaluation is judging something's value based on the available data. You can have assessment without evaluation, but you cannot have evaluation without assessment. Assessment is a broader task than evaluative testing because it involves collecting a wider range of information that must be put together to draw meaning from what was observed or measured. Of course, the first use of assessment is within the classroom, to provide information to the teacher for making instructional decisions. Teachers have always depended on their own observations and examination of student work to help in curriculum design and decision making. Teachers need ongoing support in their efforts to set high goals for student achievement.

Lately we have been hearing a lot about *authentic assessment*. The term implies evaluating by asking for evidence of the behaviors you want to produce. For assessment to be authentic, the form and the criteria for success must be public knowledge. Students need to know what is expected and on what criteria their product will be evaluated. Success should be evaluated in ways that make sense to them. It allows students to show off what they do well. Authentic assessment should search out students' strengths and encourage integration of knowledge and skills learned from many different sources. It encourages pride and may include self and peer evaluation. Having students make up some of their own questions is an effective way to differentiate assessment, especially if students aren't used to group work. Individuals could, for example, work with a partner or small group to answer student-generated questions.

In the world outside of school where people are valued for the tasks or projects they do, their ability to work with others and their responses to difficult problems or situations are what count. To prepare students for future success both curriculum and assessment must encourage this kind of performance assessment (Stenmark, 1994). Assessment of products that students produce may include portfolios, writing, group investigations, projects, interactive websites, class presentations, or verbal responses to open-ended questions. Whether it's small group class presentations, journal writing, storytelling, simple observation, or portfolios, alternative assessment procedures pick up many things that students fail to show on pencil-and-paper tests.

THE PORTFOLIO AS A TOOL FOR UNDERSTANDING

A portfolio is best described as a container of evidence of someone's skills and dispositions. More than a folder of a student's work, portfolios represent a deliberate, specific collection of an individual's important experiences and accomplishments. The items are carefully selected by the student and the teacher to represent a cross section of a student's creative efforts. It isn't just the best stuff; it's what is most important to all concerned. Portfolios can be used as a tool in the classroom to bring students together, to discuss ideas, and provide evidence of understanding. The information accumulated also assists the teacher in diagnosing learners' strengths and weaknesses. It is clearly a powerful tool for gaining a more detailed understanding of student achievement, knowledge, and attitudes.

The portfolio assessment process helps students become aware of their learning history and the development of their reasoning ability. Prospective teachers can find out a lot about themselves by sketching the most important events and efforts in their school days. As students become directly involved in assessing progress toward learning goals, the barrier between the learner and the assessment of the learner is lowered. Through critical analysis of their own work—and the work of peers—students gain insight into many ways of thinking about and resolving problems.

Portfolios are being used by teachers to document students' development and focus on their growth over time (Costantino, De Lorenzo, & Kobrinski, 2006). The emphasis is on performance and application, rather than on knowledge for knowledge's sake. Portfolios can assist teachers in diagnosing and understanding student learning difficulties. This includes growth in attitudes, thinking, expression, and the ability to collaborate with others. There is clearly more to learning than multiple-choice tests. Assessing the student over time (with portfolios) brings academic progress into sharp focus and promotes reflection on the larger issues of teaching and learning.

Advantages of Using Portfolios with Struggling Students

It is important that teachers examine the reasons for using portfolios. If the primary purpose is to evaluate students for the purpose of assigning grades, then teachers should consider having students prepare a portfolio to be submitted at the end of the grading period. Other reasons for this type of portfolio include: evaluating the effectiveness of our instruction and showcasing what has been accomplished by students. Following are some advantages of using portfolio assessment with struggling students:

- Provides organized, authentic, and continuous information about students.
- Structures learning information in an effective way for communicating with parents and administrators.
- Encourages struggling students to claim responsibility for their learning.
- Provides teachers with information as to the thinking processes used.
- Measures growth over time.

When portfolios are only used for a final evaluation, it is likely that student involvement will be minimal. They produce the required content. If the purpose is to assess ongoing work, students are more likely to participate in planning, selecting criteria, and evaluating their portfolios. This generates a feeling of pride and ownership for underachieving students (Hales & Marshall, 2004).

Linking Assessment with Instruction

Portfolios are proving useful in linking assessment with instruction at every level because they allow students and teachers to reflect on their movement throughout the learning process (Mumme, 1990). They also provide a chance to look at what and how students are learning while paying attention to students' ideas and thinking processes. We do not suggest that the "pure" objectivity of more traditional testing has no place in the classroom. Rather we must respect its limits and search for more connected measures of intellectual growth. But there is no question that when coupled with other performance measures, like projects, portfolios can make an important contribution to differentiated instruction.

Rules for Assessing and Evaluating

1. Conduct all assessment and evaluation in the context of learning teams. Teachers must assess each student's achievement, but it's far more effective when it takes place in a collaborative setting.
2. Provide continual feedback and assessment. Learning groups need continual feedback on the level of learning of each member. This can be done through quizzes, written assignments, or oral presentations.
3. Develop a list of expected behaviors:
   Prior to the lesson _____

During the lesson _____
Following the lesson _____

4. Directly involve students in assessing each other's learning. Group members can provide immediate help to maximize all group members' learning.

5. Avoid all comparisons between students that are based solely on their academic ability. Such comparisons will decrease student motivation and learning.

6. Use a wide variety of assessment tools (Lane & Beebe-Frankenberger, 2004).

As Carol Tomlinson has pointed out, assessment and differentiated instruction are inseparable.

> *In the differentiated classroom, assessment is ongoing and diagnostic. Its goal is to provide teachers day-to-day data on students' readiness for particular ideas and skills, their interests, and their learning profiles.*

—Carol Tomlinson

SUMMARY AND CONCLUSION

There are far too many struggling students who could either stay in school or become a dropout statistic. In just about every classroom, there are students who have trouble learning certain subjects—especially math and science. Some are motivated to learn, many aren't. A differentiated approach helps teachers identify the needs of all their students and adapt instructional plans to maximize the success of each learner. Even while looking for factors that get in the way of student achievement, it is possible for teachers to create classroom routines that support differentiation. When it comes to understanding struggling students, we need to talk more about responsibility and less about blame. It will take serious discussion between serious people seeking serious solutions to move the majority of underachieving students in the direction of viewing education as the way to light up their future.

From music and movies to the television and computer game industry, powerful corporations have contributed to the erosion of culture and sold out our youth by celebrating ignorance and creating a culture of anti-intellectualism. Of course, there is plenty of blame to go around. Some of us are directly responsible for the education of American elementary and middle school students. For some the responsibility is indirect. But it's important to remember that we all share some of the blame for the behavioral problems that often plague students who struggle with schoolwork. The achievement gap between schools will never be bridged until parents and students accept their share of responsibility for behavior at school.

Teacher expectation is as important as parental support. Educational attainment and upward mobility have twin pillars of success: human capital and social capital. Social capital has a lot to do with environmental and parental support. Human capital has a lot to do with a teacher's impact on a student's education. Teachers matter. The scientific literacy and numeracy problem is exacerbated by the ever-continuing shortage of teachers who are well trained in those subjects. This inevitably affects the quality of instruction. So teachers have a big role to play, especially when it comes to unmotivated students. But nothing less than a sustained societal commitment is required to make sure that all students succeed in the classroom and beyond.

Differentiated instruction can make any teacher's classroom more responsive to the needs of students who struggle with math and science. DI offers a road map to principles that can guide instruction and points to ways that teachers can modify or adapt math and science content. Along the way, performance assessment, like portfolios, can help students demonstrate what they have learned. Students' personal interests, learning profiles, and curiosity about a specific topic or skill are major considerations in differentiated learning and related assessment strategies.

While building on group cooperation, the differentiated classroom provides many different avenues for learning math and science. By having the opportunity to collaboratively explore ideas even unmotivated students tend to respond to appropriate challenges and enjoy learning about math and science. Flexible grouping and pacing, tiered assignments, performance assessment, and other factors associated with DI can bring fresh energy to math and science instruction in any classroom. With all the positive possibilities, it is little wonder that many educators now view differentiated instruction as an important ally in meeting the needs of students with increasingly diverse levels of prior knowledge, learning styles, interests, and cultural backgrounds.

Differentiated instruction has proven to be a solid asset for teachers trying to reach students who struggle with math and science (Jacobs, 2004). Clearly, it is a good way to meet specific individual and small group needs in the regular classroom. DI is an organized, yet flexible, way of adjusting teaching and learning to meet students where they are and help them achieve. In a differentiated classroom, teachers often use instructional strategies that build on multiple intelligence theory, cooperative group work, and portfolio assessment to meet unique learning and assessment needs. As teachers go about helping students become self-reliant and motivated learners, it can be an exciting adventure for everybody.

Language makes us human.
Art and culture push the boundaries of human understanding.
Science and its mathematical tools help us understand the natural world.

Technology makes us powerful.
And being in community with others can make us free.

QUESTIONS FOR TEACHERS AND PROSPECTIVE TEACHERS

1. The brain is a parallel processor. Have students think about how a camera sees the entire picture within the frame. The brain is like a camera: it takes in sensory information and transfers it to memory. That is why memories rush in when you hear a particular song, eat a certain food, or smell an odor. Have students write a question based on sensory information, let's try food. What does your brain think of when you think popcorn? Write all the senses, connections you made, your emotions, the places you think of, and your personal reflections.
2. Have students write about their preferred learning style. Give examples.
3. Encourage students to think of a subject they are having difficulties with. Go back to the multiple intelligences. Have students pick one. Some examples for the topic of math: Intelligence—verbal linguistic; activity—use creative dramatics to act out problems. Intelligence—intrapersonal; activity—develop self-understanding of math anxiety, learn to use appropriate self-talk and de-stressing techniques. Think of all the ways you're smart in math. Intelligence—interpersonal; activity—work in groups to play a math game such as cribbage or a video game like Pac-Man on the computer.

REFERENCES AND RESOURCES

Armstrong, T. (2000). *Multiple intelligences in the classroom,* 2nd ed. Alexandria, VA: Association for Supervision and Curriculum Development.

Benjamin, A. (2003). *Differentiated instruction: A guide for elementary teachers.* Portland, OR: Eye on Education, Incorporated media.

Bransford, A., Brown, L., & Cocking, R. (eds.) *How people learn: Brain, mind, experience.* Washington, DC: National Academy Press.

Browne, M. N. & Keeley, S. M. (2000). *Asking the right questions: A guide to critical thinking* (6th ed.) Upper Saddle River, NJ: Prentice Hall.

Bruce Mao Design and the Institute without Boundaries. (2004). *Massive change.* New York, NY: Phaidon Press Limited.

Costantino, P., De Lorenzo, M., & Kobrinski, E. (2006). *Developing a professional teaching portfolio: A guide for success.* 2nd ed. Boston, MA: Allyn and Bacon (Pearson Education, Inc.).

Feuerstein, R. (1980). *Instrumental enrichment: An intervention program for cognitive modifiability.* Baltimore, MD: University Park Press.

Gardner, H. (1983). *Frames of mind.* New York, NY: Basic Books.

Gardner, H. (1993). *Creating minds.* New York, NY: Basic Books.

Gardner, H. (1997). Reflections on multiple intelligences: The theory in practice. *Phi Delta Kappan,* 78(5), 200–207.

Gardner, H. (1997). Multiple intelligences as a partner in school improvement. *Educational Leadership,* 55(1), 20–21.

Hannaford, C. (1995). *Smart moves: Why learning is not in your head.* Arlington, VA: Great Ocean Publishers.

Hales, L. & Marshall, J. (2004). *Developing effective assessments to improve teaching and learning.* Norwood, MA: Christopher-Gordon Publishers, Inc.

Herbert, E. A. (2001), *The Power of Portfolios: What Children Can Teach Us About Learning and Assessment.* San Francisco, CA: Jossey-Bass.

Jackson, A. & Davis, G. (2000). *Turning points 2000: Educating adolescents in the 21st century.* New York, NY: Teachers College Press.

Jacobs, H. (ed.) (2004). *Getting results with curriculum mapping.* Alexandria, VA: Association for Supervision and Curriculum Development.

Jenson, E. (2005). *Teaching with the brain in mind.* 2nd ed. Alexandria, VA: Association for Supervision and Curriculum Development.

Lane, K. & Beebe-Frankenberger, M. (1994). *School-based interventions: The tools you need to succeed.* Boston, MA: Pearson Education.

Starr, L. (2004). *Strategy of the week.* Wallingford, CT: Education World. http://www.educationworld.com/a_corr/strategy/strategy042.shtml This online site is a place where teachers can share ideas and lesson plans.

Sprenger, M. (1999). *Learning & memory: The brain in action.* Alexandria, VA: Association for Supervision and Curriculum Development.

Stenmark, J. K. (1994). *Assessment Alternative in Mathematics: An Overview of Assessment Techniques that Promote Learning.* Berkeley, CA: University of California, Berkeley, Lawrence.

Sternberg, R. (1988). *The triarchic mind: A new theory of human intelligence.* New York, NY: Viking Press.

Sternberg, R. (1997). What does it mean to be smart? *Educational Leadership,* 54(6), March, 20–24.

Tomlinson, C. & Kalbfleisch, L. (1998). Teach me, teach my brain: A call for differentiated classrooms. *Educational Leadership,* 56(3), 52–55.

Tomlinson, C. & Cunningham Edison, C. (2003). *Differentiation in practice: A resource guide for differentiating curriculum, grades 5–9.* Alexandria, VA: Association for Supervision and Curriculum Development.

Tomlinson, C. (2003). *Fulfilling the promise of the differentiated classroom: Strategies and tools for responsive teaching.* Alexandria, VA: Association for Supervision and Curriculum Development.

Tucker, P. & Stronge, J. (2005). *Linking teacher evaluation and student learning.* Alexandria, VA: Association for Supervision and Curriculum Development.

5

Reaching Reluctant Math Students

Mathematical Reasoning and Collaborative Problem Solving

> A state legislator in Wisconsin objected to the introduction of daylight savings time because the extra hour of daylight would cause curtains and other fabrics to fade more quickly.
>
> —John Paulos

Quite a few people have an aversion to mathematics and feel that they would be better off if they could avoid it. As a result, all kinds of misguided ideas stem from policymakers and citizens who don't have a clue when it comes to applying mathematical principles. At school, there is often just as much misunderstanding when it comes to the difference between arithmetic and mathematics. Traditionally, math instruction focused primarily on the computational skills of arithmetic: addition, subtraction, multiplication, and division—along with whole numbers, fractions, decimals, and percentages. Arithmetic matters. But today there is general agreement that a deep understanding of mathematics is much more than facts, figures, and computation (NCTM, 2000).

The challenge for teachers today is to impart mathematical reasoning and problem-solving skills. And, along the way, help students develop a positive and confident attitude toward mathematics.

This chapter provides a framework for teaching mathematics and introduces you to the National Council of Teachers of Mathematics Standards. We build on the standards and describe some of the mathematical content and processes that all students should learn. The chapter also examines

- The nature of math, mathematical reasoning, and reluctant learners.
- Collaborative learning, math inquiry, and building new knowledge.

- The NCTM standards and the implications for underachieving students.
- Problem-solving strategies and activities for implementing the standards.
- Ideas for helping students who are struggling with math instruction.

Typically, students bring widely varying backgrounds to their math lessons and teachers work hard to accommodate this diversity. On one level, we believe that all students have the potential to learn mathematics. On another level, we have to admit that at least some of our students arrive so unprepared that they encounter academic difficulties. Everyone from math educators to textbook writers has been working hard to develop creative and innovative ways to meet the mathematical needs of such students. Students with attention deficits, memory problems, motor disabilities, and visual and auditory difficulties require special accommodations in the math classroom to reach their potential (White, 2004). It goes well beyond physical and environmental difficulties. In today's diverse elementary and middle school classrooms, we often find English-language learners and others who simply need further basic math instruction.

With some struggling students, it is not a question of language proficiency or disability, but a question of motivation and attitude. But whatever the source of difficulty, providing reluctant math learners with a strong mathematics program will be easier if you modify instruction, build teamwork skills, and tap into the natural strength of each student (Benjamin, 2003). And remember, it is best to make sure that even the most reluctant learner understands what it means to know and do mathematics in and out of school.

THE NATURE OF MATHEMATICS

Mathematics may be defined as

1. A method of thinking and asking questions. How students make math-related plans, organize their thoughts, analyze data, and solve problems is doing mathematics. People comfortable with math are often comfortable with thinking. The question is the cornerstone of all investigation. It guides the learner to a variety of sources revealing previously undetected patterns. These undiscovered openings can become sources of new questions that can deepen and enhance learning and inquiry.
2. A knowledge of patterns and relationships. Students need to recognize the repetition of math concepts and make connections with ideas they

know. These relationships help unify the math curriculum as each new concept is interwoven with former ideas. Students quickly see how a new concept is similar or different from others already learned. For example, students soon learn how the basic facts of addition and subtraction are interrelated ($4+2=6$ and $6-2=4$). They use their observation skills to describe, classify, compare, measure, and solve problems.

3. A tool. Mathematics is the tool mathematicians use in their work. It is also used by all of us every day. Students come to understand why they are learning the basic math principles and ideas that the school curriculum involves. Like mathematicians and scientists, they also will use mathematics tools to solve problems. They will learn that many careers and occupations are involved with the tools of mathematics.

4. A puzzle (fun). Anyone that has ever worked on a puzzle or stimulating problem knows what we're talking about when we say mathematics is fun. The stimulating quest for an answer prods one on toward finding a solution.

5. An art. Defined by harmony and internal order, mathematics needs to be appreciated as an art form where everything is related and interconnected. Art is often thought to be subjective, and by contrast objective mathematics is often associated with memorized facts and skills. Yet the two are closely related to each other. Students need to be taught how to appreciate the mathematical beauty all around them. For example, exploring fractal instances of math in nature. (A fractal is a wispy tangled curve that seems complicated no matter how closely one examines it. The object contains more, but similar, complexity the closer one looks.) A head of broccoli is one example. If you tear off a tiny piece of the broccoli and look at how it is similar to the larger head you will soon notice that they are the same. Each piece of broccoli could be considered an individual fractal or a whole. The piece of broccoli fits the definition of fractal appearing complicated; one can see consistent repetitive artistic patterns.

6. A language, a means of communicating. Mathematics requires being able to use special terms and symbols to represent information. This unique language enhances our ability to communicate across the disciplines of technology, statistics, and other subjects. For example, a struggling learner encountering $3 + 2 = 5$ needs to have the language translated to terms he or she can understand. Language is a window into students' thinking and understanding. Our job as teachers is to make sure students have carefully defined terms and meaningful symbols. Statisticians may use mathematical symbols that seem foreign to some of us, but after taking a statistics class, we too can decipher the mathematical language. It's no different for children. Symbolism, along with visual

aids such as charts and graphs are an effective way of expressing math ideas to others. Students learn not only to interpret the language of mathematics but to use that knowledge.

7. Interdisciplinary. Math works with the big ideas that connect subjects. Mathematics relates to many subjects. Science and technology are the obvious choices. Literature, music, art, social studies, physical education, and just about everything else, makes use of mathematics in some way. If you want to understand what you are reading in the newspaper, for example, you need to be able to read the charts and the graphs.

Reluctant learners claim they're just not interested in mathematics, working in groups. Discussing the seven ways that math is used every day can change their views. The following activities may help students discover what math is all about.

Activities That Help Reluctant Groups Define Mathematics

1. Mathematics as a method of thinking. List all the situations outside of school in which your group used math during the past week.
2. Math as a knowledge of patterns and relationships. Have your group show all the ways fifteen objects can be classified into four piles so that each pile has a different number of objects in it.
3. Math as a tool. Solve this problem using the tools of mathematics: Will an orange sink or float in water? What happens when the orange is peeled? Do the experiment with your group and explain your reasoning.
4. Math is having fun, solving a puzzle. With a partner play a game of cribbage (a card game in which the object is to form combinations for points). Dominoes is another challenging game to play in groups.
5. Math is an art. With a small group of students, design a fractal art picture. (A fractal is a tangled curve that seems complicated. The object contains more, but similar complexity.) A head of broccoli or a pine cone are some examples.
6. Math is a language. Divide the class into small groups of four or five. Have the group brainstorm about what they would like to find out from other class members (favorite hobbies, TV programs, kinds of pets, and so forth). Once a topic is agreed on, have them organize and take a survey of all class members. When the data are gathered and compiled, have groups make a clear, descriptive graph that can be posted in the classroom.
7. Math is interdisciplinary. With a group, design a song using a rhythmic format that can be sung, chanted, or rapped. The lyrics can be written and musical notation added.

COLLABORATIVE MATH INQUIRY

Collaborative inquiry is a way of teaching that builds on group interaction and students' natural curiosity. Inquiry refers to the activities of students in which they develop knowledge and understanding of mathematical ideas. This active process involves students in asking questions, gathering data, observing, analyzing, proposing answers, explaining, predicting, and communicating the results (Stephen et al., 2004).

Collaborative inquiry is supported, when students have opportunities to describe their own ideas and hear others explain their thoughts, raise questions, and explore various team approaches. Within a small group setting, students have more opportunities to interact with math content than they do during whole class discussions. The role of the teacher is to help students become aware of how to ask questions and how to find evidence. As teachers move away from a "telling" model to "structured group experiences", they encourage students to interact with each other and value social relationships as they become informed investigators.

The challenge for the teacher is to set up group work that engages students in meaningful math activities. Today even struggling students are being challenged to think and work together to solve problems. The next step is helping them feel secure as they go about applying their understandings.

We want all students to be involved in high-quality engaging mathematics instruction. High expectations should be set for all, with accommodations for those who need them. Students will confidently engage in mathematics tasks, explore evidence, and provide reasoning and proof to support their work. As active resourceful problem solvers, students will be flexible as they work in groups with access to technology. Students value mathematics when they work productively and reflectively as they communicate their ideas orally and in writing (NCTM, 2000).

This is not a highly ambitious dream, but part of the vision set forth in the National Council of Teachers of Mathematics Standards 2000 document. In this chapter, we will try to help teachers clarify the new mathematics standards, as well as offer suggestions for effective mathematics teaching.

NCTM STANDARDS FOR SCHOOL MATHEMATICS

The standards are descriptors of the mathematical content and processes that students should learn. They call for a broader scope of mathematics studies, pointing out what should be valued in mathematics instruction. The ten standards describe a comprehensive foundation of what students should know and be able to do. They state the understandings, knowledge, and skills required of elementary and middle school students.

All students should be provided with the opportunity to learn significant mathematics. The Principles and Standards for School Mathematics strengthen teachers' abilities to do that by including information about the way students develop mathematical knowledge. The standards include content (addressing what students should learn) and process (addressing aspects of doing mathematics). The content standards (number and operations, algebra, geometry, measurement, data analysis, and probability) describe the foundations of what students should know. The process standards (problem solving, reasoning and proof, communicating, making connections, and representing data) express ways of using and applying content knowledge.

The goals articulated by the standards can be responsive to accelerated changes in our society, our schools, and our classrooms. Individual teachers can make alterations for students within their classrooms, but the school itself must have a coherent program of mathematics study for students (Adams, 2000). No curriculum should be carved in stone at any level; rather it must be responsive to the lessons of the past, the concerns of the present, and the human and technological possibilities of the future.

IMPLEMENTING THE CURRICULUM STANDARDS

The next section of this chapter connects the standards to classroom practice by presenting few sample activities for each standard. The intent is not to prescribe an activity for a unique grade level, but to present activities that can be used in many grades.

Number and Number Operations Standard

Concepts and skills related to number are a basic emphasis for struggling students. Teachers should help reluctant learners strengthen their sense of number, moving from initial basic counting techniques to a more sophisticated understanding of numbers, if they are to make sense of the ways numbers are used in their everyday world. Our number system has been developing for hundreds of years. The modern system we use today had many contributions by numerous countries and cultures (Reys et al., 2003).

There are four important features of the number system:

1. Place value. The position of a numeral represents its value, for example, the numeral "2" in the numbers 21, 132, 213 represents different ways of thinking about the value of the number 2. In the first case, 2 represents two tens or 20, in the second case, 2 represents two ones or 2, and in the third case, 2 represents two hundreds or 200.

2. Base of ten. Base in the number system means a collection. In our number system, ten is the value that determines a new collection. Our number system has ten numerals: 0, 1, 2, 3, 4, 5, 6, 7, 8, 9. This collection is called a base ten system.

3. Use of zero. Unlike other number systems, our system has a symbol for zero. Encourage students to think about the Roman numeral system. The reason it is so cumbersome to use today is that it has no zero.

4. Additive property. Our number system has a specific way of naming numbers. For example, the number 321 names the number 300 + 20 + 1.

Place value is one of the most important concepts in the elementary and middle school. Solving problems that involve computation includes understanding and expressing multidigit numbers. Yet knowing when to exchange groups of ones for tens, or what to do with a zero in the hundreds place when subtracting, for example, confuses many students who then struggle with the step-by-step subtraction problem. Students are helped by solving real-world problems with hands-on materials such as counters, base ten blocks, and place value charts. Students must create meaning for themselves by using manipulatives (Kilpatrick et al., 2001).

The following place value activities are designed to get reluctant learners actively involved.

Grouping by Tens or Trading

Struggling students need experiences in counting many objects, trading for groups of tens, hundreds, and thousands; and talking together about their findings. Students need many models. Bean sticks and base-ten blocks are two models widely used by teachers. But students also need piles of materials (rice, beans, straws, counters, and unifix cubes) to practice counting, grouping, and trading.

Ask students to group by tens as they work. This makes the task of counting easier for students, counting by tens also helps students check errors in their counting. But most important, sorting by tens shows students how large amounts of objects can be organized. Some common errors related to place value include not regrouping when necessary or regrouping in the wrong place (Kamii, 2000).

Trading Rules

The base-ten system works by trading ten ones for one ten, or the reverse, trading one ten for ten ones, ten tens for one hundred, ten hundreds for one thousand, and so on. Base-ten blocks are a great ready-made model in teaching this principle. Encourage students to make their own model.

Building models with popsickle sticks and lima beans works equally well. Or if teachers wish to have students use construction paper and scissors, students can make their base-ten models by cutting out small squares of paper and pasting ten squares on a strip to form a ten. Then after completing ten tens, paste the ten strips together to make a hundred and then paste the hundreds together to form a thousand. It is time-consuming work, but well worth the effort.

Proportional models such as base-ten blocks, bean sticks, and ten strips provide physical representation. In all the examples just mentioned, the material for ten is ten times the size of the unit; the hundred is ten times the size of the ten; the thousand is ten times the size of the hundred; and so on. Metric measurement provides another proportional model. Meter stick, decimeter rods, and centimeter cubes can be used to model any three-digit number. Nonproportional models such as money do not exhibit a size relationship, but present a practical real-life model. Because both types of models are important and should be used, we recommend starting students with proportional models, as they're more concrete and help learners to understand the relationships more clearly.

Teaching Place Value

It is important that students think of numbers in many ways. A good place to start is to pass out a base-ten mat with the words "ones," "tens," and "hundreds." Also pass out base-ten blocks to each of the students (units, longs, flats). The units represent ones, longs represent tens, and flats represent hundreds. Now have the students build the number they hear. If, for example, the teacher says the number 42, the students take four long rods (tens) and place them on the tens column of their mat, and place two units in the ones column. Encourage students to test their skill in a small group by thinking of a number, verbalizing it, and then checking other students' mats.

Fractions

Fraction concepts are among the most complicated and important mathematical ideas that students encounter. Perhaps because of their complexity, fractions are also among the least understood by students. Some of the difficulties may arise from the different ways of representing fractions: spoken symbols, written symbols, manipulative materials, pictures, and real-world situations. It is difficult for struggling students to make sense of these five ways of representing fractions and connecting them in meaningful ways. Learners need many chances to work with concrete materials, observe and talk about fractional parts, and relate their experiences to science and mathematical notation. One helpful activity is to have students make a fraction kit.

Make a Fraction Kit

This introductory activity introduces fractions to students. Fractions are presented as parts of a whole.

Materials: Each student needs seven different 3 in. × 18 in. strips of colored construction paper, a pair of scissors, and an envelope to put a set of fraction pieces labeled as follows: 1, 1/2, 1/3, 1/4, 1/8, 1/12, 1/16.

Procedures: Direct students to cut and label the strips:
1. Have students select a colored strip. Emphasize that this strip represents one whole, and have students label the strip 1/1 or 1.
2. Ask students to choose another color, fold it in half, cut it, and then label each piece 1/2. Talk about what 1/2 means (1/2 means 1 piece out of 2 total pieces).
3. Have students select another color, and have them fold and cut it into four pieces, labeling each piece 1/4. Again discuss what 1/4 means (1 piece out of 4 total pieces, compare the 4 pieces with the whole).
4. Have students fold, cut, and label a fourth colored strip into eighths, a fifth strip into twelfths, and a sixth strip into sixteenths. Now each student has a fraction kit. Encourage students to compare the sizes of the pieces and talk together about what they discover. For example, students can easily observe that the fractional piece 1/16 is smaller than the piece marked 1/4. This is a good time to introduce equivalent fractions. "How many 1/16 pieces would it take to equal 1/4? What other fractional pieces would equal 1/4?" Explaining equivalence with a fraction kit makes fractions more meaningful (Burns, 2001).

Algebra Standard: Patterns and Functions

Patterns are everywhere in everyday life. People organize their home and work activities around patterns. The inclusion of patterns and functions in elementary and middle school opens many possibilities for math instruction. Teachers can connect many ideas in mathematics to student's background knowledge by encouraging them to describe patterns and functions in their own language to help them represent those ideas with mathematical symbols. For example, if a student has described a pattern such as "each object is 3 more than the last one, they can symbolically represent their idea as n (the object) and describe the nth object as $n + 2$. So patterns and functions naturally lead to an understanding of functions in algebra. In the activities that follow, we will explore only a few types of patterns and functions and ways to describe them. The more opportunities struggling students have to describe patterns and functions with pictures, words, tables, and variables, the more power with mathematics they will have (Kennedy & Tipps, 2000).

Multiplication Activity: Using Algebra to Build Rectangles

Discuss rectangles and demonstrate how to name them, for example, 2×3 (2 rows of 3 units), 4×5 (4 rows of 5 units). Provide students with a sheet of graph paper.

Procedures: Instruct students to plan a design, creature, or scene that they could make using only rectangles. Have them cut the graph paper into rectangles. Use the whole page. Paste the rectangles onto construction paper to make their design. Write a number sentence that tells how many 1 cm $\times$ 1 cm rectangles are included in their design. Since all students started with the same size graph paper, they should all get the same answer although their equations will be different. If the class uses a 10 cm $\times$ 10 cm graph paper grid, students can write statements that show what percentage of the whole picture is represented by each part. Have students write stories about their pictures. The stories should include mathematical statements using algebraic notation (Moses & Cobb, 2001).

Multiplication Factor Puzzles Activity

Place a large sheet of butcher paper on the chalkboard. Divide the paper, labeling each part with a multiplication product (18, 20, 21, 36, 40, and so on). Divide the class into teams. Ask each team to find and cut out of graph paper all the rectangles that can be made with a given number (20, for example). Have each team label and paste their rectangles on the butcher paper under that number (Newstrom & Scannel, 1997). As a whole class, review the findings and determine if all the possible rectangles have been found for each number without duplicates (flips, rotations). List the factors for each number.

Geometry Standard

In the elementary grades, geometry should provide the experiences for students to develop the concepts of shape, size, symmetry, congruence, and similarity in two- and three-dimensional space. Reluctant learners should begin with familiar objects and use a wide variety of concrete materials to develop appropriate vocabulary and build understanding.

Construct a Chinese Tangram Puzzle

The tangram is a Chinese puzzle made from seven geometric shapes. The seven shapes can be put together in hundreds of ways. Tangrams are fun for students to work with in developing spatial concepts. The tangram puzzle is cut from a square. Having students cut their own is a good lesson in following directions.

Materials: 6-in. squares of construction paper, scissors.

Procedures (for making a tangram kit):
1. Fold the square in half. Have students cut it apart to make two triangles.
2. Have students take one triangle and fold it in half and cut.
3. Take the other triangle, and make two folds, first in half, then fold the top corner down. Cut along the folds (students should have one trapezoid and one triangle).
4. Cut the trapezoid in half.
5. Fold one trapezoid to make a square and a triangle. Cut.
6. Fold the last trapezoid to make a parallelogram and a triangle. Cut.

Exploration:
1. Use the three smallest triangles to make a square. Use the same pieces to make a triangle, a rectangle, a trapezoid, and a parallelogram.
2. Use the five smaller pieces (all but the two large triangles) to make the same shapes.
3. Repeat with all seven pieces.

Evaluation: When students have made a tangram kit of their own have them put the square together. Encourage them to share their puzzle with family and friends.

Extensions:
1. Have students explore using the pieces to make a shape of their own. Have them draw an outline around the shape on drawing paper, name it, sign it, and put it in a class tangram box so that others can solve their puzzles.
2. Area and perimeter: encourage students to compare the areas of the square, the parallelogram, and the large triangle. Then, compare their perimeters. Have students record their findings.

Measurement Standard

Concepts and skills in the measurement standard deal with making comparisons between what is being measured and a standard unit of measurement. Students acquire measuring skills through firsthand experiences. It is important to remind students that measurement is never exact, even the most careful measurements are approximations. Students need to learn to make estimates when measuring.

Measurement tools and skills have many uses in everyday life. Being able to measure connects mathematics to the real-world environment. Being able to use the tools of measurement: rulers, measuring cups, scales, thermometers, meter sticks, and so on—and to estimate with these tools, are essential skills for students to develop.

Instruction in measurement should progress through these attributes of measurement: length, weight/mass, volume/capacity, time, temperature, and area. Within each of these areas students need to begin making comparisons with standard and nonstandard units. In upper grades, more emphasis can be placed on using measurement tools to measure.

Sample Measurement Activity: Body Ratios

Students need direct concrete experiences when interacting with mathematical ideas. The following activities are designed to clarify many commonly held misconceptions.

Finding the Ratio of Your Height to Your Head

How many times do you think a piece of string equal to your height would wrap around your head? Many struggling students have a mental picture of their body, and they make a guess relying on that perception. Have students make an estimate, then have them verify it. Few make an accurate guess based on their perceptions.

Comparing Height with Circumference

Have students imagine a soft drink can. Then have them think about taking a string and wrapping it around the can to measure its circumference. Have students guess if they think the circumference is longer, shorter, or about the same height as the can. Encourage students to estimate how high the circumference measure will reach. Then have the students try it. Like the previous activity, many students guess incorrectly. The common misperception is that the string will be about the same length as the height of the can. There is a feeling of surprise or mental confusion when they discover that the circumference is about three times the height of the can. Struggling students feel more confident when they see fellow classmates searching for a correct answer. Repeat the experiment with other cylindrical containers. Have students record their predictions and come up with a conclusion (Burns, 2001).

Group Activity: Estimate, Measure, and Compare Your Shoes

Materials: Unifix cubes, shoes.

Procedures: Estimate how many unifix cubes would fit in your shoe. Write your estimate. Choose a volunteer to take off his or her shoe. Then students are instructed to estimate how many unifix cubes would fit in the shoe. When finished with the estimate, have students actually measure the shoe using unifix cubes. Students record the measurement. Pass the shoe to the next group, they estimate and record the actual measurement. Continue passing the shoes around the class until students have recorded estimates and actual measurements of the shoes from each of the groups.

Evaluation: Instruct students to compare the shoes. Have students explain what attribute of measurement they used. Encourage students to think of another way to measure the shoes. Explain how it might be more accurate (Battista, 2002). Struggling students are actively engaged in estimating and measuring each other's shoes.

Metric Perimeter using Cuisinaire Rods

Materials: Cuisinaire rods, centimeter paper.

Procedures:
1. Have students use one red rod (2 cm), two light green rods (3 cm), and one purple rod (4 cm).
2. Arrange the rods into a shape on centimeter-squared paper in such a way that when students trace around it, they draw only on the grid paper lines.
3. Students should cut out the shape and have it remain in one piece. Make several different shapes this way.
4. Trace each and record its perimeter. Try to get the longest and the shortest perimeter.

Data Analysis and Probability Standard

It is difficult to listen to the news on television or pick up a newspaper without noticing the extensive use of charts, graphs, probability, and statistics. Following are a few suggestions for teaching struggling students some elementary concepts for probability and graphing.

The study of data analysis, statistics, and probability invites students to collect, organize, and describe information. Students communicate data through tables, graphs, and other representations. Probability and statistics are mathematical tools for analyzing and drawing conclusions about data.

Classifying and Predicting

Give students a list of statements and ask them to sort them into three piles labeled "certain," "uncertain," and "impossible." Use statements such as the following:

- Tomorrow it will rain.
- I will get 100 percent on my next spelling test.
- Tomorrow we will all visit Mars.
- If I flip a coin, it will either land heads or tails.

As the students classify the statements, discuss with them the reasons for the classifications. When they have finished, ask them to further classify the uncertain statements as either likely or unlikely. In doing this, students are predicting the outcome. Encourage students to give examples of activities and experiments to clarify their thinking. As a follow-up activity, have students come up with their own list of statements to classify into categories and offer their predictions. Reluctant learners become active math participants.

Predicting Coins and Colors

Ask students to predict whether a coin will land on heads or tails. Flip the coin and show the result. Ask students to predict the outcome of several flips of the coin. Discuss if one flip seems to have an influence on the next flip. Events are called independent if one event has no effect on another. Give each student a penny and ask them to make a tally of the heads and tails out of ten flips. Talk about such terms as "equally likely," "random," and "unbiased." Clearly explain the terms. If a student seems confused have him or her work with a partner.

Show the students a spinner with three colors (red, yellow, blue). Spin the spinner a few times to show that it is a fair spinner. Ask students to predict the number of times they could expect to get yellow if they spin the spinner thirty times. Can they find a formula for predicting the number of times a color will come up? If the probability of landing on each color is equally likely, they can write the probability of landing on any one color as the number of favorable outcomes or the total number of outcomes.

In the example of the spinner, the total number of outcomes is three because there are three colored sections altogether. Therefore, the probability of getting yellow is one out of three or 1/3. Ask the students to predict the number of times they could expect to get yellow if they were to spins the spinner thirty times.

Try the experiment using different colors and different numbers of spins. Can the students find a formula for predicting the number of times a color will come up?

Exploring Sports Statistics

The following are the salaries of five professional basketball players: $80,000, $80,000, $100,000, $120,000, and $620,000, The players are complaining about their salaries. They say that the mode of the salaries is $80,000 and that they deserve more money for all the games they play. The owners claim the mean salary is $200,000 and that this is plenty for any team. Which side is correct? Is anyone lying? How can students explain the difference in the reports?

Ask students to look in newspapers and magazines for reported averages. Are there any discrepancies in the reports? Bring in reports for discussion in class. Even slow readers respond enthusiastically to this sports challenge. Encourage students to read any reported statistics carefully (Whitin & Whitin, 2000).

Data Investigation Exercises that Empower Learners

In the future we will all be called upon to approach and solve problems not even envisioned today. A good preparation in mathematics provides the language, the tools, and the computational techniques needed to get the job done. Understanding the conceptual bases of mathematics, having the ability to communicate mathematical ideas to others, and demonstrating mathematical competence will be more important than ever.

A mathematics investigation is more demanding than a problem or an exercise. Sometimes they are used to introduce and learn mathematical concepts. More often investigations are project-like culminating activities that help students integrate what they are learning into a comprehensible whole. Like the problem, the investigation lets struggling students use several different approaches. It requires students to generate and structure the problem—creating a context that invites sustained work.

Problem Solving Standard

Problem solving has been central to elementary mathematics for nearly two decades. Problem solving refers to engaging in a task where the solution is not known. George Polya, a well-known mathematician, devised a four-step scheme for solving problems: understand the problem, create a plan or strategy, follow through with the approach selected, check back. Does it make sense?

Problems are teaching tools that can be used for different purposes. The solutions are never routine and there is usually no right answer because of the multitude of possibilities. Strategies include guessing and checking, making a chart or table, drawing a picture, acting out the problem, working backward, creating a simpler problem, looking for patterns, using an equation, using logic, asking someone for help, making an organized list, using a computer simulation—or come up with your own idea; take a risk.

Teachers should model the problem-solving strategies needed for thinking about mathematics content or responding to particular math problems. Modeling might include the thinking that goes into selecting what strategy to use, deciding what options are possible, and checking on their progress as they go along. Reluctant learners can catch on quickly if guided through this process. Following are a few problem-solving activities:

Present Interesting Problems

Present a problem to the class. Have students draw pictures of what the problem is about, or act out the problem, or have one student read the problem leaving out the numbers. Once students begin to visualize what the problem is about, they have much less difficulty solving it. Students should work in small groups when arriving at strategies and when solving the problems. Students should write how they solved it and discuss and check their answers with other groups.

The following is a sample problem to present to the class:

One day Farmer Bill was counting his pigs and chickens.
He noticed they had 60 legs and there were 22 animals in all.
How many of each kind of animal did he have?

This is a fun problem for struggling students if they can draw a picture of the animals and think about what the problem is asking. Ask students to provide the following information:

Record your strategy below:
Solve the problem another way:

Communication Standard

Outside the classroom, real-world problems are rarely solved by people working alone. People work in groups and pool their knowledge. Cooperative group learning is a way to help students develop communication skills. Through listening and talking students learn to express ideas and compare them to others. Students listen to explanations and solutions of their peers and obtain information from books and electronic sources. Throughout the elementary and middle school years students develop mathematical language using precise terms to describe math concepts and procedures.

Connections Standard

The connections standard emphasizes the many relationships between mathematics topics and everyday life. Important connections for struggling students are between the hands-on, intuitive mathematics that students have learned through their own experiences and the mathematics they are learning in school. Students' ability to experience meaningful mathematics is based on strong connections in applying math content to out of school situations.

Making Connections (Addition and Subtraction)

When students are learning about the operations of addition and subtraction, it is helpful for them to make connections between these processes and the world around them. Story problems help them see the actions of joining and separating. Using manipulative and sample word problems gives them experiences in joining sets, and figuring the differences between them. By pretending and using concrete materials, learning becomes more meaningful. Tell stories in which the learners pretend to be animals or things.

Building Connections across Disciplines

In elementary and middle school, students should be developing the processes of scientific inquiry and mathematical problem solving. This includes inferring, communicating, measuring, classifying, and predicting. The kinds of investigations that connect the two disciplines are problems like these:

1. How many ways can you sort your bag of buttons?
2. Make a Venn Diagram using your buttons. Students may need help understanding what a Venn Diagram is. Again, modeling and getting struggling students involved by working with a group dispels confusion.
3. Classify the buttons (by light and dark colors, small to large in size, number of ridges, number of patterns, number of holes) (Andrews & Trafton, 2002).

Representation Standard

Representing ideas and connecting them to mathematics is the basis for understanding. Representations make mathematics more concrete. A typical elementary classroom has several sets of manipulative materials to improve computational skills and make learning more enjoyable.

Base-ten blocks will be used in these activities to represent the sequence of moving from concrete manipulations to the abstract algorithms. Students need many chances to become familiar with the blocks, discovering the vocabulary (1's = units, 10's = longs, 100's = flats) and the relationships among the pieces. The following activities will explore trading relationships in addition, subtraction, multiplication, and division.

Banker's Game (Simple Addition)

In this activity small groups of students will be involved in representing tens. The game works best by dividing the class into small groups (four or five players and one banker). Each player begins with a playing board divided into units, longs, and flats. Before beginning, the teacher should explain the use of the board. Any blocks the student receives should be placed on the board in the column that has the same shape at the top. A student begins the game by rolling a die and asking the banker for the number rolled in units. They are then placed in the units column on the student's board. Each student is in charge of checking his or her board to decide if a trade is possible. The trading rule states that players may have more than nine objects in any column at the end of their turn. If anyone has more than nine, the player must gather them together and go to the banker and make a trade, (for example, ten units for one long). Play does not proceed to the next player until all the trades have been made. The winner is the first player to earn five tens. This game can be modified by using two dice and increasing the winning amount.

Take Away Game (Subtraction)

This game is simply the reverse of the Banker's Game. The emphasis here is on representing the regrouping of tens. Players must give back in units to the bank whatever is rolled on the die. To begin, all players place the same number of blocks on their boards. Exchanges must be made with the banker. Rules are quickly made by the students (for example, when rolling a six, a player may hand the banker a long and ask for four units back). It is helpful for students to explain their reasoning to one another. The winner is the first to have an empty playing board. Students should decide in their group beforehand whether an exact roll is necessary to go out or not.

Teaching Division with Understanding

Base-ten blocks bring understanding to an often complex algorithmic process. The following activity is a good place to start when introducing and representing division.

1. Using base-ten blocks have students show 393 with flats, rods, and units.
2. Have the students divide the blocks into three equal piles.
3. Slowly ask students to explain what they did. How many flats in each pile, how many rods, how many units?
4. Give students several more problems. Some examples: Start with 435 and divide into three piles. Encourage students to explain how many flats, rods, and units they found at the end of all their exchanges. In this problem, one flat will have to be exchanged for ten rods (tens), and then, the rods divided into three groups. One rod remains. Next, students will have to exchange the one rod for ten units, and then, divide the units into three groups. No units are left in this problem. Continue doing more verbal problems, pausing and letting students explain how they solved them. What exchanges were made? It is helpful to have students work together trying to explain their reasoning, correcting each other, and asking questions (Burns, 1988).
5. After many problems, perhaps in the next class session, explain to the students that they're now ready to record their work on paper still using the blocks. The teacher shows two ways to write the problem: $435 \div 3 =$ and $435/3 =$. Then, the teacher asks the students three questions and waits until all students have finished with each question.

    Question 1: How many 100's in each group? (Students go to their record sheet above the division symbol of the problem. They answer one flat, so they record 1 on their sheet).

    Question 2: How many in all? Students check how many cubes are represented, they answer three hundred, so they record 300 on their sheet.

    Question 3: How many are left? Students return to the problem and subtract $435 - 300 = 135$.

    Now the problem continues with the tens, then the ones. Again, they start over asking the three questions each time (Burns, 1988).
6. For advanced students, this seems like an elaborate way of doing division. By using manipulative and teaching with understanding, beginning division makes sense to elementary students. Teachers can introduce shortcuts later to make more advanced division easier and faster.

Students learn best when they are actively engaged in meaningful mathematics tasks using hands-on materials. Such a mathematics classroom encourages students' thinking, risk-taking, and communicating with peers and adults about every day experiences.

SAMPLE ACTIVITIES

In an effort to link the mathematics standards to classroom practice, a few sample activities are presented. The intent is not to prescribe an activity for a unique grade level, but to present activities that could be modified and used in many grades.

Activity 1. Estimate and Compare

Objectives:

In grades K-4, the curriculum should include estimation so students can Explore estimation strategies.

Recognize when an estimate is appropriate.

Determine the reasonableness of results.

Apply estimation in working with quantities, measurement, computation, and problem solving.

Math and science instruction in the primary grades tries to make classifying and using numerals an essential part of classroom experience. Children need many opportunities to identify quantities and see relationships between objects. Students count and write numerals. When developing beginning concepts, students need to manipulate concrete materials and relate numbers to problem situations (Small et al., 2004). They benefit by talking, writing, and hearing what others think. In the following activity students are actively involved in estimating, manipulating objects, counting, verbalizing, writing, and comparing.

Directions:

1. Divide students into small groups (two or three). Place a similar group of objects that are color coded in a container for each group. Pass out recording sheets divided into partitions with the color of the container in each box.
2. Have young students examine the container on their desks, estimate how many objects are present, discuss with their group, and write their guess next to the color on the sheet.
3. Next, have the group count the objects and write the number they counted next to the first number. Instruct the students to circle the greater number.
4. Switch cans or move to the next station and repeat the process. A variety of objects (small plastic cats, marbles, paper clips, colored shells, etc.) add interest and are real motivators.

Activity 2. Adding and Subtracting in Real-life Situations

Objectives: In early grades the mathematics curriculum should include concepts of addition and subtraction of whole numbers so that students can

Develop meaning for the operations by modeling and discussing a rich variety of problem situations.

Relate the mathematical language and symbolism of operations to problem situations and informal language.

When struggling students are learning about the operations of addition and subtraction, it's helpful for them to make connections between these processes and the world around them. Story problems using ideas from science help them see the actions of joining and separating. Using manipulatives and sample word problems gives them experiences in joining sets, and figuring the differences between them. By pretending and using concrete materials, learning becomes more meaningful.

Directions:
1. Divide students into small groups (two or three).
2. Tell stories in which the learners can pretend to be animals, plants, other students, or even space creatures.
3. Telling stories is enhanced by having students use unifix cubes or other manipulatives to represent the people, objects, or animals in the oral problems.
4. Have students work on construction paper or prepare counting boards on which trees, oceans, trails, houses, space stations, and other items have been drawn.

Activity 3. Solving Problems

Problem solving should be the starting place for developing struggling students' understanding. Teachers should present word problems for students to discuss and find solutions working together, without the distraction of symbols. The following activities attempt to link word problems to meaningful situations.

Objectives: Students will
Solve problems.
Work in a group.
Discuss and present their solutions.

Directions:
1. Divide students into small groups (two or three).
2. Find a creative way to share 50¢ among four students. Explain your solution. Is it fair? How could you do it differently?
3. The students in your class counted and found there were 163 sheets of construction paper. They were given the problem of figuring out how many sheets each child would receive if they were divided evenly among them.
4. Encourage students to explain their reasoning to the class.

5. After discussing each problem, show the students the standard notation for representing division. Soon you will find students will begin to use the standard symbols in their own writing.

Activity 4. Using Statistics for Supermarket Shopping

Statistics is the science or study of data. Statistical problems require collecting, sorting, representing, analyzing, and interpreting information.

Objectives: Students will
 Collect, organize, and describe data.
 Construct, read, and interpret displays of data.
 Formulate and solve problems that involve collecting and analyzing data.

Problem:
1. Your group has $2.00 to spend at the market. What will you purchase?
2. Have groups explain and write down their choices.
3. Next, have groups collect data from all the groups in the class.
4. Graph the class results.

THE INTERACTIVE FUTURE OF MATH INSTRUCTION

Instruction in mathematics has become much more than knowing how to balance a checkbook or estimating how long it will take to get to a new location. Over the last few decades, both teaching methods and subject matter content have changed. So have the textbooks. Teachers of mathematics no longer teach computation and procedures in isolation from the situations that require those skills. In today's schools, students learn to perform mathematics computations by working together to put these skills into practice (Cavanagh et al., 2004).

Over the last three decades the term *arithmetic* has faded while mathematics inquiry, mathematical reasoning, and problem solving have moved front and center. Whether it's asking questions, gathering evidence, making conjectures, formulating models, or building sound arguments, this is mathematics today. As the National Council of Teachers of Mathematics' most recent guidelines point out, basic arithmetic skills must not be neglected. Problem solving and inquiry may be the keys to mathematics instruction in the twenty-first century, but computational skills like addition, subtraction, multiplication, division, fractions, and mental arithmetic still provide the foundation.

To help their students achieve a deeper understanding, more attention is being given to application and social interaction. Collaborative inquiry and problem-solving activities have become important up-to-date avenues to deep knowledge in mathematics. Now, students must be able to use a wide range of mathematical tools to solve math-related problems (Small et al., 2004). Knowing mathematics means being able to use it in purposeful ways. It also means being able to understand the role that mathematics serves in society.

NEW IDEAS ON TEACHING AND LEARNING

There is general agreement that a constructive, active view of learning must be reflected in the way that math and science are taught (Van de Walle, 2004). Classroom mathematics experiences should stimulate students, build on past understandings, and explore their own ideas. This means that students have many chances to interpret math ideas and construct understandings for themselves. To do this, struggling students need to be involved in problem-solving investigations and projects that engage thinking and reasoning. Working with materials in a group situation helps reinforce thinking. Students talk together, present their understandings, and try to make sense of the task.

Some of the newest methods for teaching mathematics in active small group situations include writing about how they solved problems, keeping daily logs or journals, and expressing attitudes through creative endeavors such as building or art work (Whitin & Whitin, 2000).

With the renewed emphasis on thinking, communicating, and making connections between topics, students are more in control of their learning. With collaborative inquiry, students have many experiences with manipulatives, calculators, computers, and working on real-world applications. There are more opportunities to make connections and work with peers on interesting problems. The ability to express basic math understandings, to estimate confidently, and check the reasonableness of their estimates are part of what it means to be literate, numerate, and employable.

Whether it's making sense of newspaper graphs, identifying the dangers of global warming, or reading schedules at work, mathematics has real meaning in our lives. The same might be said for using the calculator, working with paper and pencil, or doing mental mathematics, students must master the basic facts of arithmetic before they can harness the full power of mathematics. Unfortunately, simply learning to do algorithms (the step-by-step procedures used to compute with numbers) will not ensure success with problems that demand reasoning ability. The good news is that the curriculum is changing to make mathematics more interactive and relevant to what students need to know in order to meet changing intellectual and societal demands. And it is doing this, without dropping the underlying structure of mathematics.

Teachers have found that the more opportunities students have to participate with others, the more likely they are to learn to do mathematics in knowledgeable and meaningful ways. Quite simply, struggling students learn more if they have opportunities to describe their own ideas, listen to others, and cooperatively solve problems. All collaborative or cooperative learning structures are designed to increase student participation in learning, while building on the twin incentives of shared group goals and individual accountability.

HINTS FOR HELPING STRUGGLING STUDENTS UNDERSTAND MATHEMATICS

- Introduce math concepts in real-world settings.
- Develop an understanding of the math operations (adding, subtracting, multiplying, dividing) by tapping into students' curiosity.
- Use differentiated instruction to allow for students' learning styles.
- Integrate ideas with the mathematics standards.
- Plan stimulating lessons.
- Rewrite textbook materials to reflect reluctant learners' interests.
- Let learners explore materials before they use them.

In a world filled with the products of mathematical inquiry, knowing about this subject is more important than ever. Being naive or afraid of mathematics can be a real problem in school, in the workplace, and for citizens in a democracy. It is also a problem if students don't have a clue about how math impacts their day-to-day lives.

Peer support also helps students feel more confident and willing to make mistakes that go hand-in-hand with serious inquiry. So, whether you want to paint it in the subtle hues of collaborative inquiry or the day-glow colors of cooperative learning, student learning teams are a powerful way to approach mathematics instruction for reluctant math students.

SUMMARY AND CONCLUSION

This chapter stressed investigations, problems, and collaborative activities that are interesting for all students—and especially attractive for struggling students. We emphasized problem solving, communication, collaborative learning, deductive reasoning, and making connections because these are all part of what twenty-first-century math instruction is about.

Mathematics is more than a language for describing the natural world. It can also used to describe common events in everyday life and complex events in science, technology, business, and just about everything else. Understanding the subject puts people at an advantage in school, in the workplace, and as citizens in a democracy. The central concern here is with elementary and middle school students, and their need to learn mathematics for complex and common applications. The mathematics curriculum is continually changing to reflect the needs of students with diverse learning needs. In fact, the diversity of today's students requires a differentiated approach to instruction to meet societal demands and the mathematical needs of the twenty-first century.

The National Council of Teachers of Mathematics and the Mathematical Sciences Education Board suggest changes in what mathematics we teach, how it is taught, and to how to get struggling students involved. Incorporating the standards into national and state standards gives their suggestions broad seal of approval. The involvement and approval of the major professional organizations further amplifies the impact. So it is little wonder that mathematics instruction is shifting the emphasis from an elaborate study of procedures toward paying more attention to a deeper understanding of the central ideas of mathematics.

An understanding of concepts, proficiency with skills, and a positive attitude all have roles to play in mathematical literacy (numeracy). Seeing math as part of the wider world, rather than simply dry problems or dull textbooks, is crucial for involving reluctant learners. As they gain mathematical reasoning skills, struggling students are much more likely to have a positive attitude toward math. For everyone in the classroom: with competency comes confidence and an increased willingness to learn math content.

In tomorrow's schools, both teachers and students will be expected to exhibit new ways of interacting and thinking about mathematics. Much of what we do in the future will be based on the best of today's commonsense, classroom-proven approaches that work for teachers at any grade level. Differentiated instruction and collaborative problem solving are good examples. Both are particularly helpful for teachers who are trying to provide struggling students with experiences that can enable them to acquire mathematical knowledge.

As you go about matching math instruction to the readiness, interests, and talents of all students, the result is likely to be the development of a natural sense of community in the classroom. This can all help provide social support for recognizing the relationship of mathematical problems to life outside of school. And it can generate student confidence in their ability to understand and apply mathematics. The goal: to give students an appreciation of the power, beauty, and fascination of mathematics—and help them become mathematically empowered.

The teaching of a mathematical topic can begin with a problem situation that embodies key aspects of the topic, and mathematical techniques are developed as reasonable responses to reasonable problems. The learning of mathematics in this way can be viewed as a movement from the concrete (real world problem) to the abstract (symbolic representations).

—Thomas Schroeder

QUESTIONS FOR TEACHERS AND PROSPECTIVE TEACHERS

1. What is a real-world experience a teacher could use to engage students in a discussion about understanding math operations (adding, subtracting, multiplying, dividing)?
2. List key steps a teacher would take when helping students with a subtraction error. Select a computation task that engages students' interests and intellect.
3. Design a question or activity that focuses on estimation and problem solving in a way that promotes the investigation and growth of mathematical ideas.
4. How would you focus on helping struggling students make sense of math and see the subject in a more positive light?
5. The attitude of fear and dislike of math are often related. Design a math lesson that involves collaborative reasoning in a way that is somehow intrinsically interesting, surprising, and esthetically pleasing.

REFERENCES AND RESOURCES

Adams, D. & Hamm, M. (1998) *Collaborative inquiry in science, math and technology.* Portsmouth, NH: Heinemann.

Adams, T. (2000). Helping children learn mathematics through multiple intelligences and standards for school mathematics. *Childhood Education 77,* 86–92.

Andrews, A. G. & Trafton, P. R. (2002). *Little kids powerful problem solvers: Math stories from a kindergarten classroom.* Westport, CT: Heinemann.

Battista, M. T. (2002). Learning in an inquiry-based classroom. In J. Sowder & B. Schappelle (eds.), *Lessons learned from research* (pp. 75–84). Reston, VA: National Council of Teachers of Mathematics.

Benjamin, A. (2003). *Differentiated instruction: A guide for elementary school teachers.* Larchmont, NY: Eye On Education.

Burns, M. (1988). *Mathematics with manipulatives.* Six videotapes. White Plains, NY: Cuisinaire Company of America.

Burns, M. (2001). *About teaching mathematics: A K-8 resource.* White Plains, NY: Math Solutions Publication.

Burris, A. (2005). *Understanding the math you teach: Content and methods for prekindergarten through grade 4.* Upper Saddle River, NJ: Pearson Education.

Cavanagh, M., Dacey, L., Findell,C., Greenes, C., Sheffield, L., & Small, M. (2004). *Navigating through number and operations in prekindergarten–grade 2.* Reston, VA: National Council of Teachers of Mathematics.

Johnson, D. & R. Johnson. (1990). Using cooperative learning in math. In N. Davidson (ed). *Cooperative learning and mathematics*, (p. 122). Menlo Park, CA: Addison-Wesley.

Kamii, C. (2000). *Young children reinvent arithmetic: Implications of Piaget's theory.* New York, NY: Teacher's College Press.

Kennedy, L. & Tipps, S. (2000). *Guiding children's learning of mathematics.* Belmont, CA: Wadsworth/Thomas Learning.

Kilpatrick, J., Swafford, J., & Findell, B. (eds.) (2001). *Adding it up: Helping children learn mathematics.* Washington, DC: National Academy Press.

Moses, R. P. & Cobb, Jr., C. E. (2001). *Radical Equations: Math Literacy and Civil Rights.* East Sussex, UK: Beacon Press.

National Council of Teachers of Mathematics (NCTM). (2000). *Principles and standards for school mathematics.* Reston, VA: NCTM.

Newstrom, J. & Scannel, E. (1997). *The big book of team building games.* San Francisco, CA: Jossey-Bass.

Paulos, J. (1988). *Innumeracy: Mathematical illiteracy and its consequences.* New York, NY: Hill and Wang.

Polya, G. (1957). *How to solve it.* 2nd ed. Princeton, NJ: Princeton University Press.

Posamentier, A. (2005). *What successful math teachers do, grades 6–12: 79 research strategies for the standards-based classroom.* Thousand Oaks, CA: Sage Publications.

Reys, R., Lindquist, M., Lamdin, D., Smith, N., & Suydam, M. (2003). *Helping children learn mathematics.* New York, NY: John Wiley & Sons.

Schroeder, T. & Lester, F. (1989). Developing an understanding in mathematics via problem solving. In Trafton, P. (ed.), *New directions in elementary school mathematics.* Reston, VA: NCTM.

Small, M., Sheffield, L. J., Cavanagh, M., Dacey, L., Findell, C. R., & Greenes, C. E. (2004). *Navigating through Problem Solving and Reasoning in Grade 2.* Reston, VA: National Council of Teachers of Mathematics (NCTM).

Stephen, M., Bowers, J., Cobb, P., & Gravemeijer, K. (2004). *Supporting students' development of measuring conceptions: Analyzing students' learning in social context.* Reston, VA: NCTM.

Van de Walle, J. (2004). *Elementary and middle school mathematics: Thinking developmentally.* 5th ed. Boston, MA: Pearson Education.

White, D. (2004). By way of introduction: Teaching mathematics to special needs students. *Teaching Children Mathematics*, 11(3), 116–117.

Whitin, P. & Whitin, D. (2000). *Math is language too: Talking and writing in the mathematics classroom.* Reston, VA: National Council of Teachers of Mathematics; Urbana, IL: National Council of Teachers of English.

RESOURCES

The National Council of Teachers of Mathematics Standards

Principles
- Equity
- Curriculum

- Teaching
- Learning
- Assessment
- Technology

Standards for School Mathematics
- Number and Operations
- Algebra
- Geometry
- Measurement
- Data Analysis and Probability
- Problem Solving
- Reasoning and Proof
- Communication
- Connections
- Representation

6

Science for All Students

Collaborative Inquiry, Active Involvement, and Struggling Students

> Science teaching should change . . . with classrooms becoming a community in which all students learn science through inquiry and active involvement.
>
> —National Science Education Standards

Science is an exciting and interesting system of knowing about the world and beyond. Scientific knowledge is based on information gathered by observing, experimenting, and collaborative inquiry. At the elementary and middle school levels, it is best to learn science by doing science in association with others. It always helps when teachers use a variety of classroom practices that closely attend to students' prior knowledge, learning styles, and social comfort zones. And, as good teachers will tell you, it's best not to assume that one student's optimum path for learning is identical to anyone else's. Since there can be no intelligent inquiry in a vacuum, teachers sometimes have to provide information, generate excitement, and suggest questioning possibilities. Still, early on, all students should be encouraged to ask their own big questions.

Here we will explore the nature of science, the science standards, and how scientific inquiry affects struggling students at the elementary and middle school levels. Collaborative inquiry is part of every science program. Inquiry involves curiosity, posing questions, and actively seeking answers. Observing, measuring, collecting, and classifying are a part science that comes naturally to many students. It's a pain for others. So we suggest some motivating approaches to learning science for those who would rather avoid the subject. This can be done without hindering high-achieving students. Of course, it is up to the teacher to provide ways for each individual to learn science as deeply and quickly as possible.

It is a good idea to relate the scientific processes and related inquiry skills to just about every aspect of classroom life. So, a sampling of activities are provided to help teachers open up the possibilities for cutting across subject matter boundaries to get at the big ideas of science. This chapter also

- Explores how collaborative learning is related to the scientific process.
- Examines scientific inquiry and its implications for struggling students.
- Identifies how elementary and middle school students learn science.
- Suggests activities and methods based on the national science standards.
- Explores ways to help reluctant learners get excited about science.

When it comes to struggling students, it is best to minimize the learning problems and maximize the opportunity to participate in a skill-oriented inquiry science program.

An important goal of science instruction is to open the minds of all students and expand their perception and appreciation of the very nature of life—water, rocks, plants, animals, people, and other elements of the world. As students' scientific understandings about the world in which they live develop, their scientific curiosity, interest, and knowledge will be amplified.

THE CHANGING SCIENCE CURRICULUM

The past quarter century has seen many pressures to reinvent the goals of science education and change how the subject is taught. At the same time, the technological products of science have sparked changes in the practices of working scientists, the economy, and how people live and work. The impact on the culture is dramatic. Technology shapes culture and culture returns the favor. At a personal level, a student's social culture shapes just about everything. Those with high social capital tend to do better than those with low social capital. Teamwork skills, home environment, health, and economics all have a lot to do with it. But teachers can make a big difference. In the differentiated classroom, teachers attend to the differing social and academic needs of diverse learners.

In an effort to respond to these conditions, new science standards have been identified to update the traditional concepts and principles of science the disciplines (biology, chemistry, earth science, and physics) (National Academy Press, 1996).

Do these changes represent a reinvention of goals or curricula? The most important change in science education is in the nature of science itself. Research in the sciences today is concerned with finding solutions to personal and social problems, rather than focusing on theories related to the natural world. The school problems we face today are more difficult and involved than ever before. We need to recognize that a new culture is emerging. Today's culture is defined by a global economy, an information era, differing family structures, a society that is knowledge-intensive effecting a new world of work, and new developments in how we think about learning (Howe, 2000).

An active curriculum for the twenty-first century should have the power to make a difference in the lives of struggling students and in the society where they live. The science curriculum for the new century has

1. Greater depth and less superficial coverage.
2. Focuses on problem solving.
3. Emphasizes skills and knowledge of the subject.
4. Provides for individual differences.
5. Contains a common core of subject matter.
6. Is closely coordinated to related subjects such as mathematics.
7. Is part of an integrated curriculum.
8. Is attuned to personal relevance (ASCD, 2000).

The new curriculum also provides for individual differences for those students having difficulties. There should be many ways of displaying and transferring knowledge. Most curriculum organizers stress verbal modes, many effective teachers add visual representations such as a directional chart (like a road map or web diagram). Teachers should provide a scaffolding structure at the beginning of the year; this includes offering suggestions, cues, and explanations. As the year progresses, struggling students are able to solve problems on their own. This scaffolding approach recognizes multiple intelligences and is designed to accommodate for individual differences (Thomas, 2003).

The new curriculum offers a common core of subject matter. A common curriculum for all students draws students together. A fragmented curriculum such as tracking separates students based on ability or career goals. The traditional curriculum tracked and dispersed students in different directions. In responding to individual differences, the new curriculum for all students leads to unity and builds character among students (Weiss and Pasley, 2004).

Another characteristic is that the science curriculum is closely coordinated to related subjects such as mathematics. The mathematics curriculum supports and closely relates to the science curriculum. The various developmental levels of the subject are also coordinated so the 3rd grade science content builds on the 2nd grade content and leads to the 4th grade science curriculum.

Instead of separate subjects, now elementary and middle school science are part of an integrated curriculum. Selected integration results in better achievement and improved attitudes (Glatthorn, 2000). The focus of the curriculum on active learning emphasizes results. This means improved learning for all students. A quality learning curriculum is teacher friendly, with clear objectives, and less attention given to mindless activities. The new curriculum is also attuned to personal relevance. This includes technology amid the various disciplines, giving students the tools they need to improve society (ASCD, 2000).

THE EXCITING WORLD OF SCIENCE EDUCATION

Science can be the most exciting experience for elementary and middle school students and teachers if it is taught as an active hands-on subject where students learn through doing. Science provides imaginative teachers many opportunities for helping to teach students who struggle with science. This has been complicated in the past. Science terms seemed nearly impossible to understand. Many students felt science was boring. (Really, very, boring). How are teachers going to help students trudge their way through it, or pass the tests? For elementary and middle school students struggling with their science textbooks, for those who aren't naturally drawn to the sciences or for whatever reason can't seem to connect ideas to knowledge comprehension, it is a major problem. We want these students to know they are not alone (Schultz, 2002).

STRATEGIES FOR HELPING STUDENTS
WHO STRUGGLE WITH SCIENCE

Many strategies are based on the idea that teachers adapt instruction to student differences (Benjamin, 2003). Today teachers are determined to reach all students, trying to provide the right level of challenge for students who perform below grade level, for gifted students, and for everyone in between. They are working to deliver instruction in ways that meet the needs of auditory, visual, and kinesthetic learners while trying to connect to students' personal interests. The following strategies will be helpful.

Use a Collaborative Approach with Inclusive Students

Collaborative learning is a "total class" approach that lends itself to inclusion (Wang & Birch, 1987). It requires everyone to think, learn, and teach. Within a cooperative learning classroom, there will be many and varied strengths among students. Every student will possess characteristics that will lend themselves to enriching learning for all students. Sometimes these "differences" may constitute a conventionally defined "disability," sometimes it simply means the inability to do a certain life or school-related task. And sometimes it means, as with the academically talented, being capable of work well beyond the norm. Within the collaborative learning classroom, such exceptionality need not constitute a handicap.

Collaborative learning with inclusive students is not simply a technique that a teacher can just select and adopt in order to "accommodate" a student with a disability within the regular classroom. Making significant change in the classroom process is going to require that teachers undergo changes in the ways that they teach, and in the ways they view students. This means creating comfortable, yet challenging, learning environments rich in diversity. The goal is collaboration among all types of learners. In mixed-ability groups, the emphasis must be on proficiency rather than age or grade level as a basis for student progress.

Active collaboration requires a depth of planning and a redefinition of planning, testing, and classroom management. Perhaps most significantly, collaborative learning values individual abilities, talents, skills, and background knowledge. Within a collaborative learning classroom, conventionally defined "disabilities" fade into the heterogeneity of expected and anticipated differences among all students.

Form Multiage Flexible Groups

Schools have tried to meet the needs of struggling and advanced learners by pulling them out of regular classrooms. This has resulted in many problems. Struggling students will experience more long-term success by being placed in heterogeneous classes unless teachers are ready and able to meet them at their point of readiness and systematically escalate their learning until they are able to function as competently and confidently as other learners. To maximize the potential of each learner, educators need to meet each student at his or her starting point and ensure substantial growth during each school term. Classrooms that respond to student differences benefit virtually all students. Being flexible in grouping students gives students many options to develop their particular strengths and show their performance (Tomlinson, 1999).

Set Up Learning Centers

A learning center is a space in the class that contains a group of activities or materials designed to teach, reinforce, or extend a particular concept. Centers generally focus on an important topic; and use materials and activities addressing a wide range of reading levels, learning profiles, and student interests.

A teacher may create many centers such as a science center, a music center, or a reading center. Students don't need to move to all of them at once to achieve competence with a topic or a set of skills. Have students rotate among the centers. Learning centers generally include activities that range from simple to complex.

Effective learning centers usually provide clear directions for students including what a student should do if he or she completes a task, or what to do if they need help. A record-keeping system should be included to monitor what students do at the center. An ongoing assessment of student growth in the class should be in place, which can lead to teacher adjustments in center tasks.

Develop Tiered Activities

These are helpful strategies when teachers want to address students with different learning needs. For example, a student who struggles with reading from a science textbook or has a difficult time with complex vocabulary needs some help in trying to make sense of the important ideas in a given chapter. At the same time, a student who is advanced well beyond grade level needs to find a genuine challenge in working with the same concepts.

Teachers use tiered activities so that all students focus on necessary understandings and skills but at different levels of complexity and abstractness. By keeping the focus of the activities the same, but providing different routes of access, the teacher maximizes the likelihood that each student comes away with important skills and is appropriately challenged.

Teachers should select the concepts and skills that will be the focus of the activity for all learners. Using assessments to find out what the students need and create an interesting activity that will cause learners to use an important skill or understand a key idea is part of the tired approach. Teachers should also think about, or actually draw, a ladder that places the student on a skill level (the top step represents learners with very high skills, the bottom step is for learners with low skills and complexity of understanding). It is important to provide varying materials and activities. Teachers match a version of the task to each student based on student needs and task requirements. The goal is to match the task's degree of difficulty and the students' readiness (Tomlinson & Cunningham Edison, 2003).

Make Learning More Challenging

Research indicates that alternative strategies that address the causes of poor performance offer hope for helping students succeed (Benjamin,

2002). Challenging strategies put more emphasis on authentic problems where students are encouraged to formulate their own problems on a topic they're interested in, and work together to solve it. Problems are connected to the "real world" and allow time for discussion and sharing of ideas among students.

Have a Clear Set of Standards

Integrating standards into the curriculum helps make learning more meaningful and interesting to reluctant students. Having a clearly defined set of standards helps teachers concentrate on instruction and makes clear to students the expectations of the class. Students come to understand what is expected and work collaboratively to achieve it. Challenging collaborative groups to help each other succeed is another way to avoid poor performance by reluctant students (Center for the Study of Teaching and Policy, 2001).

Expand Learning Options

Not all students learn in the same way or at the same time. Teachers can expand learning options by differentiating instruction. This means teachers reaching out to struggling students or small groups to improve teaching in order to create the best learning experience possible (Tomlinson, 1999).

Introduce Active Reading Strategies

There is an approach that uses "active reading" strategies to improve students' abilities to explain difficult text. This step-by step process involves reading aloud to yourself or someone else, as a way to build science understandings (Schultz, 2002). Although most learners self-explain without verbalizing, the active reading approach is similar to that used by anyone attempting to master new material: the best way to truly learn, is to teach, to explain something to someone else.

THE CHANGING SCIENCE CURRICULUM

Today, active science learning in the elementary and middle schools is changing the boring textbook process. It contributes to the development of interdisciplinary skills. For example, the overlap in science and mathematics is obvious when you look at common skills. Many of the best models in science education involve having students work in cross-subject and mixed-ability teams. Teachers begin by making connections between science, mathematics, and real-world concerns (a good example would be those found in the newspaper). The live action of science education and literacy are in the hands of teachers.

To use and understand science today requires an awareness of what the scientific endeavor is and how it relates to our culture and our lives. The National Council on Science and Technology Education identifies a scientifically literate person as one who recognizes the diversity and unity of the natural world, understands the important concepts and principles of science, and is aware of the ways that science, mathematics, and technology depend on each other (Atkin & Atkin, 1989; Jackson & Davis, 2000).

> Scientific literacy implies that a person can identify scientific issues underlying national and local decisions and express positions that are scientifically and technologically informed.
>
> —National Science Education Standards

REVIEWING THE NATIONAL SCIENCE CONTENT STANDARDS

The classroom must be the focus of the Science Education Standards. The content standards outline what students should know, understand, and be able to do. The standards are described as follows:

- Linking the science ideas and process skills.
- Applying science as inquiry.
- Becoming aware of physical, life, earth, and space science through activity-based learning.
- Using science understandings to design solutions to problems.
- Understanding the connection of science and technology.
- Examining and practicing science from personal and social viewpoints.
- Discovering the history and nature of science through readings, discussions, observations, and writings (National Research Council, 1996).

Inquiry in the Science Standards and the Process Skills

The inquiry skills of science (often referred to as inquiry processes) are acquired through a questioning process. As we discussed in chapter two, this question about inquiry directs the searcher to knowledge, whether newly discovered by the individual or new ideas not explored before in the field. Inquiry also raises new questions and directions for examination. The findings may generate ideas or suggest connections or ways of expressing concepts and interrelationships more clearly. The process of inquiry helps struggling students grow in content knowledge and the processes and skills of the search. It also invites reluctant learners to explore anything that interests them. Whatever the problem, subject, or issue may be, any inquiry that is done with enthusiasm and with care will use some of the same thinking processes that are used by scholars who are searching for new knowledge in their field of study.

Inquiry processes form a foundation of understanding and are components of the basic goals and standards of science and mathematics. These goals are intertwined and multidisciplinary providing students many opportunities to become involved in inquiry. Each goal involves one or more processes (or investigations). The emphasis clearly has shifted from content toward process. The inquiry process approach includes the major process skills and standards as outlined in the activities that follow:

Science Activities Based on the Science Standards

To enliven the curriculum, the authors introduced their pre-service teachers to integrating curriculum content by using the National Science Education Standards. The pre-service teachers were to design a science lesson based on the standards and the science process skills (Adams & Hamm, 1998; Hamm & Adams, 1998).

Activity 1. Mystery Liquids Experiment

Inquiry Skills: Hypothesizing, experimenting, and communicating.

Science Standards: Inquiry, physical science, science and technology, personal perspectives, written communications.

Description: In this exploring activity, students are experimenting with chemicals and doing physical science work. They are learning to use tools found in the lab and becoming familiar with the safety rules of science, mathematics, and technology. Review with the students the properties of matter (solids and liquids), then present them with the mystery compound (made from cornstarch and water).

Background Information:
Facts about solids—
Do not change shape easily.
Will not allow other solids to pass through easily.
Are usually visible.
Have a definite shape.
Become liquid when heated.

Remain solid when cooled.
Facts about liquids—
Change shape easily (take the shape of the container).
Will allow a solid to pass through easily.
May be visible or invisible.
Have a definite shape.
Become gaseous when heated.
Become solid when cooled.

Introduce the activity by talking about liquids, define the characteristics of a liquid. Have students think of all the liquids they encounter every day. Present the problem and the rules to the class.

Problem: Have students try to find out what the four mystery liquids are.

Rules:
1. Each liquid is a household substance that may or may not have been colored with food coloring to hide its identity.
2. Students are limited to using only their sense of sight to do this experiment. Absolutely no smelling, tasting, or touching the liquids! Students should experiment by manipulating.
3. For safety reasons, caution students they are NOT TO SMELL, TOUCH, OR TASTE the chemicals.
4. Each medicine dropper may be used to pick up only one liquid. We do not want contamination!

Purpose: Students will experiment with a cornstarch and water mixture trying to discover some of the properties of the magic mixture. Students will perform a variety of experiments to decide whether the magic compound is a solid or a liquid.

Materials: 1 box of cornstarch, 1 cup of water, 1 aluminum pie tin, 2 paper cups, and student worksheets or science/math journal.

Background Information: To make the mystery compound, mix 1 box of cornstarch with 1 cup of water. Food coloring can be added if you choose. The magic matter mixture has properties of both a solid and a liquid. Students make a prediction about the mysterious matter mixture, record their observations, and then use data to support that prediction.

Procedures:
1. Review the properties of matter. Ask the question, "Is the magic matter a solid or a liquid?"
2. Pass out materials and allow students to "play" with the substance for a few minutes and record their observations.

3. Have students conduct the experiments with the mystery compound and record their results on their worksheets or in their science/math journal.
4 Instruct students to analyze their data, answer the question, and support their conclusion.

Data (Observation) Sheet:
1. Color
2. Texture: what does it look and feel like?
3. What is its shape?
4. What does it smell like?

Experiment: Do each test. Record your results.
1. The quick finger poke test. Have students try to poke their finger into the mystery matter so that the tip of their finger touches the bottom of the pan. In order to make sure that this is the quick finger poke test, try to touch the bottom of the pan in 1 second. (Like their finger is touching a hot stove!)
2. The slow finger poke test. Have students try to poke their finger into the mystery matter so that the tip of their finger touches the bottom of the pan. In order to make sure that this is the slow finger poke test, try to touch the bottom of the pan in 10 seconds. (Like their finger is moving in slow motion.)
3. Shape test. Put some mystery matter into one paper cup. Have students check to see if the mystery matter takes the shape of the cup or if it stays in its first shape.
4. Pour test. Try to pour the mystery matter from one cup to another.
5. Bounce test. Hold the mystery matter about 12 inches from the desk. Drop the mystery matter. Does it bounce?
6. Ball test. Have students try to form the mystery matter into a ball. Check to see if it holds its shape for 5 seconds.
7. Heat test. Students should let the teacher know when their group gets to this point. The teacher will do this experiment for the group or the group may wish to try it with teacher supervision. Make a container out of foil. Fashion a bump on one side to clip on a clothespin. Put a small amount of the mystery matter in the container over a votive candle.
8. Cool test (after heat test). Let the mystery matter cool to room temperature.
9. Shatter test. The teacher will do this experiment for the group or the group may choose to try it with teacher supervision. Have students put the mystery matter in waxed paper on the table to see if they can shatter it with the hammer.

Results:
1. Encourage students to write a description of the activity.
2. Explain how the group went about solving the problem.
3. Record each experiment on a pie graph stating the chemical and your guesses.

Evaluation:
1. Share the results.
2. Write about what the group learned from the activity.
3. Give some follow-up suggestions for how the activity could be improved. Encourage struggling students to work with their group and follow the procedures.

Follow-up:
Have students work together to write answers to these questions.
1. How did the mystery matter act as a solid? As a liquid?
2. What are some reasons that they can think of why this material would act in this way?
3. What are some ways students might use this material?
4. Make a circle graph of the results.
5. Can they think of another test to try?

Activity 2. Demonstrating the Behavior of Molecules

Inquiry Skills: Observing, comparing, hypothesizing, experimenting, and communicating.

Science Standards: Inquiry, physical science, science and technology, personal perspectives, and written communications.

Background Information an Description: This activity simulates how molecules are connected to each other and the effect of temperature change on molecules. Students usually have questions about the way things work. The questions students naturally ask such as "Why does ice cream melt? "Why does the tea kettle burn my hand?" "Where does steam come from?" and "Why is it so difficult to break rocks?" Explain that molecules and atoms are the building blocks of matter. Heat and cold energy can change molecular form. The class is then asked to participate in the "hands-on" demonstration of how molecules work. This is a great opportunity for struggling students to participate and perhaps assume leadership as a group leader. Before beginning the demonstration explain that matter and energy exist and can be changed, but not created or destroyed. Ask for volunteers to role play the parts of molecules. Direct students to join hands to show how molecules are connected to each other, explaining that these represent matter in a solid form. Next ask them to "show what happens when a solid becomes a liquid." Heat causes the molecules to move more rapidly so they can no longer hold together. Students should drop hands and started to wiggle and move around. The next question is "how do you think molecules act when they become a gas?" Carefully move students to the generalization that heat transforms solids into liquids and then into gases. The class enjoys watching the other students wiggle and fly around as they assume the role of molecules turning into a gas. The last part of the demonstration was the idea than when an object is frozen, the molecules have stopped moving altogether. The demonstration and follow-up questions usually spark a lot of discussion and more questions.

Activity 3. What Will Float?

Inquiry Skills: Hypothesizing, experimenting, and communicating.

Science Standards: Inquiry, physical science, science and technology, personal perspectives, and written communications.

Description: The weight of water gives it pressure. The deeper the water, the more pressure. Pressure is also involved when something floats. For an object to float, opposing balanced forces work against each other. Gravity pulls down on the object, and the water pushes it up. The key to floating is the object's size relevant to its weight. If it has a high volume and is light for its size, then it has a large surface area for the water to push against. In this activity, students will explore what objects will float in water. All students should try to float some of these objects.

Materials:
large plastic bowl or aquarium
bag of small objects to test: paper
   clips, nails, keys, etc.
spoon
oil-based modeling clay

large washer
salt
ruler
paper towels
kitchen foil, 6 in. square

Procedures:
1. Have the students fill the plastic bowl half full with water.
2. Direct the students to empty the bag of objects onto the table along with the other items.
3. Next, have students separate the objects into two groups: the objects that will float, the objects that will sink. Encourage students to record their predictions in their science and math journals.
4. Have students experiment by trying to float all the objects and record what happened in their science and math journals.

Evaluation: Have students reflect on these thinking questions and respond in their math and science journals. Encourage students to work together helping students who are having trouble expressing their ideas.

1. What is alike about all the objects that floated? Sank?
2. What can be done to sink the objects that floated?
3. What can be done to float the objects that sank?
4. How can a piece of foil be made to float? Sink?
5. Describe how a foil boat can be made.
6. How many washers will the foil boat carry?
7. What could float in salt water that could not float in fresh water?
8. Encourage students to try to find something that will float in fresh water and sink in salt water.

(This activity was adapted from *Science in Elementary Education*, Peter Gega, 1994.)

Activity 4. Exploring Water Cohesion and Surface Tension

Inquiry Skills: Hypothesizing, experimenting, and communicating.

Science Standards: Inquiry, earth science, science and technology, personal perspectives, and written communications.

Description: Students will determine how many drops of water will fit on a penny in an experiment that demonstrates water cohesion and surface tension.

Materials: One penny for each pair of students, glasses of water, paper towels, eye droppers (one for each pair of students).

Procedures: Have students work with a partner. As a class, have them guess how many drops of water will fit on the penny. Record their guesses on the chalkboard. Ask students if it would make a difference if the penny was heads or tails. Also record these guesses on the chalkboard. Instruct the students to try the experiment by using an eyedropper, a penny, and a glass of water. Encourage students to record their findings in their science journals. Bring the class together again. Encourage students to share their findings with the class. Introduce the concept of cohesion. (Cohesion is the attraction of like molecules for each other. In solids and liquids the force is strongest. It is cohesion that holds a solid or liquid together. There is also an attraction among water molecules for each other.) Introduce and discuss the idea of surface tension. (The molecules of water on the surface hold together so well that they often keep heavier objects from breaking through. The surface acts as if it is covered with skin.)

Evaluation, Completion, and /or Follow-up: Have students explain how this activity showed surface tension. Instruct students to draw what surface tension looked like in their science journal. What makes the water drop break on the surface of the penny? (It is gravity.) What other examples can students think of where water cohesion can be observed? (Rain on a car windshield or window in a classroom, for example.) Even disinterested students can relate to this activity if drawn into the conversation.

Activity 5. Experimenting with Surface Tension: Soap Drops Derby

Inquiry Skills: Hypothesizing, experimenting, and communicating.

Science Standards: Inquiry, physical science, science and technology, personal perspectives, and written communications.

Description: Students will develop an understanding that technological solutions to problems, such as phosphate-containing detergents, have intended benefits and may have unintended consequences.

Objective: Students apply their knowledge of surface tension. This experiment shows how water acts like it has a stretchy skin because water molecules are strongly attracted to each other. Students will also be able to watch how soap molecules squeeze between the water molecules, pushing them apart and reducing the water's surface tension.

Background Information: Milk, which is mostly water has surface tension. When the surface of milk is touched with a drop of soap, the surface tension of the milk is reduced at that spot. Since the surface tension of the milk at the soapy spot is much weaker than it is in the rest of the milk, the water molecules elsewhere in the bowl pull water molecules away from the soapy spot. The movement of the food coloring reveals these currents in the milk.

Grouping: Divide class into groups of four or five students.

Materials: Milk (only whole or 2% will work), newspapers, a shallow container, food coloring, dish washing soap, a saucer or a plastic lid, and toothpicks.

Procedures:
1. Take the milk out of the refrigerator 1/2 hour before the experiment starts.
2. Place the dish on the newspaper and pour about 1/2 inch of milk into the dish.
3. Let the milk sit for a minute or two.

4. Near the side of the dish, put one drop of food coloring in the milk. Place a few colored drops in a pattern around the dish. What happened?
5. Pour some dish washing soap into the plastic lid. Dip the end of the toothpick into the soap, and touch it to the center of the milk. What happened?
6. Dip the toothpick into the soap again, and touch it to a blob of color. What happened?
7. Rub soap over the bottom half of a food coloring bottle. Stand the bottle in the middle of the dish. What happened?
8. The colors can move for about 20 minutes when students keep dipping the toothpick into the soap and touching the colored drops.

Follow-up Evaluation: Students will discuss their findings and share their outcomes with other groups. Struggling learners, along with the rest of the class are usually excited by the soap drops derby. Explain what the soap box derby is (a race down a hill by kids using a wooden platform). In this case the soap drops are racing in many directions. Today, NASCAR is a good example of car races. Have struggling students along with the rest of the group explain what a "soap drops derby" is.

Activity 6. Create a Static Electric Horse

Inquiry Skills: Hypothesizing, experimenting, and communicating.

Science Standards: Inquiry, physical science, science and technology, personal perspectives, and written communications.

Objectives and Description:
1. Students will have an opportunity to explore static electricity.
2. No previous knowledge of static electricity is necessary.
3. Students will learn through fun, hands-on experimentation more about the concepts of static electricity, (positive and negative charges).

Materials: 1 inflated balloon for each student, scissors, tag board horse patterns, colored tissue paper, and crayons or markers.

Procedures:
1. Short introduction focusing on the horses and a mystery question: Ask students if they think they could make a paper horse move without touching it? (No mention yet of static electricity concepts.)
2. Teacher describes how to construct the horse:
   Fold the paper in half and trace the horse pattern on one side of tissue paper. (Trace forms are passed out.)

Fold both halves of tissue paper together, cut out pattern—making sure to leave the horse joined together at the top of its head and tail. Decorate (color) both sides of the horse.

3. Teacher describes how to "electrify" the paper horse:
   Students place their horse on smooth surface.
   They rub a balloon over their hair a few times.
   Students hold the balloon in front of the horse.
4. The teacher passes out the balloons.
5. Next the teacher instructs the students to get in groups of four or five sitting around the table.
6. Now students "electrify" their horses and have short races across tables.
7. After the races have ended, have a class discussion on what happened between balloon and horse.
8. Ask students to describe their views. Then add the scientific explanation describing static electricity: the outer layer of electrons from atoms on the hair are rubbed off and cling to the atoms of the balloon, producing static electricity. When students hold the positively charged balloon close to the uncharged (negatively charged) horse, there is a strong attraction between them—and the horse races toward the balloon.

Evaluation:
1. Instruct students to write in their journal about their experiment.
2. Some possible assignments:
   - In their own words, have students explain the connection between the horse, the balloon, and static electricity. For students struggling to write about "their horse" or afraid to construct a horse for themselves, have them work with the small group and come up with a group statement of the experiment.
   - Have students write a short story about their horse in the race.
   - Illustrate the "electric" horse race, provide commentary.
   - Have the group write an article for the school newspaper describing their experiment.

Post-Assessment: Assessment is based on observing the students and from reading their written/illustrated journals about their experiments.

Activity 7. Rainforest Interdependence

Inquiry Skills: Hypothesizing, experimenting, and communicating.

Science Standards: Inquiry, life science, science and technology, personal perspectives, and written communications.

Description: This inclusive science activity is designed for all students, but it's an ideal lesson to use for Limited English Proficient (LEP) learners. It encourages the students to come together and establish themselves as groups; speaking and writing is not mandatory! The only adaptation required in this activity is a simple color coding of the identifying cards, which will enable the student to visualize what other students (plants and animals) he or she is connected with, rather than just reading the card. Additional adaptations might include: pictures of the plant or animal on the cards that show the actual relationship, or more color coding, by matching the color of the yarn to the color of the cards. The student will be able to see his or her group members by the colors, pictures, and yarns and understand the interrelationships, without having to read the card.

This is a valuable lesson—not only for LEP students, but also for students with other language deficiencies and all students within the classroom. The exceptional student will not be singled out, and all the students can benefit by the simple color classification. The color coding and pictures serve to reinforce the written relationships, and the students will receive graphic, physical examples of the purpose of the activity to show interdependence. The activity will also help increase social interaction within the classroom, and might help break down the barrier caused by the difference in language.

The evaluation and conclusion to this activity will be for students to discuss and then write their reaction to, or interpretation of, what occurred when the connections were broken. This will be an opportunity for the student and his or her classmates to artistically describe the lesson.

Objectives:
1. Students will follow directions, participate in all activities, and work cooperatively with their classmates.
2. Students will discuss, as a class, their feelings about this activity.
3. Students will draw a picture of the interdependence of the rain forest.
4. Students will utilize some of the information that has been gained in the previous lessons.

Materials: Plant and animal cards pasted on 3 × 5 index cards, pictures of rain forest plants and animals, yarn (3-yard pieces) for three pieces per student, paper, and other art supplies.

Preparation:
1. Teachers, aides, or student helpers will cut and paste pictures of plant and animal cards onto 3 × 5 cards for each student.
2. Pictures or books of rain forest plants and animals should be available for reference if needed.
3. Move the desks to the edges of the classroom so that the students can move around.

Procedures:
1. Distribute one card to each student.
2. Pass out several long pieces of yarn to each student.
3. Each student will read his or her card and then find the person or people who have a related card.
4. When a match or relationship is made, the students then attach themselves with a long piece of yarn (tie around wrist). More than two students can be connected. Example: Kapok tree will be attached to parrots, insects, etc.
5. If a student wants more information, direct them to the pictures and other reference material.

Evaluation:
1. The class will discuss, while still connected, how it feels to depend on the other organisms.
2. Instruct students to guess what part of the rain forest their plant or animal lives in: canopy, under story, or forest floor?
3. Have students reflect on these questions:
   What plant or animal did you represent?
   What do you depend on for food or shelter?
   How does it feel to have so many connections?
   What did you learn from this activity?
   Would you like to live in a rain forest? Why?
4. The teacher may then cut several pieces of the yarn that are attached to the Kapok tree and ask the class:
   What would happen if the Kapok tree is cut down?
   What other animals would be affected?
5. After discussing the effects of the destruction of a part of this delicate ecosystem, the students may come up with some other ideas.

Activity 8. *Experimenting with Ramps*

Inquiry Skills: Observation, prediction, measurement, data recording

Standards: Inquiry, physical science

Description: Students will compare how objects go down inclined planes (slides, ramps)

Objectives: Students will learn about the concept of balance. A balance is a way of physically comparing two objects or groups of objects. Students will develop and extend their understanding of balance as they construct and use ramps (slides) that convey the important concept of how balance works. They will compare how objects go down the ramps (slides).

Procedures:

1. Form the class into groups of four.
2. Give each group a block and a ramp (paper towel roll cut lengthwise).
3. Show the group how to make a slide by taping a ramp to a block.
4. Have the students make slides, making sure they are identical (the slopes form the same angle). Then have the group of students align their slides along the edge of a table. Use a block to form a barrier at the other end of the table.
5. Set out objects for students to test their slides (paper clips, balls, marbles, dice, cylinder-shaped blocks, paper towel rolls, penny, rocks, masking tape rolls). Students will record their predictions of the objects that will reach the barrier and those that won't. Encourage struggling students to record their predictions with a partner and state their reasons. Test all the objects.

Evaluation: Have students explain how this activity showed balance. Have students write their reflections. Discuss which objects reached the barrier and which did not. Have students describe and compare the distance each traveled.

Activity 9. Recyclable Materials Construction by Sally Morey SFSU Student

Science Standards: Science inquiry, physical science, science and technology, math and science coordination, and problem solving.

Science Inquiry Skills: Observation, prediction, measurement, data recording.

Description: "Hands-on technology" describes the exciting things that happen during technological problem solving when students develop and construct their own "best" solution. This middle school activity moves beyond conducting experiments or finding solutions to word problems (all students doing the same task at the same time). In "hands-on technology" students are not shown a solution. Typically, this results in some very creative designs.

Using the tools and materials found in a normal middle school technology education laboratory, students design and construct solutions that allow them to apply the process skills. The products they create and engineer in the technology lab often use a wide range of materials such as plastics, woods, electrical supplies, and so forth. During the course of solving their problem, students are forced to test hypotheses and frequently generate new questions (Hamm & Adams, 1998). This involves a lot of scientific investigation and mathematical problem solving, but it is quite different from the routine classroom tasks. In this activity, a problem is introduced to the class. Working in small groups of four or five students their challenge is to plan a way of coming up with a solution. Students are to document the steps they used along the way. Some suggestions: have struggling students brainstorm and discuss with friends, draw pictures, show design ideas, use mathematics, present technical drawings, work together, and consult with experts.

Background Information: The best construction materials are strong, yet lightweight. Wood is unexpectedly strong for its weight, and therefore well suited for many structures. Larger buildings often use steel-reinforced concrete beams, rather than wood, in their construction. However, steel and concrete are both heavy, presenting problems in construction. A lighter material would be a great alternative and a best seller in the construction industry. This could be done by reinforcing the beam with a material other than steel—ideally, a recyclable material.

Problem: Design the lightest and strongest beam possible by reinforcing concrete with one or more recyclable materials: aluminum cans, plastic milk jugs, plastic soda bottles, and/or newspaper. Students must follow the construction constraints. The beam will be weighed. Then it will be tested by supporting it at each end, and a load will be applied to the middle. The load will be increased until the beam breaks. The load divided by the beam weight will give the load-to-weight ratio. The designer of the beam with the highest load-to-weight ratio will be awarded the contract.

Construction Limits: The solution must
1. Be made into a reusable mold that the student designs.
2. Result in a beam 40 cm (or approx. 16 inches) in length that fits within a volume of 1050 cubic cm (approx. 64 cubic inches).
3. Be made from concrete and recyclable materials.

Objectives:
1. Groups of students will plan and design their beam.
2. Groups will work on their construction plans.
3. Students will design and construct their beam.
4. Students will gather information from a variety of resources and make sketches of all the possibilities they considered.
5. Students will record the science, mathematics, and technology principles used.

Procedures:
1. Divide students into small groups of three or four students.
2. Present the problem to the class.
3. Students will discuss and draw out plans for how to construct a beam. All students should be part of this process.

4. Students will design a concrete beam reinforced with recycled materials.
5. Students will work together to construct, measure, and test the beam.
6. Students will present their invention to the class.

Evaluation: Students will document their work in a portfolio that includes
Sketches of all the possibilities their group considered.
A graphic showing how their invention performed.
Descriptions of the process skills used in their solution.
Information and notes gathered from resources.
Thoughts and reflections about this project. Reluctant students may need assistance in their designs. Encourage them to work together on their construction.

Activity 10. How I See Who I Am: Personal Reflections

Inquiry Skills: Hypothesizing, experimenting, and communicating.

Science Standards: Inquiry, life science, science and technology, personal perspectives, and written communications.

Description: This activity is designed to help the students think about themselves and teach communication skills. Hand out a copy of the following worksheet to the class. Tell the students to complete each sentence. Assign students to pairs. All students fill out a sheet and discusses it with their partner.

How I See Who I Am Worksheet

Name
Today I feel
I get angry when
My idea of a good time is
School is
I can't understand why
I wish teachers
I like to read about
On weekends I
I don't know how
I wish people wouldn't
I'd rather read than
My greatest disappointment was
I feel proud when
I would like to be
I wish I could

I look forward to
I wish someone would help me to
I'd read more if
The kinds of stories I like are
If I were a teacher, I would
If I had three wishes, they would be

Evaluation: Have the students trade papers with other partnerships and make up new sentences. Then, have them complete each other's "How I See Who I Am" worksheets. Struggling students benefit by observing and comparing themselves with others.

HINTS FOR HELPING DISINTERESTED LEARNERS

Nearly all educators agree with the goal of differentiated instruction, but teachers may not have strategies for making it happen. Here are a few hints that teachers can use to enhance instruction:

1. Assess students. The role of assessment is to foster worthwhile learning for all students. Performance assessments, informal assessment tools such as rubrics, checklists, and anecdotal records are some assessment strategies that are helpful for students with learning problems. Teachers may use a compacting strategy. This strategy encourages teachers to assess students before beginning a unit of study or development of a skill (Tomlinson, 1999).
2. Create complex instruction tasks. Complex tasks are
   * Open-ended,
   * Intrinsically interesting to students,
   * Uncertain (thus allowing for a variety of solutions),
   * Involve real objects, and
   * Draw upon multiple intelligences in a real world way.
3. Use television in the classroom. Television's wide accessibility has the potential for making learning available for students who do not perform well in traditional classroom situations. It can reach students on their home ground, but the most promising place is in the classroom.
4. Use materials and activities that address a wide range of reading levels, learning profiles, and student interests. Include activities that range from simple to complex, from concrete to abstract.
5. Use science notebooks. Science notebooks are an everyday part of learning. The science notebook is more than a record of collected data and facts of what students have learned. They are notebooks of students' questions, predictions, claims linked to evidence, conclusions,

and reflections. A science notebook is a central place where language, data, and experiences work together to produce meaning for the students. Notebooks support differentiated learning. They are helpful when addressing the needs of disinterested students. In a science notebook even students who may have poor writing skills can use visuals such as drawings, graphs, and charts to indicate their learning preferences. There is ongoing interaction in the notebooks. For teachers, a notebook provides a window into students' thinking and offers support for all students (Gilbert & Kotelman, 2005).

6. Provide clear directions for students. Teachers need to offer instructions about what a student could do if he or she needs help.
7. Use a record-keeping system to monitor what students do.
8. Include a plan for ongoing assessment. Teachers use ongoing assessment of student readiness, interest, and learning profile for the purpose of matching tasks to students' needs. Some students struggle with many things, others are more advanced, but most have areas of strengths. Teachers do not assume that one set of skills fits all students.

SUMMARY AND CONCLUSION

One of the important new goals of American education is to prepare scientifically literate citizens. This means preparing students who can make use of scientific knowledge and connect the implications of science to their personal lives and to society. Scientific literacy also involves having a broad familiarity with today's scientific issues and the key concepts that underlie them. As far as the schools are concerned, this means organizing scientific inquiry around real-life problems—the kind that can elicit critical thinking and shared decision making. Inquiry today involves curiosity, observation, posing questions, and actively seeking answers.

The recognized importance of a scientifically literate citizenry has resulted in national efforts to reform science education. Instructional strategies include concrete, physical experiences, and opportunities for students to explore science in their lives. Today's science has an emphasis on ideas and thinking skills. This involves sequencing instruction from the concrete to the abstract. Students are actively involved in the learning process, developing effective oral and written communication skills. Frequent group activity sessions are provided where students are given many opportunities to question data, to design and conduct real experiments, and to carry their thinking beyond the class experience. Students raise questions that are appealing and familiar to them, activities arise that improve reasoning and decision making. Collaborative learning has become the primary grouping strategy where learning is done as a cohesive group in which ideas and strengths are shared (Sherman, Richardson, & Yard, 2005).

Science can be an exciting experience for students and teachers when it is taught as an active hands-on subject. Connecting with other disciplines can provide many opportunities for integration with other subjects. Teachers need subject matter knowledge that is broad and deep enough to work with second language learners and others who may have difficulty with their schoolwork. This often requires improving language and broad-based literacy development possibilities to get at content. It may take some effort to gain insights into others' experiences and ways they may be encouraged.

To understand and use science today requires an awareness of how science connects language and technology domains and how it relates to our culture and our lives. Good science teachers are usually those who have built up their science knowledge base and developed a repertoire of current pedagogical techniques. By focusing on real investigations and participatory learning, teachers move students from the concrete to the abstract as they explore themes that connect science, math, and technology.

Teaching strategies include many participatory experiences and opportunities for students to explore science in their lives. The emphasis on inquiry involves posing questions, making observations, reading, planning, conducting investigations, experimenting, providing explanations, and communicating the results. Students develop effective interpersonal skills as they work together, pose questions, and critically examine data. This often means designing and conducting real experiments that carry their thinking beyond the classroom. As instruction becomes more connected to students' lives, enriching possibilities arise from inquiring about real-world concerns.

All students can learn science and should have the chance to become scientifically literate. This was one of the themes in the National Science Education Standards (NRC, 2000). The standards emphasize the processes of science and give a great deal of attention to cognitive abilities such as logic, evidence, and extending that knowledge to construct explanations of natural phenomena. Scientific literacy should begin in the early grades, where students are naturally curious and eager to explore. Another theme in the standards is that science is an active process. Getting students actively involved in the process or the doing of science moves students along the road to scientific awareness.

Learning the fundamentally important facts, concepts, and skills of science certainly matters. But just as fundamental is the disciplined use of knowledge: inquiry and problem solving. Concepts and inquiry are both fundamental skills that students must begin developing early on. Outside of school, scientific truth is elusive in a culture that is being swamped with stuff that looks like information but is often something a little more suspicious. Being able to use the scientific method (processes) to sort things out would certainly help. Also, skeptical inquiry skills are needed to sort through the multimedia collage of material that passes by students in the wink of an eye.

At school the basics of science and scientific reasoning must go hand-in-hand if we are going to motivate all of our students to learn science. In the differentiated classroom, teachers work to elicit students' current understanding of scientific ideas and move students at least a little bit away from everyday ways of talking about natural phenomena to more scientific ways of examining and discussing subjects. With the help of collaborative inquiry and investigative experiences, even the more reluctant learners can be motivated to learn how to apply scientific processes and recognize where their thinking is breaking down. The traditional approach of feeding struggling students a diet rich in basic skills is a recipe for disaster. No matter how well it's done, the old chalk, talk, and memorize routine will not go a long way toward engaging disinterested students. There has to be some joy, excitement, and interaction in the process of learning science and becoming scientifically literate.

REDEFINING SCIENCE EDUCATION IN THE TWENTY-FIRST CENTURY

There is no question that the science education experienced by students today is strongly influenced by the national standards, professional associations textbooks, and state requirements. State agencies generally have more influence than federal agencies. But the basic school structure is largely under local control. Schoolboard members, teachers, and parents have a major say in deciding what science gets taught and how it gets taught. We could all use a better vocabulary to address the future of science education. But in the meantime, it is important to recognize that total agreement may not be possible and that the major players have to collaborate if science instruction is going to shine.

Increasingly, schools are mixing ability groups, cultures, and second language learners. Teachers must provide different routes to content, activities, and products to meet an increasingly diverse set of student needs. In general, motivation is enhanced when the science curriculum is made more meaningful with collaborative inquiry into real-life situations and problems (Abruscato, 2004). Along the way, students can learn that the organizing principles of science apply to local and global phenomena. In response to calls for all students to achieve higher standards of scientific knowledge, there are corresponding pressures to expand access to higher-level science classes. More and more nontraditional students are finding themselves in rigorous science classes. As a result, in today's demanding school environment a one-size-fits-all delivery system just won't get the job done (Martin, 2006).

In today's social environment, it is no longer enough to provide some youth with a quality science curriculum (in preparation for college) and others with the bare outlines of scientific facts. Now, every student must be involved in inquiry-based science instruction. Struggling students, like everyone else, must be involved a process of asking questions, exploring, and making connections that lead to discovery. Active science learning connects students with the past, the present, and the science-influenced world of tomorrow. The basic idea is to make sure that all students acquire the appropriate level of scientific knowledge and scientific understanding.

Teachers are increasingly connecting learning about science to responsible citizenship and self-understanding. Goals include using scientific knowledge in making wise decisions and solving difficult problems related to life and living. The subject is becoming more interdisciplinary; for example, some of the new research fields emerging include biochemistry, biophysics, plant engineering, terrestrial biology, and neurobiology to name a few. Some of these changes are reflected in the standards and in the textbooks. At every grade level, science has dimensions that extend to the social sciences as well as ethics, values, and law (Greene, 2003).

Meeting the needs of struggling students requires finding relationships among science, technology, and students' life experiences. Suggestions are needed for meeting the adaptive needs of students in a changing world. Educators have long recognized that science education should not be isolated from human welfare or social and economic progress. "Learning to learn" has also been viewed as essential for preparing students for the world in which they will live (National Research Council). It is our belief that the best way to do this is to teach science in a way that challenges all students intellectually. And it is just as important to structure lessons so that every student develops and sustains a high level of curiosity and engagement.

Clearly, science education should reflect human values and emphasize responsibility for the natural world. It should also help all students understand that they are part of a global community (the National Science Education Standards). When it comes to struggling students, there are many problems, but there are also powerful opportunities. Teachers can really make a big difference. But before the power of knowledgeable teachers can be unleashed, we must be sure that they build up their informal ideas and have the ability to make informed judgments. The nation has to be sure that there are enough high quality teachers to arrange the science classrooms of the future. Effective instructors are the key because, in the final analysis, what goes on in the classroom comes down to the teacher and his or her level of professional competency.

Science distinguishes itself from other ways of knowing and from other bodies of knowledge through the use of empirical standards, collaborative inquiry, logical arguments, and skepticism.

—National Research Council

QUESTIONS FOR TEACHERS AND PROSPECTIVE TEACHERS

1. Why are some students reluctant to participate in science lessons? What can you do to make science more attractive for all learners?
2. How might you design a science lesson that allows for differences in students' prior knowledge, learning styles, interests, and socialization needs?
3. What is your personal image of science and scientists? Draw a picture of a scientist. (You can do some of these questions with your students.)
4. Think of a science question you are curious about. How might it generate scientific interest in others?
5. Get together with someone else and compare questions. See if the two of you come up with a good question. Form a hypothesis.
6. Do some research or perform an experiment that proves or disproves your hypothesis. Present your findings to the others.

REFERENCES AND RESOURCES

Abruscato, J. (2004). *Teaching children science*. Boston, MA: Allyn and Bacon/Pearson.

Adams, D. & Hamm, M. (1998). *Collaborative inquiry in science, math, and technology*. Portsmouth, NH: Heinemann.

American Association for the Advancement of Science. (2001). *Atlas of science literacy*. Washington, DC: American Association for the Advancement of Science.

Association for Supervision and Curriculum Development (ASCD). (2000). ASCD Yearbook 2000. Brandt, R. (ed.) Education in a new era. Alexandria, VA: ASCD.

Atkin, J. M. & Atkin, a. (1989). *Improving Science Education Through Local Alliances: A Report to Carnegie Corporation of New York*. Santa Cruz, CA: ERT Association.

Benjamin, A. (2003). *Differentiated instruction: A guide for elementary school teachers*. Larchmont, NY: Eye On Education.

Benjamin, A. (2002). *Differentiated instruction: A guide for middle and high school teachers*. Larchmont, NY: Eye On Education.

Center for the Study of Teaching and Policy. (2001). *Teacher preparation research: Current knowledge, gaps, and recommendations*. Seattle, WA: Author.

Gega, P. (1994). *Science in elementary education*. 7th ed. New York, NY: Macmillan.

Gilbert, J. & Kotelman, M. (2005). Five good reasons to use science notebooks. *Science & Children*, 43(3), 28–32.

Glatthorn, A. & Jailall, J. (2000). Curriculum for the new mellenium. In Brandt, R. (ed.) *Education in a new era: ASCD Yearbook 2000*. Alexandria, VA: ASCD.

Greene, B. (2003). *The elegant universe*. New York, NY: Vintage Books.

Hamm, M. & Adams, D. (1998). *Literacy in science, technology and the language arts: An interdisciplinary inquiry*. Westport, CT: Greenwood/Hienemann.

Howe, A. (2002). *Engaging children in science*. Upper Saddle River, NJ: Merrill/Prentice-Hall.

Jackson, A. W. & Davis, G. A. (2000). *Turning points 2000: Educating adolescents in the 21st century*. New York, NY: Teachers College Press.

Loucks-Horsley, et al. (2003). *Designing professional development for teachers of science and mathematics*, 2nd ed. Thousand Oaks, CA: Corwin Press.

Martin, D. (2006). *Elementary science methods: A constructivist approach*. 4th ed. Belmont, CA: Wadsworth/Thomson.

Murphy, F. (2003). *Making inclusion work: A practical guide for teachers*. Norwood, MA: Christopher-Gordon Publishers.

National Research Council (NRC). (1996). *National science education standards*. Washington, DC: National Academy Press.

National Research Council (NRC). (2000). *Inquiry and the national science education standards*. Washington, DC: National Academy Press.

Paulos, J. A. (1991). *Beyond numeracy*. New York, NY: Alfred Knopf.

Rudolph, J. (2002). *Scientists in the classroom: The cold war reconstruction of American science education*. New York, NY: Palgrave.

Schultz, J. (2002). Learning how to learn: Science education for struggling students. *Quest*, 5(1), January, 1–3.

Sherman, H., Richardson, L., & Yard, G. (2005). *Teaching children who struggle with mathematics: A systematic approach to analysis and correction*. Upper Saddle River, NJ: Prentice Hall/Pearson.

Thomas, E. (2003). *Styles and strategies for teaching middle school mathematics*. 2nd ed. Ho-Ho-Kus, NJ: Thoughtful Education Press.

Tomlinson, C. (1999). *The differentiated classroom: Responding to the needs of all learners*. Alexandria, VA: Association for Supervision and Curriculum Development.

Tomlinson, C., & Cunningham Edison, C. (2003). *Differentiation in practice: A resource guide for differentiating curriculum*. Alexandria, VA: Association for Supervision and Curriculum Development.

Wang, M. & Birch. J. (eds.) (1987). *Handbook of special education: Research and practice, vol. 1*. London: Pergamon.

Weiss, I. & Pasley, J. (2004). What is quality instruction? *Educational Leadership*, 61(5), February, 24–28.

7

Technology and Reluctant Learners

The Motivating and Collaborative Possibilities of Powerful Tools

All of our inventions are but improved means to an unimproved end.

—Henry David Thoreau

The technological products of math and science are an increasingly powerful force in the development of civilization. So it is little wonder that understanding the implications of a world filled with the technological by-products of mathematics and science is viewed as a necessity for everyone. Technological tools have long been an intrinsic part of all cultural and educational systems. When computers came along, they amplified the influence. Educators now realize that they must be prepared to provide their students with the advantages that current technology can bring.

The purpose of this chapter is to help teachers do a better job of reaching struggling students by using technology to meet different needs and learning styles. In the TMI (too much information) digital age, there are a vast number of education-related technological problems and possibilities. The topics in this chapter range from the influence of the math and science standards to connecting students who struggle with these subjects to a technological world. It also examines

- How differentiated instruction and technology change learning.
- Methods of understanding and taking control of multiple media symbol systems.
- The process for evaluating digital software and Internet access to the world of ideas.
- The promise, pitfalls, and social effects of converging technologies.

157

We suggest injecting a little healthy skepticism into the debate, paying attention to the myths, as well as the magic.

As far as digital technology is concerned, it is important that struggling students go beyond worksheet-type on-screen experiences to engage in higher-level thinking, collaborative inquiry, problem solving, and meaningful communication. By offering some suggestions on the use of new media, we hope to shed some light on the technological implications of the standards in mathematics and science. Along the way, there are suggestions for integrating manipulatives, calculators, video, computers, and the Internet into daily lessons. A major concern is that half of all entering children now come to school with one or more risk factors in their home environment (Thomas and Bainbridge, 2001). These risks are evident in what students do at home and at school.

The term *differentiated instruction* is often applied to a variety of classroom practices that allow for the differences in student interests, prior knowledge, socialization needs, and learning styles. It can also be used to describe the degree of individual structure in a lesson, pacing, complexity, and level of abstraction. It is our belief that students need to approach math, science, and technology in different ways to more fully understand these subjects. We also believe that it is best to differentiate work with these subjects when doing so is the best means to reach students. The basic idea is that learning happens when adjustments are made so that a learner at any achievement level can make sense (meaning) out of the math and science information and concepts being taught.

Although electronic technology is the emphasis here, the standards make it clear that both high-tech (computers) and low-tech (simple manipulatives) methods are essential to problem solving in mathematics and inquiry in science. The standards also suggest ways of improving math and science instruction for all students, including those who are struggling with these subjects. Clearly, all students should have access to the same high-quality content to ensure that they meet similar learning goals. The underlying assumption is that underachieving students should not be limited to executing math rules and remembering basic science concepts. Aiming low just doesn't get the job done. When in doubt, it is best to "teach up" with strategies that engage the imagination with the help of active learning and group participation (Gregory & Chapman, 2002).

From problem solving with mathematics to understanding the natural world, technological designs and tools have constraints that limit our choices. Part of the excitement has always been not knowing when the boundaries of effectiveness will shift and where things will end up. One example of a surprise that awaits us is associated with learning about the architecture of information storage in the mind. Where science, math, and their technological associates are taking us remains something of a mystery.

Some of the consequences can be predicted. Many cannot. For example, who at the beginning of the twentieth century would have predicted the human consequences of physics and the technologies associated with atomic energy?

Technology shapes and reflects the values found in society. At school, it can isolate learners or help them join with others. In our personal and civic lives, technological tools frequently slip through our hands to limit our choices at work and erode the edges of the constitutional rights of privacy in our daily lives. On one level, digital technology and globalization empower individuals and diminish governments. On another, it can bring out the worst in human nature and diminish the imagination. Those who think that it is all good or all bad just don't get it. Heaven help those who don't want to get caught up in dealing with a glut of information. Do you dare to question the time-wasting computer-based functions, like email, that so dominate professional life these days? Of course, if you are an administrator or executive, maybe you can get a secretary to sort through it for you.

In spite of some nuisances and misplaced enthusiasm, computer-based technology is now an essential part of math and science instruction. At their out-of-school worst, they are rigidly preprogrammed arcade-like shoot-'em-ups where children frantically click on icons for instant gratification. At school, computers and the Internet can turn mathematics and science into spectator sports. As usual, digital technology is a double-edged sword. Computers can be an excellent vehicle for questioning, investigating, analyzing, simulating, and communicating. At their best, technological tools allow you to take control, solve problems, inquire collaboratively, and observe phenomena that would otherwise remain unobservable.

THE MATH AND SCIENCE STANDARDS AND UNDERACHIEVING STUDENTS

Mathematics is the language of the natural world.

—Galileo

The math, science, and technology standards view technology as a means to form connections between the natural and man-made worlds. There is general agreement that it is important to pay attention to technological design and how technology can help students understand the big ideas of science and mathematics. The standards also suggest that in the elementary grades, students should be given opportunities to use all kinds of low-tech and high-tech technology to explore and design solutions to problems. A suggested theme is helping students see the human factor and its societal implications. The laws of the physical and biological universe are viewed as important to understanding how technological objects and systems work. The standards also point to the importance of connecting students to the various elements of our technologically intensive world so that they can construct models and solve problems with technology.

Although our focus is on the math and science standards, there are also standards that relate directly to information and communication technology. The National Educational Technology Standards for Teachers suggest that within a sound educational setting, technology can enable students to become

- Capable information technology users.
- Information seekers, analyzers, and evaluators.
- Problem solvers and decision makers.
- Creative and effective users of productivity tools.
- Communicators, collaborators, publishers, and producers.
- Informed, responsible, and contributing citizens.

Through the ongoing use of technology in the schooling process, students are empowered to achieve important technology capabilities. The key individual in helping students develop those capabilities is the classroom teacher.

As the technology standards go on to suggest, it is up to the teachers to arrange the classroom environment, prepare the lessons, and provide activities that help their students use technology to learn, communicate, and creatively take part in media-related projects.

We agree with the idea that the problem-solving ability of children can be developed by firsthand experiences where they use technological tools similar to those used by mathematicians, scientists, and engineers. Of course, computers and the Internet are important. But, as the standards point out, students should also see the technological products and systems found in the relatively low-tech world of zippers, can openers, and math manipulatives. Young children can engage in projects that are appropriately challenging for them; ones in which they may design ways to fasten, ways to move, or ways to communicate more effectively. Students begin to understand the design process as well as improve their ability to solve simple problems. Even solving simple problems where they are trying to meet certain criteria, students will find elements of math, science, and technology that can be powerful aids. At higher grade levels, lessons can include examples of technological achievements where math and science have played a part. Students can also be encouraged to examine where technical advances have contributed directly to scientific progress. To consider the other side of the coin, they can look a where the products of math and science have hurt the environment and taken away jobs.

Children and young adults should have many experiences that involve math, science, and technological applications. Some of these are as simple as measuring and weighing various objects on a balance scale. This can teach math and science skills such as comparing, estimating, predicting, and recording data. What is the technology connection? A scale is one of the relatively simple technological tools used in science and mathematics for measuring mass or weight. Too frequently, however, teachers forget to mention the technological connection. Whether it's simple or complex, bathroom scales or hot new computers, the technology in our day-to-day world is often misunderstood—and it's difficult to escape.

Struggling students can be motivated by studying an existing product: to determine its function and to identify the problems it solves, the materials used in its construction, and how well it does what it is supposed to do. An old technological device, like a vegetable or cheese grater, can be used as an object for students to investigate and try to figure out what it does, how it helps people, and what problems it might solve and cause. Such student problems provide excellent opportunities to direct attention to a specific technology—the tools and instruments used in science and mathematics. In the early elementary grades, many tasks can be designed around the familiar contexts of the home, school, and community. In the early grades, problems should be clear and have only one or two solutions that do not require a great deal of preparation time or complicated assembly.

Many curriculum programs and some state guidelines suggest that teachers should integrate math and science with technology and society issues in a way that encourages a multidisciplinary analysis of problems that are relevant to the students' world. A sequence of five stages is usually involved in a technology-based problem-solving process: 1) identifying and stating the problem; 2) designing an approach to solving the problem; 3) implementing and arriving at a solution; 4) evaluating results; and 5) communicating the problem, design, and solution. In keeping with the standards document, teachers may also have elementary students design problems and technological investigations that incorporate several interesting issues in math and science. By using a variety of materials and technologies for mathematical problem solving and scientific inquiry, students can come to recognize (as John Dewey has suggested) that education is more than preparing for life; it is life itself.

Examples of Activities to Motivate Reluctant Learners

The Egg Drop

The first example includes a design activity, where students design and test a container that can keep a raw egg from breaking when dropped from five or six feet in the air. This low-tech activity should be preceded by a science unit on force and motion so that students are able to apply their knowledge of science in their design process. Students should work in small groups to plan their egg drop design. Emphasize creativity. Students are to bring materials from home to finish their design. If that problem is too difficult, have students design a container that is an egg catcher. The tasks for both activities should include: 1) work with a group; 2) brainstorm ideas; 3) sketch a design; 4) formulate a rationale; 5) assign group tasks—including cleanup crew; 6) get materials (string, paper towel rolls, styrofoam peanuts, cotton, soft packing material, etc.); 7) build the container; 8) try several tests, and 9) do a class demonstration. The presentation will be started with a discussion of what their group has done to meet the challenge. Assessment for the egg drop is not whether the egg broke, but rather how they were able to share what they found out as they tried to solve the problem and prepared for a successful attempt. It's helpful to have the class make a video of the presentation. It can be viewed again by the designers and by parents, or it can be used in other class sessions in years to come.

Designing and Building a City

Another interesting problem for middle school students is to design and build a city. Students are instructed to design a city with an efficient road network. They must also create an election process that ensures that the city council fairly represents all city residents. In addition, students must contact construction companies and make a plan for building their cities. To prepare for this challenge, students have learned about routing graphs, which are used to plan routes for mail carriers and garbage carriers so that they don't waste steps or gas unnecessarily. Contractors also use routing graphs to plan roads in new residence communities. Students collaborate in groups analyzing their decisions by writing a rationale for their design decisions. They must also make a fifteen-minute oral presentation to "sell" their cities. This project allows students to be creative in applying the science, math and technology applications they've learned. Some students have created their cities on islands, on the moon, or even underground.

Other Bright Science Activity Ideas

Other low-tech activities might include: 1) design a device to keep pencils from rolling off your desk, 2) create something that's easy to make that tastes good and would fit in your lunch box, 3) design a device that would shield your eyes from the sun, 4) create an instrument that would make lifting easier, and 5) design ways to save money on school supplies.

Understanding Communications Technology

Activity. Create a Communications Time Line

The ways in which people communicate with each other have changed throughout history. In ancient days, cave painting conveyed messages and created meaning for people. For centuries, storytelling and oral language served as the primary means of communicating information. Handwritten manuscripts were the first written for of communication, followed more recently by the printing press, telegraph, typewriter, telephone, radio, television, computers, and video cell phones. The list could go on.

Materials: Reference books, science/math journals, communication devices from home, grandparents, community, etc.

Procedures:
1. Have children research the history of communications technology and create a time line in their science/math journal.
2. Encourage students to assemble a communications time line project for display, using as many actual objects, or their representations, as they can.
3. Remind students that each time period needs to have some examples of the actual objects used and a written explanation about these communications devices.

Evaluation:
1. Direct students to choose a communications technique from the past. Teachers may wish to divide students into groups according to interests and assign each group a certain time period or technological tool used for communication.
2. Direct groups to orally (and perhaps graphically) present their communication tool to the class.
3. Teachers may extend the project by having students project what communications of the future will look like.

Awareness of Time

Time is often a difficult concept for children to grasp. Throughout modern history, people have recorded the passage of time. These activities get children involved in time measurement by using a number of old and new technological tools.

Activity. Create a Water Clock

Have children collect a variety of large cans, plastic bottles, and plastic containers. Make a small hole in the bottom of the containers (try to make all of the holes in the containers the same size). Make a paper plug or small cork to fit the hole. Fill the containers with water. Release the plugs and compare the times of each container. Encourage students to guess which one will empty first.

Follow-up Activities:
1. Have students choose common jobs that can be timed with water clocks.
2. Encourage students to make a list of things that can be timed with a water clock.
3. Instruct students to hypothesize how the size of the hole affects the water drip process.
4. Have students use a digital clock to determine how much water flows out in one minute's time from their water clock.
5. Ask students to design a system to mark their water clock to determine the time without measuring the water each time.
6. Ask students if they can make a clock another way.
7. Have students write a program for a computer to record time.

Follow-up Questions: Instruct students to respond to these questions in their science/math journal:
1. Why are clocks so important to the industrial age?
2. How are clocks used as metaphors?
3. Encourage students to speculate on the future of clocks and their role in the future.

Hypothesis Testing

Activity. Test Your Hypothesis

This technology awareness activity is designed to get students involved in the historic role of technology in today's society.

Problem: Instruct students to bring in a paper bag containing
1. One item that no one would be able to recognize (an old tool of their grandfather's, for example).
2. One item that some people may be able to identify.
3. One common item that everyone would recognize.

Procedures:
1. Divide students into small groups. Tell students that all items in their bags should be kept secret.
2. Give the students the following directions:
   There will be no talking in the first part of this activity.
   You are to exchange bags with someone else in your group.

You may then open the bag, remove one item, and write down what you think that item is.

Have students examine each item carefully. Also, have students write their reaction to how they feel about this item, what they think it may be used for, and which category this item falls into (common item, one no one would recognize, etc.).

3. Repeat with each of the items in the bags.
4. Exchange bags with other groups and go through the same procedure.
5. When students have finished examining their bags of articles and written their responses, have them meet back together in their groups and explain what they have discovered in their bags. Encourage class speculation, questions, and guesses about unidentified items. The student who brought in the unknown tool or article should be responsible for answering the questions posed, but should not give away the identity until all guesses and hypotheses have been raised.

As the standards in math and science make clear, children can learn a great deal about both subjects from the low-tech and the high-tech ends of the technology spectrum.

ELECTRONIC MEDIA AND TODAY'S TEACHING ENVIRONMENT

Educational technology changes math and science instruction by changing the classroom environment and providing opportunities for students to create new knowledge for themselves. It goes beyond the "telling" model of instruction that many underachieving students find so problematical to encourage students to learn by doing. Computer-based technology can also serve as a vehicle for discovery-based classrooms—giving students access to data, experiences with simulations, and the possibility for creating models of fundamental math/science/technology processes. Like the best teachers, today's technology can increase everybody's capacity to learn.

In one technologically savvy sixth grade classroom we visited, students were involved with software and Internet website evaluation. The teacher was using Smart Board technology to help the students with note taking and preserving student ideas. One struggling student and his partner were encouraged to write in and highlight the text. All of the students were working in pairs to construct flowcharts and graphic organizers. The homework question of the week: "What is the role of media in our society?" A more intriguing and controversial question was: "How do you have a just society when genetics is so unjust?" The teacher made sure that everyone had an online study partner. And they made sure that the students knew how to prepare a summary of their homework discussions for the teacher. Not many of us could juggle all this and integrate the result into the curriculum. But with time, practice, and a little in-service training, teachers less familiar with technology can easily become aware of the general issues and make the appropriate match between the problems they face and potential technological support.

Digital technology is transforming the social and educational environment before many of us have a chance to think carefully about what we hope to accomplish. Like everyone else, teachers are consumers of technology and they need to be able to judge critically the quality and usefulness of the electronic possibilities springing up around them. Many people outside of school think that life today is moving too fast—hyped with wireless laptops, cell phones with TV shows, podcasts, blogs, BlackBerries, and instant messages. They should try to imagine what it is like to be a teacher with struggling students, new curriculum choices, political demands, standardized tests, and whiz-bang technologies swirling around them.

UNDERSTANDING THE ROLE OF TECHNOLOGY

The research and the standards have suggested that two of the keys to success with technology involve teacher training and being able to access the quality of what students see and do while peering into a computer screen. The standards for mathematics and science suggest active, inquiry-based, and hands-on learning that uses the computer as a power tool for such things as visually exploring models, simulations, collaborative inquiry, and problem solving. It's all very motivational for reluctant learners. The real question usually revolves around how much math and science they are really learning. (For good suggestions, go to the Math Forum home page: http://forum.swarthmore.edu/index.js.html or http:mathforum.org/dr.math/.)

There are some technological negatives that should be kept in mind. To begin with, people often uncritically accept information on the Web—and they tend to accept the parameters of computer programs, even when the simulated environment is very wrong. The wired world intensifies the problem of uncritical consumers and the outsourcing of all sorts of information technology jobs. It's changing both how students learn and how they will eventually work. There is no question that digital technology and the Internet are revolutionizing the worldwide marketplace. But globalization is more than manufacturing in China, call centers in India, and the computerization of the developing world. The dark side involves accelerating the spread of everything from pornography and radical religious ideologies to the details of bomb making for a growing community of jihadists around the world. (For more information on the technological pluses and minuses, go to http: www.technorealism.org.)

In the schools of the twenty-first century, technology can have a distancing and isolating effect on youngsters who grow up with television, computers, the Internet, and video games. Sven Birkerts goes so far as to suggest that as electronic media pushes print aside, we are experiencing "the progressive atrophy of all that defines us as creatures of the spirit." In *The Gutenberg Elegies*, he suggests that we are on the verge of losing more than we know. It may be easier to get struggling students to attend to flashy movement on a video screen, but simply being motivated by a computer program or imagery on the Internet doesn't mean that students are learning something important.

In our new media-fed society, images can engage public attention with small controversies and trivial banalities. However, this same media-connected world can also provide students with the possibility for controlling and charting the course of their education and their culture. Information is not just constructed and used by a small elite but by anyone with a computer, camcorder, or television. The best of the new technology moves you out of a passive rim and into interaction with others. There is no question that new media toys, computers, and the Internet are ubiquitous. But how much of it is good for you? In 1999, the American Academy of Pediatrics recommended no screen time at all for children under the age of three. More recently, they voiced a concern that older children may be spending too much time in front of video and computer screens. The problem seems to be that the increasing use of media can displace human interaction and impede crucially important brain growth and social development.

New ways of relating to electronic information require a break from habit. Thousands of years ago, it was the written word. Next, it was the printing press. Today, it's multimedia computing and the Internet—the coming together of computers, video, sound, animation, and telecommunications. Computers are both evolutionary and revolutionary. At their best, they help you do things better while conjuring up new possibilities for critical thinking, collaboration, and creativity. As teachers struggle with school reform and underachieving students, they need all the help they can get. At its best, multiple media encourages interaction while adding a new dimension to learning by communicating meaning with vivid motion video, animation, and quality sound. A point of interest: children and young adults will often pass up passive television viewing when they can use a computer or game controller (Monaco, 2000).

People learn best if they take an active role in their own learning. Relying on a host of cognitive inputs, individuals select and interpret the raw data of experience to produce a personal understanding of reality. Ultimately, it is up to each person to determine what is attended to and what is ignored. How elements are organized and how meaning is attached to any concept is an individual act that can be influenced by a number of external agents. The thinking that must be done to make sense of perceptions ultimately transforms the "real world" into different things for different people. By motivating struggling students through the excitement of discovery, technology can assist the imaginative spirit of inquiry and make lessons sparkle. (If students want to find out about something quickly, have them check Wikipedia on the Internet.)

COMPREHENDING VIDEO MESSAGES

Parents, teachers, and other adults can significantly affect what information children gather from television. The skills learned from analyzing this visually intensive medium will apply to more advanced multimedia platforms. Students' social, educational, and family contexts influence what messages they take from the television, how they use TV, and how "literate" they are as viewers (Kress, 2003). To become critical viewers who are literate about media messages, students should being able to

- Understand the grammar and syntax of television, as expressed in different program forms.
- Analyze the pervasive appeals of television advertising.
- Compare those with similar presentations to those with similar purposes in different media.
- Identify values in language, characterization, conflict resolution, and sound/visual images.
- Identify elements in dramatic presentations associated with the concepts of plot, storyline, theme, characterizations, motivation, program formats, and production values.
- Utilize strategies for the management of duration of viewing and program choices.

Understanding media is a bit like the Olympics—you have to begin very early. Parents and teachers can engage in activities that affect children's interest in televised messages—and help them learn how to process video information. Good modeling behavior, explaining content, and showing how the program content relates to student interests are just a few examples of how adults can provide positive viewing motivation. Adults can also exhibit an informed response, point out misleading TV messages, and take care not to build curiosity for undesirable programs.

The viewing habits of families play a large role in determining how children approach the medium. The length of time parents spend watching television, the kinds of programs viewed, and the reactions of parents and siblings toward programming messages all have a large influence on the child. If adults read, and there are books, magazines, and newspapers around the house, children will pay more attention to print. Influencing what children view on television may be done with rules about what may be watched, interactions with children during viewing, and the modeling of appropriate content choices.

Whether co-viewing or not, the viewing choices of adults in a child's life (parents, teachers, etc.) set an example for children. If parents are heavy watchers of public television or news programming, then children are more likely to respond favorably to this content. Influencing the settings in which children watch TV is also a factor. Turning the TV set off during meals, for example, sets a family priority. Families can also seek a more open and equal approach to choosing television shows—interacting before, during, and after the program. Parents can also organize formal or informal activities outside the house that provide alternatives to TV viewing.

It is increasingly clear that the education of children is a shared responsibility. Parents need connections with what's going on in the schools. But it is teachers who will be the ones called upon to make the educational connections, entwining varieties of print and visual media with science, mathematics, or technology. It is possible to use the TV medium in a way that encourages students to become intelligent video consumers.

Activities That Can Help Students Make Sense of Television

1. Help students critically view what they watch.

    Decoding visual stimuli and learning from visual images require practice. Seeing an image does not automatically ensure learning from it. Students must be guided in decoding and looking critically at what they view. One technique is to have students "read" the image on various levels. Students identify individual elements and classify them into various categories, then relate the whole to their own experiences, drawing inferences and creating new conceptualizations from what they have learned. Encourage students to look at the plot and storyline. Identify the message of the program. What symbols (camera techniques, motion sequences, setting, lighting, etc.) does the program use to make its message? What does the director do to arouse audience emotion and participation in the story? What metaphors and symbols are used?

2. Compare print and video messages.

Have students follow a current event on the evening news (taped segment on a VCR) and compare it to the same event written in a major newspaper. A question for discussion may be: How do the major newspapers influence what appears on a national network's news program? Encourage comparisons between both media. What are the strengths and weaknesses of each? What are the reasons behind the different presentations of a similar event?

3. Evaluate TV viewing habits.

After compiling a list of their favorite TV programs, assign students to analyze the reasons for their popularity and examine the messages these programs send to their audience. Do the same for favorite books, magazines, newspapers, films, songs, and computer programs. Look for similarities and differences between the media.

4. Use video for instruction.

Using a VCR, make frequent use of three- to five-minute video segments to illustrate different points. This is often better than showing long videotapes or a film on a video cassette. For example, teachers can show a five-minute segment from a video cassette movie to illustrate how one scene uses foreshadowing or music to set up the next scene.

5. Analyze advertising messages.

Advertisements provide a wealth of examples for illustrating media messages. Move students progressively from advertisements in print to television commercials, allowing them to locate features (such as packaging, color, and images) that influence consumers and often distort reality. Analyze and discuss commercials in children's TV programs: How many minutes of TV ads appear in an hour? How have toy manufacturers exploited the medium? What is the broadcasters' role? What should be done about it?

6. Create a scrapbook of media clippings.

Have students keep a scrapbook of newspaper and magazine clippings on television and its associates. Paraphrase, draw a picture, or map out a personal interpretation of the articles. Share these with other students.

7. Create new images from the old.

Have students take rather mundane photographs and multiply the image, or combine it with others, in a way that makes them interesting. Through the act of observing, it is possible to build a common body of experiences, humor, feeling, and originality. And through collaborative efforts, students can expand on ideas and make the group process come alive.

8. Use debate for critical thought.

Debating is a communications model that can serve as a lively facilitator for concept building. Taking a current and relevant topic, and formally debating it, can serve as an important speech/language extension. For example, the class can discuss how mass media can support political tyranny, public conformity, or the technological enslavement of society. The discussion can serve as a blend of social studies, science, and humanities studies. You can also build the process of writing or videotaping from the brainstorming stage to the final production.

9. Include print and electronic media in daily class activities.

Using newspapers, magazines, literature, and electronic media (like brief television news clips) in daily class activities can enliven classroom discussion of current conflicts and dilemmas. Neither squeamish nor politically correct, these sources of information provide readers with something to think and talk about. And they can present the key conflicts and dilemmas of our time in a way that allows students to enter the discussion. These stimulating sources of information can help the teacher structure lessons that go beyond facts to stimulate reading, critical thinking, and thoughtful discussion. By not concealing adult disagreements, everyone can take responsibility for promoting understanding—engaging others in moral reflection and providing a coherence and focus that helps turn controversies into advantageous educational experiences.

EXPLORING MATH ACTIVITIES USING CALCULATORS

You may not be able to afford a computer for every two students, but for a tiny fraction of that cost you can still get some interesting points across with cheap calculators. The new mathematics recommendations specify that calculators should be continually made available for all students. This includes homework, class assignments, and tests. The following activities are just some suggestions for how to use calculators and computers in your class.

Activity 1. Use the Calculator to Improve
Addition and Subtraction Estimation Skills

Select two teams of students. Provide a calculator for each student. As play begins, one member from the first team says a three-digit number. A player from team two says another three-digit number. Both players silently write an estimate of the sum of the two numbers. Players are given a five-second time limit to make estimates. Then both players use the calculator to determine the sum. The player whose estimate is closest to the actual sum scores a point for the team. In case of a tie, both teams earn a point. The next player on each team assumes the same role.

The rules for subtraction are similar. One player from each team names a three-digit number. Both players then write down their estimates of the difference between the two numbers. Again, the player whose estimate is closest to the actual difference earns a point for the team. Students who engage in this activity for a while develop estimation strategies that benefit them in and out of the classroom.

Activity 2. Explore Calculator Patterns

You need a calculator. Choose a number from 2 to 12. Press the + key. Press the = key. (You should see the number you first entered.) Keep pressing the = key. Each time you press, list the number displayed. Continue until there are at least twelve numbers on your list. Write down the patterns you notice.

Activity 3. Use Calculator Multiplication Puzzlers

You need a calculator. For each problem, find the missing number by using the calculator and the problem-solving strategy of guessing and checking. Don't solve the problems by dividing; instead, see how many guesses each takes you. Record all of your guesses. For example 4 × __ = 87. You might start with 23 and then adjust. Below is a possible solution that shows you how to record:

$$4 \times 23 = 92$$
$$4 \times 22 = 88$$
$$4 \times 21 = 84$$
$$4 \times 21.5 = 86$$
$$4 \times 21.6 = 86.4$$
$$4 \times 21.7 = 86.8$$
$$4 \times 21.8 = 87.2$$
$$4 \times 21.74 = 86.96$$
$$4 \times 21.75 = 87$$

Activity 4. Solve Problems with the Calculator

How many seconds old are you? Students may need to become familiar with the directions—how many seconds in a minute, a day, a month, a year? It's good to define the parameters. How old will you be at noon today? Encourage students to take a guess. Have them write it down. Then they can use a calculator to find out. The problem requires several phases to find its solution:

1. Decide what information is needed and where to collect it.
2. Choose the numerical information to use.
3. Do the necessary calculations.
4. Use judgment to interpret the results and make decisions about a possible solution.

Activity 5. Count with a Calculator

The calculator can be used as a powerful counting tool. Important concepts of sequencing, placing value, and indicating one to one correspondence are learned through a child's physical interaction with this almost magical counting device.

To make a calculator count: enter the number 1 and press the + sign. Press the + sign again. Next press the = sign. Continue to press =. The calculator will begin counting. Each time the = sign is pressed, the next number in sequence appears on the screen. If this set of instructions doesn't work with your calculator, check its directions. The directions should indicate how to get a constant function. Follow the directions on how to get a constant and any of the counting activities will work for you.

Activity 6. Count Backward with a Calculator

A calculator can also be programmed to count backward. Start with the number 1. Next push the − sign. Push the − sign again, and then, the number you want to count backwards from appears. For example, if you wanted to count backwards from 100, enter 1 − − 100 = = = . When you press =, the calculator should show 99. Continue to press =. With each press of the = button, the next number in reverse sequence appears. This is a great way to introduce children to counting backward.

Activity 7. Skip Counting with a Calculator

A calculator can skip count also. Encourage students to count by 100's and 1000's. Or try skip counting by 3's, 5's, 7's, 9's, or whatever. You can begin counting with any number and skip count by any number. Have students try these calculator counting exercises, then make up their own. Encourage speculation about what the next number will be. Can you find a pattern?

5 + + 10 = = = =
3 + + 5 = = =

1000 − 100 = = =

Try having a counting race. How long does it take counting by 1's to count to 1000. How long would it take counting by 100's to count to 1,000,000?

CHANGING MEDIA SYMBOL SYSTEMS

Print and the video screen (or film) take different approaches to communicating meaning. Print relies on the reader's ability to interpret abstract symbols. The video screen is more direct. In both cases, thinking and learning are based on internal symbolic representations and the mental interpretation of those symbols. The impact of either medium can be amplified by the other.

Because electronic symbol systems play such a central role in modern communication, they cannot be ignored. It is important that students begin to develop the skills necessary for interpreting and processing all kinds of video screen messages. Symbolically different presentations of media vary as to the mental skills of processing they require. Each individual learns to use a media's symbolic forms for purposes of internal representation. To even begin to read, a child needs to understand thought–symbol relationships. To move beneath the surface of video imagery requires some of the same understandings. It takes skill to break free from an effortless wash of images and electronically induced visual quicksand.

Unlike direct experience, print or visual representation is always coded within a symbol system. Learning to understand that system cultivates the mental skills necessary for gathering and assimilating internal representations. Whether twenty-five plus hours a week at home (TV) or five hours a week at school (computers), the video screen is changing the texture of learning.

Each communications medium makes use of its own distinctive technology for gathering, encoding, sorting, and conveying its contents associated with different situations. The technological mode of a medium affects the interaction with its users—just as the method for transmitting content affects the knowledge acquired. Learning seems to be affected more by what is delivered than by the delivery system itself. In other words, the quality of the programming and the level of interactivity are the keys. But different media are more than alternative routes to the same end. Studies suggest that specific media attributes call on different sets of mental skills and by doing so, cater to different learning styles (Berge & Clark, 2005).

Processing must always take place and this process always requires skill. The closer the match between the way information is presented and the way it can be mentally represented, the easier it is to learn. Better communication means easier processing and more transfer. Early on, research suggested that voluntary attention and the formation of ideas can be facilitated by electronic media—with concepts becoming part of the child's repertoire. Now, new educational choices are being laid open by electronic technologies. Many schools already offer courses on the Internet and a few of them grant undergraduate and graduate degrees to cyberstudents. Skeptical educators aren't worried because they don't think cyberschools will ever catch on. Over the years, they point out, one new technology after another has made bold predictions of educational reform and has inevitably floundered. As Larry Cuban, a professor of education at Stanford University, argues, "The virtual university concept has echoes of instructional television. Both ideas came out of the impulse to somehow increase the productivity and reduce the cost of traditional education" (Lohr, 2003).

Understanding and employing these technological forces require a critical perspective that interprets new literacies from a unique and critical perspective. We would do well to remember that while certain educational principles remained constant, each step along the way—from speech to handwritten manuscripts to print—required major changes in teaching and learning.

UNDERSTANDING AND CREATING ELECTRONIC MESSAGES

Understanding the conventions of visual electronic media can help cultivate mental "tools of thought." In any medium, this allows the viewer new ways of handling and exploring the world. The ability to interpret the action and messages on a video display terminal requires going beyond the surface to understanding the deep structure of the medium. Understanding the practical and philosophical nuances of a medium moves its consumers in the direction of mastery.

Seeing an image does not automatically ensure learning from it. The levels of knowledge and skill that children bring with them to the viewing situation determine the areas of knowledge and skill development acquired. Just as with reading print, decoding visual stimuli and learning from visual images require practice. Students can be guided in decoding and looking critically at what they view. One technique is to have students "read" the image on various levels. Students identify individual elements, classify them into various categories, and then relate the whole to their own experiences. They can then draw inferences and create new conceptualizations from what they have learned. Many students can now videotape their own scenes with a camcorder, edit their work, and use the family DVD player or VCR for playback. These new "video pencils" can transform the landscape of student visual creations. They can also have a major impact on our society as once "invisible" events get put on the air.

Planning, visualizing, and developing a production allows students to critically sort out and use electronic media to relay meaning. Young multimedia or video producers should be encouraged to open their eyes to the world and visually experience what's out there. As students learn to create in a medium, they learn to redefine space and time. They also learn to use media attributes such as structure, sound, lighting, color, pacing, and imaging. Lightweight camcorders have made video photography much easier and various computer programs have done the same thing for multimedia production. By "writing" and "editing" in a digital medium, students can gain a powerful framework for evaluating, controlling, and creating in electronic media.

HOW TO CHOOSE COMPUTER SOFTWARE

Most teachers subscribe to a number of professional journals and just about every school staffroom has dozens. The journals are simple enough to give to upper grade students so that they can help with the selection. Many contain software reviews that can keep you up-to-date. Both paper and online educational technology magazines often publish an annotated list of what their critics take to be the best new programs of the year. Even some of the old reliables have been improved and put on CD-ROM or made available on the Internet. Also, district supervisors of science and mathematics often have a list of what they think will work at your grade level. Of course, you can get your class directly involved in the software evaluation process. This helps your students reach the goal of understanding the educational purpose of the activity. We like to start our workshops by having teachers work in pairs to review a few good programs that most school districts actually have. As you and your students go about choosing programs for the classroom, the following checklist may prove useful.

Software Checklist:

1. Can the software be used easily by two students working together? (Graphic and spoken instructions help.)
2. What is the program trying to teach and how does it fit into the curriculum?
3. Does the software encourage students to experiment and think creatively about what they are doing?
4. Is the program lively and interesting?
5. Does it allow students to collaborate, explore, and laugh?
6. Is the software technically sophisticated enough to built on multisensory ways of learning?

7. Is there any way to assess student performance?
8. What activities, materials, or manipulatives would extend the skills taught by this program?

The bottom line is, do you and your students like it? We suggest that teachers reserve their final judgment until they observe students using the program. Don't expect perfection. But if it doesn't build on the unique capacities of the computer, then, you may just have an expensive electronic workbook that will not be of much use to anybody. With today's interactive multimedia programs, there every reason to expect science and math programs that can invite students to interact with creatures and phenomena from the biological and physical universe. Students can move from the past to the future and actively inquire about everything from experiments with dangerous substances to simulated interaction with long dead scientists. Just don't leave out experiments with real chemicals and experiences with live human beings.

Good educational software often tracks individual progress over time and gives special attention to problem areas. Most of what you find on the Internet doesn't do that. Free Internet offerings have cut into the sale of educational software and diminished the quality. Another change is a tendency to move away from the computer platform and put educational programming on all kinds of gadgets. Even Children's Software Review has changed its name to Children's Technology Review. One of its links, littleflicker.com, is a good site for finding educational games all over the Internet.

UNDERSTANDING THE SYMBOL SYSTEMS OF THE FUTURE

Since the field of education seems to be entering a unique period of introspection, self-doubt, and great expectations, theoretical guidelines are needed as much as specific methods. To give teachers the freedom to reach educational goals means knowing what those goals are. It is dangerous to function in a vacuum because rituals can spring up that are worse than those drained away. As electronic learning devices flood our schools and homes, we need to be sure that findings are linked to practice. A close connection between these two domains requires defining educational needs in a more theoretical and practical way. If the two are not integrated, then one will get in the way of the other.

A wide range of intellectual tools can help students understand social and physical realities. Technology can be an ally in the learning process or it can be an instrument to subvert human integrity. To avoid the latter, adults and children need to have control over the technology they are using. The research suggests that for students to write well, they need to read good literature, know how to search out information, write for an actual reader, tap into their personal experiences, and cooperatively edit their material. Learning about electronic communications technology can follow a similar pattern.

Reaching students requires opening students' eyes to things they might not have thought of on their own. This means tapping into real experience, fantasies, and personal visions, with technological tools serving as capable collaborators. The combination of thoughtful strategies and the enabling features of video tools can achieve more lasting cognitive change and improved performance. With this minds-eye approach, previously obscure concepts can become comprehensible, with greater depth, at an earlier age.

Printed, written, and hand-drawn pictures (the oldest technological media) have been the cognitive tools that western culture has traditionally chosen to teach children. Good theoretical and practical techniques developed for understanding how a traditional communications medium interacts with human learning will be helpful in understanding the new media—even after we have gone beyond the current technological horizons in education. As print, computers, and video merge, children and young adults can develop explicit metacognitive strategies as they search for data, solve problems, and graphically simulate their way through multiple levels of abstraction.

THE INTERNET AND ACCESS TO THE WORLD OF IDEAS

Internet users often make the analogy of exploring the World Wide Web. The Web is a large vaguely mapped territory with unusually beautiful scenery, unfamiliar languages and customs, and treacherous and technological jungles. For computer explorers, the Web is the most exciting communications medium since people a generation ago listened to explorers of the North Pole on their crystal radios. The Web and other equipment such as portable computers, digital cameras, and satellite telephones enable us to participate in rich adventures as they happen on land, sea, air, and space. For example, one fifth grade class that we recently visited was using Google Earth; it's free software connecting satellite and aerial images with mapping capabilities. So students were getting high-resolution flyover (real time) images of everything from the Taj Mahal to troops massing in Iraq.

Things have certainly changed since the early 1990s when Mosaic unlocked the Web for ordinary users. Not only that, but search engines have been vastly improved since Netscape Navigator became one of the more popular '90s browser tools for making the Internet even more accessible. Now, we use our favorite, Firefox—and sometimes, Microsoft's Internet Explorer and Apple Computer's Safari. Downloading the latest version is a good way to get what you want for free. As Web browsers are finding their way into applications programs, the necessary software for connecting to the Internet are coming already installed in many computers. The basic idea is to get away from the more cumbersome "folder and file" system. Microsoft has woven the Internet's World Wide Web into its current Windows PC operating system. Apple Computer is doing the same thing with Safari for its Macintosh computers. In both cases, the idea is to make it easier for everybody by arranging for the computer to get the job done when it comes out of the box.

Students can retrieve images and text from information sources arranged as World Wide Web pages by clicking the mouse on highlighted words or phrases. We are now at a stage where even novices can find their way around the global Internet network—downloading images, messages, audio, and video with the click of a mouse. The Internet has become an example of how a virtual community can connect telecommunicators around the world. Educators are increasingly looking to the cyberspace reached by these data highways as they strive to make their classrooms more interactive, collaborative, and student centered.

As we put together the technological components that provide access to a truly individualized set of active learning experiences, it is important to develop a modern philosophy of teaching, learning, and social equity. While new educational communications technologies have the potential to make society more equal, they could also have the opposite effect if access is limited to those with the money for equipment. As we enter a world of computers, camcorders, interactive TV, satellite technology, and databases, the schools are usually behind the curve and find themselves trying to catch up with the more technologically sophisticated.

Electronically connecting the human mind to global information resources will result in a shift in human consciousness similar to the change that occurred when a society moved from an oral to a written culture. The challenge is to make sure that this information is available for all in a twenty-first-century version of the public library. Recently, technologically advanced libraries have sprung up in large cities like New York. Libraries that can't afford to provide free access to the Internet now charge a fee. The technology could give us the ability to impact the tone and priorities of gathering information and learning in a democratic society. Of course, every technology has the potential for both freedom and domination. Who can argue with easy access to vast troves of information? With the Internet, for example, opportunities could be lost in a land rush generated by corporations. Like other technological advances, this one can mirror back to us all sides of the human condition.

There is no doubt about the fact that the world is reengineering itself with many technological processes. The convergence of communication technologies may be one of the codes to transforming the learning process and making people more creative, resourceful, and innovative in the things they do. While learning to use what's available today, we need to start building a social and educational infrastructure that can travel the knowledge highways of the future. Experts may disagree about the ultimate consequences of innovation in electronic learning. But the development of basic skills, habits of the mind, wisdom, and traits of character will be increasingly affected—one way or another—by the technology.

CONNECTING THE CLASSROOM TO THE INTERNET WILL NOT GUARANTEE GOOD EDUCATION

One of the enduring difficulties about technology and education is that a lot of people think about the technology first and education later, if at all.

—Wiske

There is general agreement that we need a "reimagining" of public education. As Americans try to fix their schools, they find many conflicting proposals and movement in many directions. One of the more popular directions suggests linking all of the public schools to the Internet. The majority are already connected. What really matters is what students and teachers actually do with these connections. The most important thing is to ask: where are we going and what are we trying to accomplish?

Will learning online become an enormous boon or an enormous bane for education? Caught between promise and misplaced technological enthusiasm, it depends on where you are coming from. Those who propose connecting to the Internet suggest that it will give students access to an incredible array of learning tools. Opponents say that the new technology promotes trivial pursuits rather than disciplined learning. Skeptics argue that the Internet will distract children from learning—while fans counter with pointing out how it can expand and enrich the way many subjects are taught. Both groups agree that students should learn to use their minds well, communicate effectively, and grow as social beings.

NEW MEDIA REALITIES CREATED BY NETWORKING TECHNOLOGIES

There are studies that point to some potential benefits when students and teachers use new computer-based technology and information networks. For example:

- Computer-based simulations and laboratories can be downloaded and help support national standards (especially in subjects like math and science) by involving students in active and inquiry-based learning.
- Networking technology, like the Internet, can help bring schools and homes closer together.
- Technology and telecommunications can help include students with a wide range of disabilities in regular classrooms.
- Distance learning, through networks like the Internet, can extend the learning community beyond the classroom walls.
- The Internet may help teachers continue to learn—while sharing problems/solutions with colleagues around the world.

Since the "Net" is rarely censored, it is important to supervise student work or use a program that blocks adult concerns. We suggest that teachers keep an eye on what students are doing and make sure that the classroom is offline when a substitute teacher is in. A program like NetNanny is another way to prevent children from accessing inappropriate material. Just as with libraries and bookstores, it is important not to restrict the free flow of information and ideas. There can be a children's section without bringing everyone down to the intellectual level of a seven year old.

In today's world, children grow up interacting with electronic media as much as they do interacting with print or people. They are engaged. But does this mean that they are learning anything meaningful or that they are making good use of either educational or leisure time? The Internet, like other electronic media, can distract students from direct interaction with peers—inhibiting important group, literacy, and physical exercise activities. The future may be bumpy, but it doesn't have to be gloomy. Good use of any learning tool depends on the strength and capacity of teachers. The best results occur when it is informed educators who are driving change rather than the technology itself.

Sailing through the crosscurrents of a technological age means harmonizing the present and the future, which means much more than reinventing the schools. It calls for attending to support mechanisms. Successfully sailing through the crosscurrents of our transitional age requires the development of habits of the heart and habits of the intellect. Thinking about the educational process has to precede thinking about the technology.

Rapid changes in information technology are resulting in less and less of a difference among the television screen, the computer screen, and telephone-linked networks. In fact, connecting a cable modem to the cable TV line (if the cable company does its part) results in much faster communication and quick acting full-motion video. When "online" is "on-cable," it becomes even easier to swap email, participate in electronic chat groups, and quickly roam around the Web. This can all be done at lightning speed when compared to the snail's pace of information that flows through modems connected to old copper telephone lines.

Possibilities for intelligent use of the computer-based technologies may be found in earlier media. For example, when television first gained a central place in the American consciousness, the sociologist Leo Bogart wrote that it was a "neutral instrument in human hands. It is and does what people want." The same thing might be said about today's multimedia and telecommunications technologies. The Internet and other computer-controlled educational tools may have great promise. But anyone who thinks that technological approaches will solve the problems of our schools is mistaken.

As we venture out onto the electronic road ahead, we should remember the words of T. S. Eliot: "Time present and time past are both perhaps contained in time future, And time future is contained in time past."

NEW TECHNOLOGIES, THE INTERNET, AND EDUCATIONAL PRIORITIES

The Internet is just one example of how linked multimedia computers can help us weave a new community—or waste a great deal of time. If linking the classroom to the Internet is going to have positive results, we need a clear set of educational priorities before we select the technologies to advance those priorities. In addition, teachers need training to properly harness the technology for instructional purposes. The notion that positive things happen by simply putting the technology in the classrooms and connecting to the Internet is wrong. The technology only helps children learn better if it is part of an overall learning strategy.

It is important to remember that learning works best within the context of human relationships. When it comes to the using educational technology wisely, we would do well to remember that just about everything that happens in the classroom must be filtered through the mind of the teacher. In recognition of this fact, the National Educational Goals project recognizes the need for "the nation's teaching force to have access to continual improvement of their professional skills". As technological potential and hazard intrude on our schools, there is general agreement that teachers need high-tech in-service training to deal with the explosion of electronic possibilities.

As teachers look for ways to engage students with the technology, they must ask themselves, "What is the problem to which this can be applied?" It may sometimes be a Faustian bargain—something important is given and something important taken away. The quality of the technological content, the connection to important subject matter, and a recognition of the characteristics of effective instruction are central factors in determining instructional success. School is, after all, a place where students should come into contact with caring adults and learn to work together in groups.

PROMISE, PITFALLS, AND SOCIAL EFFECTS

The two founding fathers most interested in education, Thomas Jefferson and Benjamin Franklin, both believed in spreading schooling widely among the people. Franklin wanted to train students to enter the world of work. Jefferson believed in teaching students "how to work out their greatest happiness" as citizens.

The purpose of the public schools?

To promote the joy of learning for its own sake,
To promote large inclusive narratives for all students to believe in,
To be preparatory arenas for civic life, or
To enter the economic world with concrete workplace skills.

The tension of these sometimes conflicting purposes is still with us. But whatever combination of views you accept, our educational structures need to connect with changing media realities.

Do technological triumphs signal new possibilities or do they represent a culture in decline? A central fact of the last twenty years is that technological change and globalization have enriched the most powerful while severely hurting the less educated half of the American population. In the *End of Work*, Jeremy Rifkin, writes about the danger of social unrest as we get a growing class of technological "have nots" who are more separated than ever from a core of knowledge workers. As retrenchment in social and educational spending takes place, a technological underclass is growing up that is outside of the bounds of common humanity. Worse yet, our obligation to each other is no longer reflected by our government and other social and educational institutions.

Technological powerlessness can add to cumulative social neglect and exacerbate the aftereffects of social discontent. The process should be enough to send shivers down the national spine. We are not just witnessing sins of omission and commission, but a reminder of how cumulative neglect can harm everything from character to altruism and compassion. Recent surveys have shown that learning online has become yet another socioeducational fault line, with minority and low-income students less likely than students in wealthier school districts to have classroom access to computers and the Internet. What is needed is a new vision or a technologically connected vision of excellence in a vital new curriculum that includes all children.

We have to ask some basic questions about the values inherent in any new technology. What social or educational problems will it solve and how will it create other problems that we might need to prepare for? As we sort out technological myths from promising possibilities, the challenge is to arrange the technology so that it will help children manage both their technological and social lives with intelligence. How can we go about inventing a technologically intensive education that inculcates basic social competencies such as cooperation, self-control, self-awareness, reasoning, and empathy?

Technological innovations are bound to influence how we shape our social connections and how we develop socially responsible behavior. As Richard Sclove points out in his book *Democracy and Technology,* "People are prone to resign themselves to social circumstances established through technological artifice and practices that they might well reject if the same results were proposed through a formal political process." When it comes to the schools, using any technology needs to be part of an overall learning strategy or it will not enlarge educational opportunities or cultivate social responsibilities.

What happens when students spend more and more time in cyberspace? Everyone enters school a little like an exposed photographic negative. Education can develop and focus the possibilities in almost any direction. Social intelligence and traditional academics are all part of the mix. Whether it is Albert Speer's Nazi Germany or Robert McNamara's Viet Nam, being the best and the brightest does not guarantee high moral values or great wisdom. Social intelligence and empathy are also needed. As Oliver Wendell Holmes said about Franklin Roosevelt: "He has a second class intellect and a first class temperament." Developing social intelligence is central to democracy and can contribute to academics while adding to the traditional aspects of intelligence.

Making sure that social responsibility and civic competence are part of a students' daily life in school means we must expand our vision of the curriculum and revisit some of the classical roles assigned to education in the past. For example, networking technology can assist in the process by fostering group communication with students from different schools and backgrounds. Computer-controlled networks can also help draw us together or scatter us into a million electronic communities that isolate us from others. We can gain access to badly needed information or get buried under an avalanche of information so deep that it blurs what is worth remembering. Children are even more vulnerable to what may be destructive or enriching. What does it mean to reintroduce social responsibility into the technologically intensive educational environment of the late twentieth century?

Teachers can contribute to helping students develop social responsibility when they teach many subjects by incorporating social skills like cooperation, group communication, and a sense of living in a learning community. They can also work with students to create ground rules for treating others with caring and respect. The Internet may help by merging public issues with citizenship education and personal development—helping young people recognize the importance of a life that contributes to the public good. Technology can redefine our concept of the social group. Membership in an electronic group may confer the status of "citizen of the world" or make the recipient the final dumping ground for a glut of email. When we get two hundred email messages in a day (at work), we just erase them all (without reading them) and assume that if the message is important, the sender will contact us directly.

If children just consume the educational equivalent of international junk mail, then electronic networking may well become a colossal waste of time. Some teachers see the Internet as a major expansion of textbooks, libraries, and global communications. Others see students spending large chunks of time going after trivial bits of information rather than developing the skills of critical judgment and analysis. Are both right?

What will it take to open a vast array of new learning possibilities for children? Promoting high-technology will not help much if American schools are in a state of disrepair. To begin with, we need to recognize that the educational structures and lessons that our machines fit into are more important than the technology itself. Even the best schools are just beginning to shape teaching materials for the Internet. Teachers are just beginning to learn how to steer students towards well-organized websites. As many are finding out, having a motivating thing to do on the side is fairly easy, but bringing the Internet into the core of the curriculum is much harder.

Today's technological and marketplace changes in communications are sweeping and profound. In many respects, the Internet is becoming part of a new and larger canvas—more personalized two-way street that is altering how we learn, work, play, and live. Technological literacy is viewed by the public as important. They are right. Elements of electronic learning most certainly will be part of our future. And if the schools do not participate in shaping new media, then they are bound to be shaped by it. We just have to learn how to sort out the promise from the pitfalls and not assume that either computers or the Internet will guarantee good schooling.

CONVERGING TECHNOLOGIES AND SHAKING THE BACON

The convergence of broadcast television, cable, computer, telephone, video games, educational software, and publishing offers opportunities to entertain for profit, to inform, and to educate. The explosion of technological advances can enslave our youth with mindless video games (in an attempt to stave off boredom) or empower them to learn and to think in new and interesting ways. Even leisure time should be held to a higher standard than "killing time." It should concern itself with replenishing the spirit—for example: a discussion of ideas, attending a fine arts event, watching good films or theater, listening to music, or hiking. According to the Centers for Disease Control and Prevention (in Atlanta), nearly twice as many students were not active as similar groups were fifteen years ago. They also found correlations among economic class, television watching time, weight gain, and a lack of exercise. The void left when the homework is finished and the chores done is often filled by sitting in front of the television set, playing video games, or surfing the Internet. The result is a lot of obese and unhealthy children. Why not raise expectations and use the communications tools at hand to enhance healthy physical recreation, the enjoyment of the arts, and lifelong learning? Isn't it possible to structure new media systems so that they enable students to become physically active, intellectually curious, and informed citizens?

On the eve of the twenty-first century, there is a race in the communications' industry to merge two-way telecommunications, computers, and television in order to offer new digital entertainment and information services. Satellite dishes the size of a pizza are already competitive with the cable TV industry, and new interactive TV services are being provided by regional telephone companies. The process will redefine the nation's watching and thinking habits. Fiber optics, digital transmission, wireless technology, and a trove of multimedia choices will change not only what Americans experience but how they experience it. A major focus: how to provide more choices and how to make the interactive experience just as new and exciting as when television and computers first came out.

Through the integration of computer and television technologies, the concept of "application" will be replaced with the concept of "channel." This integration will enable the "user" or the "viewer" to store, control, and electronically travel through a vast array of choices. In the future, the system could include an "intelligent assistant" to record programs you might want—without being told.

There is a need for user-friendly electronic program guides to help customers navigate the expanding and confusing market of information and communications software. Writing will continue to be important. A bad example is the typical software manual written by a computer expert. It usually fails to clearly communicate to the uninitiated, because the writer lacks training in boiling down intricate operations into concise and easily understandable steps. Articulate and highly trained writers who have taught inexperienced customers new software programs would be the best candidates for composing such manuals. To help them develop clear technological writing skills, we have had students try their hand at rewriting some of the technological directions they come across—occasionally sending the result to the hardware or software manufacturer.

When it comes to regular classroom math and science writing assignments, computers can be a great aid for helping children learn to write well across the disciplines. At the pre-writing stage, students can gather information and stimulate possibilities; during writing phase, sharing a social context can affect their awareness of how their work communicates with others; and during the revision phase, they can learn to revise and edit their early drafts. When it comes to student video productions, the writing and doing stages are a little like going to the grocery store to get the best ingredients. The editing phase is more like putting everything together and cooking the meal. Whether it's electronic or on paper, motivation can be enhanced by making sure that the students share the result with others. Also, when publication or showing is involved, the final result is bound to be more professional looking.

THE VIDEO GAME AS A NEW FORM OF NARRATIVE

The video game industry is now approaching the movie industry in size and the boundaries between the two are sometimes blurred. Games are made from movies and there are even movies about games. Set designers, directors, actors, and special effects technicians often move back and forth between the two media. For example, the landscape of Myst, a popular CD-ROM video game, weaves images, narrative, and sound to present a surreal kind of interactive science fiction story. The player moves, touches objects, unravels mysteries, and solves puzzles in an alternative universe. Sony, Microsoft, and Nintendo are facing growing competition from new game machines and services that deliver games over the telephone line. Video game makers are entering into agreements with telephone companies, satellite systems, and Internet service providers. By using accessory devices, it is possible for players in different locations to compete against each other.

New categories of computerized exploration and entertainment make use of voices, personalities, and images of familiar characters from TV, the movies, and politics. Many movies, like *The Day After Tomorrow*, miss clear opportunities to make scientific points—or they simply convey bad science to make a dramatic point. *Jurassic Park* is an example of a movie that connects to realistic video games that, among other things, challenge players to collect different types of simulated dinosaur eggs based on clues. Because you can view the game through the eyes of your character, it gives you the impression of three-dimensionality. Coming face-to-face with T. Rex, Triceratops, and even Velociraptors, the player can save the lawyer in *Jurassic Park* or arrange for several other people to be eaten.

"Game" is becoming a misnomer for experiences that can appeal to every type of individual. Video games are rapidly becoming much more than flat screen fun and games for twelve-year-old boys. The latest software is often stored on high-capacity CD-ROM storage media and exploits the latest powerful hardware to give realistic graphics and moving video. Very realistic animation and moving video activities are taken from programs such as *Snow White, Star Trek,* or fighter plane simulations developed for the military. TV or movie actors can see their likenesses go through all kinds of antics that are based on decisions made by the user. A program from Sony and Disney transfers the actual animation cells from the Disney movies (like *Aladdin*) to the screen and creates picture-perfect animation. Home computers equipped with the CD-ROM players, stereo sound, Internet connection, and the latest interactive software are now available to over half of the children and teenagers in America.

In the fast-growing world of massively multiplayer online games, today's students often play out virtual roles that revolve around fantasy or medieval kingdoms and galaxies far, far away. Many of these Internet games require the user to pay a subscription fee before they can move into a virtual economy and cybersociety in a way that can blur the lines between fantasy and reality. If you don't have the patience, time, or skill to reach higher levels of participation, you can outsource it to the Chinese who will trash some of the ogres, gnomes, and trolls for you. In fact, there are more than 100,000 full-time young Chinese gamers working in factories with posters of Magic Land and World of Warcraft hanging on the walls. They get paid to do the dirty work. And you get to play all kinds of roles and plunder make-believe treasures. Need a babysitting service for your virtual kingdom while you are away? Go for a chat on QQ, the popular Chinese messaging service.

Interactive storytelling techniques will allow plot lines to evolve in almost infinite directions. Characters can be programmed to surprise us in ways that have never been programmed or written. Credit card sized devices have been developed that allow players to insert new characters into their favorite games. For example, Philips, the European electronics company, has released an interactive mystery novel-movie called *Voyeur* that lets the user go into any room they choose in a house, collect evidence, call in the police, or even get shot by a full-motion video character if a mistake is made. As an interactive mystery using real actors, it is no more violent than a typical young adult mystery novel. But why not use the same technology to graphically enter into more edifying experiences?

Millions of Americans got their first glimpse of virtual reality technology when Sega of America, the U.S.-based arm of the Japanese video game maker, released its home "VR" equipment for its Genesis video game. By putting on glove controllers and a helmet-like device, players found themselves inside the game. Instead of manipulating images on a flat screen, players can move their bodies around, pivot up, and duck down as they capture or escape villains. Head-mounted displays have separate liquid crystal display screens for each eye to create three-dimensional effects and stereo earphones for high quality sound. When certain gloves are used, wearers can feel their hands grip objects.

Game makers are marketing powerful compact-disk systems and headsets (goggles and stereo headphones) and new virtual reality games. The latest Xbox is a more conventional example of today's possibilities. Game play is a way to create narrative at a time when more established story vehicles like network television, movies, newspapers, and books are in decline. To advance as a serious media form, video games will have to do a better job of storytelling, character development, and intellectual/emotional development in the same way they have enhanced action and images. As far as teaching math and science is concerned, this technology has the potential to become a powerful lever in motivating even the most disinterested student. As video play occupies more and more of our students' imaginative life, one can only hope that this technology will be turned to better storytelling and at least some educational purposes.

Computer-based simulation game technology is a more tested and purposeful relative of video games. From theme park attractions to simulated surgery in virtual operating rooms, this technology has moved through its infancy and into childhood. Some of the applications that have been developed for the military involve what has been called "telepresence," which gives the operator the sensation of putting his or her hands and eyes in a remote location. On a more civilian note, one could just as easily send a geological probe to Jupiter's moon Europa or take a robotic submersible to the bottom of an ocean on earth. Today's simulation technology allows you to control the action, view the surroundings, search for strange creatures, and sometimes even feel what the robot feels. At some point, the multisensory world of virtual reality will advance to the point where it will enable people to see, hear, smell, and touch objects.

THE NEW AND LARGER CANVAS OF TECHNOLOGY

Harmonizing the present and the future means more than reinventing the schools. It means attending to support mechanisms. To successfully sail through the crosscurrents of our transitional age requires the development of habits of the heart and habits of the intellect. In today's world, children grow up interacting with electronic media as much as they do interacting with print or people. Does being engaged by electronic media mean that children are making good use of leisure time or learning anything meaningful? The future may be bumpy, but it doesn't have to be gloomy. Technology does open up some possibilities. Parents, teachers, and programming are the foundations upon which possibilities can be built. In schools, the technology can also play a role in reexamining what to teach and how to teach it. It can also end the isolation of the teacher and the student.

To avoid creating a technological underclass in schools, most states have set up organizations to provide technological support for their public schools. Recognizing that the impact of technology on the schools grows as teachers come to better understand it, some states have provided teachers with a computer and school-related software to use at home. This beats being embarrassed by students who know more about the technology than most adults. At the school district level, administrators are noticing how corporations upgrade their personnel. One of the results is that teachers are being given a series of two-day technology workshops in pleasant surroundings—rather than the usual after school crunch.

To get things right at the classroom level, it is best to have informed educators, rather than the technology itself, drive the school use of educational technology. Whether there is definitive evidence of the educational benefits of multimedia or just how academic computing can improve learning are not the only issues. Since the technology pervades our society, students must be familiar with it. Yes, we know, this argument is a little like saying that since cars are so much a part of our culture, we should give driver's education a central role to play in the curriculum. Still, technology, especially computer technology, is a proven motivator for engaging struggling students in math and science learning (Berge & Clark, 2005).

Just because many underachieving students like certain aspects of electronic learning (computers for example), there is no guarantee that they are learning a great deal. New communication technologies can be used to help students understand imagery, solve problems creatively, and apply these solutions to real-life situations. It takes some effort, but the engaging can be made more meaningful. When interactive information technology is properly integrated with the science and mathematics curricula, it engages the students' imaginations, helps them understand concepts, and opens doors to a knowledge-intensive society.

BLURRING THE EDGES OF REALITY

As technology progresses, the difference between the real and the unreal can become blurred. For example, online children can, for example, play games where they make ninety-degree turns on a motorcycle at two hundred miles an hour, defying the laws of physics. The make-believe physics of *Star Trek* and other science fiction movies allows "starships" to exceed the speed of light (which seems to be the natural speed limit in the universe). Although some past scientific theories have been proven wrong, if you really count on making it to warp speed, then you are going to be very disappointed.

Unlike science fiction and philosophy, or religious beliefs, mathematics and science rely on testability and consensus. The scientific method leaves little room for the supernatural. Some theories get changed and others are discarded, but math and science have proven to be useful tools in predicting natural events and gaining some measure of control over what is going on around us. In film and literature, you can have fun with mythical alternative universes and other creative falsehoods that are not verifiable. Are creatures from outer space coming by to check us out? These extraterrestrial visits are not taken seriously by scientists for the simple reason that there is no evidence of them. While there may be a probability of something intelligent way out there, years of searching have turned up no proof of it.

To develop intelligent life, a stellar system needs many things, including a great deal of time in a supportive environment. Concentrations of heavy elements (like carbon and oxygen) and liquid water are just two examples of things that become available only long after a galaxy gets going. And just because you get a little simple one-cell life going doesn't mean that you are going to get much else. One thing is for sure, the distances are so vast that it's almost impossible for creatures to get here from there. Whether life in the universe is special or ubiquitous is a dramatic question for inquiry that will draw many students into the study of mathematics and science.

If we find that life started in at least two places in this solar system, then, it probably happened in others. How often life gets transformed to higher life forms is the logical next question. Mars might serve as an example. Signs of primitive life have been detected in a meteorite. But in spite of spacecraft from this planet visiting the place, there is no evidence that higher life forms ever existed there. Mars landers have analyzed the Martian soil for evidence of bacteria or other living creatures and found not a trace. More recent visits have looked for fossils to see if biology arose at about the same time, independently, on both Mars and Earth. The results have not been conclusive.

The evolution of the human race shows how much the element of chance and time influence the development of intelligent life. When science applies its technological tools to the fossil record, we find that it took billions of years to get from simple organisms to us. Even complicated life forms do not insure the development of what we think of as higher intelligence. The dinosaurs, for example, were around for 150 million years and didn't even come close. In fact, the *New York Times* reported that only about half of the American population knows that humans did not live at the same time as dinosaurs (Kristof, 2005). About the same time, it was reported that only one in five Americans have ever taken a physics course. The nation may lead the world in scientific research, but three out of four Americans haven't heard that the universe is expanding (Holt, 2005).

In spite of all the Nobel prizes, Americans on the whole do not seem to care much for math and science. Some subjects do, however, seem to generate interest. We now know that there are plenty of other stars out there with planets circling around them. So there is a fair probability of something smart someplace. But given the many thousands of years (at best) that it really takes to get to where the little green guys might live, it seems unlikely that anyone is going to go around tormenting aliens. Still, tall tales and fictional stories that speculate about alternative universes can be interesting. Just don't confuse them with objective reality. For example, our students had great fun speculating about advanced life in the water under the ice crust of Jupiter's moon Europa. We took a few known facts and developed some great science fiction. In this part of the universe, water seems to be a prerequisite for life. On Earth, the ocean doesn't go more then seven miles deep, even in a few midocean trenches. But Europa is completely covered with water, some of it sixty miles deep. The problem is that the surface is an icy wasteland with a few slushy cracks that suggest that there might be liquid water underneath. The biological attraction of this Jovian satellite is that scientists suspect that it has a hot core and the possibility of inner waters. Although it is far from certain, some love to speculate about alien life forms evolving for billions of years under the crust. To find out, we need to go back and do some drilling. Spacecraft have gotten close and mapped the surface, but it will take a geological probe to figure out what is under the ice sheets. In the meantime, let's have some fun with it. Tall tales, based on thin evidence, have often made for good stories. It is when we see myths, metaphors, allegories, and flights of fancy as scientific truth that bad things happen.

There are many unexplored possibilities. And there are just as many over-the-edge experiments waiting to shatter models of reality. But when it comes to dealing with mathematics and science, certain rules apply. There are various levels of confidence. But this does not mean that fallacies have to be tolerated. One of the most misunderstood properties of modern science is the notion that nothing can be proved as absolutely true or false. Now that's false. If a theory makes predictions about the universe that consistently fail the test of experiment, then it is, as far as math and science are concerned, always wrong, period.

An element of skepticism is a natural part of the scientific process. Sometimes this flies in the face of public opinion. Just because there are many people who believe in something doesn't make it so. Although the ancient Greeks had used mathematics (primarily geometry) to calculate the circumference of the Earth, by the Middle Ages much of this knowledge had been lost and most people believed that the Earth was flat. They were wrong—the Earth was proven to be fairly round when the technology came along that allowed people to travel around it.

THE FINE LINE BETWEEN FUN, FOOLISHNESS, AND INSIGHT

In a recent edition of the *New York Times*, Nicholas Kristof wrote: "At a time when only 40 percent of Americans believe in evolution, and just 13 percent know what a molecule is, we're an argument at best for 'mediocre design.'" He also pointed out that one-fifth of Americans still believe that the Sun goes around the Earth rather than the other way around. These examples illustrate a profound illiteracy about math and science in a century where some of the most important choices that will be facing us require knowledge of these subjects. The good news is that the Flat Earth Society had attracted few converts.

Nonsense masquerading as scientific truth is amplified by our media-wired world. Whether it is the result of honest ignorance, religious fundamentalism, personal greed, or corporate moneymaking, the impact of pseudoscience on our democracy is chilling. Selective opposition to scientific evidence is often more strategic than philosophical. Has your electricity ever gone out? Do you know why? When power is treated as a commodity, money becomes more important than reliability. It costs less to wait until something totally breaks down, rather than replacing equipment that is worn out, yet still working. Massive power grids are good for the power company, but they only have to fail in one place and customers from Canada to Mexico are offline. If citizens knew what was going on, the chances of backup systems being in place would probably be much better—and profits for the provider would be lower. Whether by accident or design, the power companies are but one example of folks who would rather keep the public in the dark (literally and figuratively) than involve them in technological decision making. Avoid an informed discussion—or bore them to death with trivial details—and they will switch channels. Power "brownouts" and the many billions of dollars wasted on unusable atomic power plants are just two examples of an uneducated public leaving it to these "experts."

Being skeptical does not have to get in the way of the search for truth. One of the most important intellectual tools that the scientific method bestows on us is a well-defined procedure for exposing the increasingly blatant nature of scientific falsehoods propagated by the mass media. Technology may be a neutral instrument in human hands, but it is good at blurring images of the physical and biological universe. This is particularly true of the electronic media. American TV news reporters have to present both sides of a controversy, even if one side is utter nonsense. Fooling the gullible is not only easier, it is more likely. Alien creatures crash in New Mexico. Sure . . . our new multimedia systems provide a dramatic and gripping platform. But who provides the content?

In our multimedia age, the technology of computers, iPods, television, telephone, cable, and satellite communications are converging, making a lot of money, and failing to do much for our children. Under pressure from the public at least one of these multimedia giants—the television industry—agreed to three hours of educational programming a week. The loopholes in the Children's Television Act are being closed so that reruns of *Leave It to Beaver, GI Joe,* and *The Jetson's* will no longer be considered educational. Similar steps need to be taken across the whole range of multiple media. The rapid expansion in the number of websites offering video podcasts may indicate how bored some people are with standard commercial TV. A growing number of middle school students are willing to seek alternatives online or even create a site of their own. This is especially true now that TiVo can be used to watch some of these Web videos on home television sets.

We are ushering in a brave new world in which technology can be used for more then promoting foolishness. It can be used for gathering information, mathematical problem solving, scientific inquiry, and testing a wide range of real-world possibilities. When it comes to educational technology, sometimes learning actually does take place. For example, by using the Internet and the World Wide Web for distributed learning, educational institutions, companies, and government agencies can deliver information and training to students worldwide in less time and at lower cost. At school, elementary and middle school students can tap into the rapidly evolving technological environment and use simulations to electronically explore time, space, insights, and falsehoods in every corner of the planet. It would be helpful if they knew the difference.

Early on, users of the Internet viewed advertisements as reprehensible. The typical Internet user of yesteryear was a scientist or educator looking for something true, interesting, and important. Now, nearly everybody has access and the content is like the wild west. Anything goes. Companies are even scrambling to set up what *MacWorld* magazine once called "suck 'em in young and cheap" advertisements. These things are not ads, they're minuses. Since today's children often have a say in purchases, advertisers love to develop the "nag" factor. Ads for junk foods can have a powerful effect on children, family purchases, and the rate of childhood obesity. Younger children are the most vulnerable. If only we could invent a reliable way to block the exploitation. For now, the best thing we can do is encourage teachers who want their students to use the Internet at school to do everything possible to keep an eye on what they are doing—while helping them avoid the worst of what the Internet has to offer.

There are filtering programs for the Internet that do a fair job of blocking certain content. Although there doesn't seem to be a way to block all the ads, filtering software can at least protect students from the cretins and nasty folks out there. Censorship doesn't seem to be the answer. And you don't want to reduce everything in the world to the intellectual level of elementary and middle school students. What we need is a little intellectual depth for those of all ages to choose from.

There is no question but that today's technology plays a role in distracting students (especially those who are at risk academically) from their studies. What could be more powerful than understanding how math, science, and technology can reveal some of the realities we are faced with. In fact, understanding these subjects creates the potential for how reality could, or should be. It goes beyond the schools because we all (including the mass media) have a responsibility to support a culture that supports thought and imagination.

A little programming that makes some intellectual demands on everyone involved would be welcome. Especially now that everything from computers to cell phones can have so many video links the potential is there for moving us from the old lowest common denominator (TV) culture to a first choice electronic culture. As the possibilities develop, what goes on the television screen will come from a visual bookstore of possibilities. Let us hope that it is well stocked with something worth reading and that users know how to take control of their own viewing. Simply opening up the choices doesn't automatically make for high quality programming or intelligent video consumers. Even with more than three hundred channels, there still may be nothing worth watching. What the United States lacks is what nearly every other industrialized country has: a communications policy that tempers market forces in all media with requirements that the technology has to contribute something to informing, nurturing, educating, and protecting children.

DIFFERENTIATION, TECHNOLOGY, AND INTERESTING GROUP WORK

> Education and its technological tools are a regulation of the process of coming to share in the social consciousness.
>
> —John Dewey

Differentiation, collaborative learning, and the Internet are natural partners. To access a good sample of recommended Internet resources try www.filamentality.com and search for "DI Using Technology." But whether you are online or offline, it's important to remember that students come to whatever they are doing or reading with different levels of prior knowledge. To find good activities, we often use WebQuests. These are investigative activities on the Internet that are educator created and peer reviewed. A few free examples: www.webquest.org and www.discoveryschool.com. If you are willing to pay for a subscription, www.webquestdirect.com.au is a good service.

A simple lesson for mixed-ability groups: everyone reads or does the same math, science, or technology problem, activity, or section of text. Each student finds a partner and does some Internet research that they will bring back to the small group. We sometimes have upper grade students explore the medium itself by going online to read reviews of related books. *The Google Story* by David Vise and *The Search* by John Battelle are good examples. (Although the Google Book Search Library Project has made a vast number of books online, they seem to have avoided these two.) "Disruptive technology" is a good topic for student exploration. Disruptive technology, like Google, shakes things up by changing the way that students, adults, and business operate. Advertising and price comparisons change business practices. Information from the outside world is readily available for students. And individuals can "google" their own genes to get information about the world inside.

After discussions in small collaborative groups, projects or work assignments can be brought back to the whole class and each group shares their findings. Sometimes, a group may want to put their findings online or post their book reviews at www.amazon.com. Wikipedia has open editing, so students can put some things there. This online encyclopedia is very timely, but the accuracy is mixed. So we tell students that it's a good starting point, but that it shouldn't be their only source.

As a close associate of problem solving, math and collaborative inquiry in science and technology-based instruction is dramatically changing how students and teachers go about doing their work. New technologies give teachers powerful tools for offering a customized curriculum in a social context. The digital Thinking Readers, for example, are full-text computerized books that provide built-in supports that include individualized learning and reciprocal (student to student) teaching. We like using KWL charts with them. It has three columns labeled: know, want to know, learned. Just before reading, two students work together to put down what they know about a subject. In the second column, they write what they want to know. After they explored a math or science-related passage, they write what they learned in a third column. This builds on prior knowledge and teamwork. It also brings a focus to the work. To communicate the work to everybody, we sometimes have student partnerships put their work on large pieces of paper so that they can be taped up, explained, and seen by everybody in a whole class discussion.

When it comes to struggling students and digital technology, it is important to provide multiple options—like practicing skills, accessing information, and working with peers to engage with math and science materials. It is also important to go well beyond lectures and printed materials because they can fail to reach some students—especially underachieving students. Collaborative groups are another way to help less motivated students by encouraging them to take on different roles, share resources, and help themselves and others learn. Although technology has something to offer, it takes a commitment to critical thinking, social interaction, and at least some hard work to learn math and science.

When students are actively engaged with ideas and other students, the natural power of teamwork accommodates more types of learning than the old chalk-and-teacher-talk model. It has always been true that when interesting questions are raised in learning groups, those involved tend to lead each other forward. Struggling learners may need to take conscious steps to activate prior knowledge. This can be done as a small group reviews what's been covered out loud and on paper. Collaborative learning of this type is effective because the framework of the strategy is good for all students. The research also suggests that somewhat collaborative learning groups result in more cross-cultural friendships and have some positive effect on intergroup relations (Slavin, 1995). With an increasingly diverse student talent pool, learning to advance through the intersection of different points of view is more important than ever.

While aiming high, teachers have to be realistic about what children and young adults can achieve. To help struggling students, teachers need to focus on the math or science concept(s) that they want to teach. The next step is figuring out how different kinds of learners are going to show an understanding of the concepts covered. When it comes to active small group learning, it takes the right mix of students because one child with a serious emotional problem can undo a group—or even the whole class. In general, at the elementary and middle school levels, mixed-ability groups work well. When underachieving students are all placed in the same class, their negative behaviors can feed off each other. The integration of disinterested students with those who are doing well with math and science gives many of them their best chance to flourish. But remember, it's just as bad to say that Jane is bored as to say that Johnny can't do math or science. So, teachers must provide extra enrichment for their high achieving students so that they stay challenged and their parents stay cooperative.

TECHNOLOGICAL PROMISES AND UNDERACHIEVING STUDENTS

Besides altering how we learn, play, live, and work, technology has become a powerful tool for doing mathematics and science. It can even help puncture some of the colorful balloons of mathematical nonsense and pseudoscience. But if our faith in technology simply becomes a powerful ideology, we miss the point. It can be magical, but it is not the main purpose in life or a silver bullet for educational improvement. Technology is an important thing, but not the only thing. If computer-based learning is to be healthy, then, we have to ask some challenging questions about it. A little skepticism will improve the product. Experienced teachers know that educational shortcuts from film-strips to videotapes have promised a lot and delivered little or nothing. Digital technology promises more. But to quote Jane Austen, "when unquestioned vanity goes to work on a weak mind it produces every kind of mischief."

Applications derived from math and science help drive technology, and technology returns the favor. Technology expands as mathematics and science call for more sophisticated instrumentation and techniques to study phenomena that are unobservable by other means due to danger, quantity, speed, size, or distance. As technology provides tools for investigations of the natural world, it expands mathematical and scientific knowledge beyond preset boundaries. It is important to convey some excitement about this expanding knowledge in the classroom. To do a good job of this requires teachers to use all the technological help that they can get to soften subject matter boundaries and engage underachieving students in a study of the physical and biological universe. It works best if you can go beyond one-shot assignments and weave technological possibilities into the fabric of the classroom.

Broad societal problems often get in the way of American students learning math, science, and technology. Even those coming from homes where parents stress achievement have their values undermined when the youth subculture scorns academic achievement (Steinberg, Brown, & Dornbusch, 1996). In an era of globalization, Americans will be increasingly find themselves facing stiff competition from people in other countries. Today's global realities require people who are intellectually curious, cognitively flexible, and able to synthesize knowledge across disciplines.

There is general agreement that the United States has the best universities in the world. But the American public school system leaves many of its students unable to compete. The good news is that many universities are coming to the view that the world of education has to be viewed as a whole if the talent pool is to go on to do great things. As far as math, science, and technology are concerned, there are a growing number of university officials and corporate executives who say that the failure to produce students well prepared in these subjects is undermining the country's production of scientists and engineers and putting the nation's economic future at risk. So, it's not just the teacher education professors—more people than ever seem interested in sharing responsibility for improving the K-12 system.

Changing the attitudes and improving the mediocre performance of American students are either at or near the top of just about everybody's societal "to do" list. Surveys consistently show that despite a general lack technological, mathematical, and scientific literacy, the public is convinced of the overall value of knowing about these subjects. It is also clear that for better or for worse, the technological products of math and science are revolutionizing the daily lives of all Americans. It is just as clear that most of our schools are not preparing either teachers or students to navigate around in a technologically intensive world. The National Science Foundation has gone so far as to suggest that unless more of our best and brightest go into teaching—and in-service teachers receive more support, training, and resources—many struggling students are going to be left "homeless in the universe"(National Science Foundation, 1996).

TEACHERS HOLD THE KEYS TO TOMORROW

To get the educational job done in math, science, and technology, we need teachers who can help students from diverse backgrounds gain the competencies needed for identifying, analyzing, and solving mathematical and scientific problems. With the high-tech explosion of possibilities, it is important to remember that curriculum connections to the world of numbers and the natural world must be filtered through the mind of the teacher. It is also time to make sure that students who struggle with math and science become engaged with these subjects. Clearly, investment in "human ware" beats investment in "software" every time.

In the hands of competent teachers, technology is a powerful lever for adding power to math and science instruction. It can amplify learning and motivate underachieving students (Berge & Clark, 2005). And it can contribute to collaborative learning activities that provide many possibilities for creative engagement. Computers and the Internet give us access to more people and more information. This makes critical thinking and teamwork skills more important than ever.

Like the fields of mathematics and science, technological and social progress is usually incremental. Spectacular new approaches and theories are relatively rare events and will continue to be so. However, you can be sure that to live, learn, and work successfully in an increasingly complex and technological world, everyone must understand and make full use of technological tools. Teachers may wish to communicate with peers, parents, and the larger world community. However, we suggest not accepting instant messages from students and reserving your personal email address for professional activities. Teachers can, however, use the full range of available technology to enhance their productivity and improve their professional practice. Lifelong learning and personal change are facts of life in the twenty-first century. When teachers are supported and well prepared, they can walk in the world with such confidence and enthusiasm that they don't have to fear the unhappiness of change.

In the future, educators are bound to find themselves focusing more on how schools can enhance math and science learning for students who come from a variety of families, economic situations, and linguistic environments. In tomorrow's schools, learners will be even more socially, culturally, and educationally diverse than they are today. A key motivator is bound to be using a variety of instructional models that draw upon technology, group collaboration, and the learning dispositions of students. As far as math and science are concerned, one of the goals will continue to be generating more enthusiasm for learning, problem solving, and collaborative inquiry.

When it comes to using technology to help students who struggle with math and science, the key is the content of technology-assisted lessons and how both are connected to what is going on in the classroom. There is little question that technological tools can be powerful levers in the hands of thoughtful and informed teachers. For teachers to lead students into a future that is useful requires orchestrating learning conditions in a way that brings out the best in everybody. It is teachers, after all, who must make appropriate choices about technology systems, resources, and services. And it is teachers who must implement a variety of instructional and grouping strategies in a way that meets the diverse needs of learners.

> The future is not some place we are going to, but one we are creating. The paths to it are not found but made, and the activity of making them changes both the maker and the destination.
>
> —John Schaar

QUESTIONS FOR TEACHERS AND PROSPECTIVE TEACHERS

1. How might technology help teachers differentiate instruction?
2. Why is it important to help students understand media symbol systems?
3. What are some of the pluses and minuses associated with technology?
4. How do the math and the science standards relate to technology?

REFERENCES AND RESOURCES

Battelle, J. (2005). *The search: How google and its rivals rewrote the rules of business and transformed our culture.* New York, NY: Portfolio (Penguin Group).

Berge, Z. & Clark, T. (eds.) (2005). *Virtual schools: Planning for success.* New York, NY: Teachers College Press.

Bianculli, D. (1992). *Taking television seriously.* New York, NY: Continuum.

Birkerts, S. (1995). *The Gutenburg elegies: The fate of reading in an electronic age.* New York, NY: Faber and Faber.

Brooks-Young, S. (2002). *Making technology standards work for you: A guide for school administrators.* Eugene, OR: International Society for Technology in Education.

Buckingham, D. (2003). *Media education: Literacy, learning, and contemporary culture.* Cambridge, UK: Polity Press.

Bull, G. & Bell, L. (eds.) (2005). *Teaching with digital images: Acquire, analyze, create, communicate.* Eugene, OR: International Society for Technology in Education.

Burke, J. (2002). *Tools for thought.* Portsmouth, NH: Heinemann.

Carr-Cellman, A. (2005). *Global perspectives on E-learning.* Thousand Oaks, CA: Sage Publications.

Cole, D. (2006). *Game industry research.* San Diego, CA: DFC Intelligence.

Egan, K. (2005). *An imaginative approach to teaching.* San Francisco, CA: Jossey-Bass.

Eisner, E. (2002). *The arts and the creation of the mind.* New Haven, CT: Yale University Press.

Fabos, B. (2004). *Wrong turn on the information superhighway: Education and the commercialization of the Internet.* New York, NY: Teachers College Press.

Friedman, B. (2004). *Web search savvy: How to find anyone or anything on the Internet.* Mahwah, NJ: Erlbaum.

Gordon, D. (ed.) (2003). *Better teaching and learning in the digital classroom.* Cambridge, MA: Harvard Education Press.

Gregory, G. & Chapman, C. (2002). *Differentiated instructional strategies: one size doesn't fit all.* Thousand Oaks, CA: Corwin Press.

Holt, J. (2005). Madness about a method: How did science become contentious and politicized. *New York Times Magazine,* December 11, 2005.

Kist, W. (2005). *New literacies in action: Teaching and learning in multiple media.* New York, NY: Teachers College Press.

Kress, G. (2003). *Literacy in the new media age.* London, UK: Routledge.

Kristof, N. (2005). *New York Times,* December 6, 2005.

Lohr, L. (2003). *Creating graphics for learning and performance: Lessons in visual literacy.* Upper Saddle River, NJ: Merrill.

McKibben, B. (1992). *The age of missing information.* New York, NY: Random House.

Monaco, J. (2000). *How to read a film: The world of movies, media, and multimedia.* New York, NY: Oxford University Press.

National Research Council. (2000). *National science education standards.* Washington, DC: National Academy Press.

National Science Foundation. (1996). *Homeless in the universe.* Washington, DC: National Science Foundation.

Norton, P. & Wilburg, K. (2003). *Teaching with technology: Designing opportunities to learn.* Belmont, CA: Wadsworth/Thomson Learning.

Slavin, R. (1995). Cooperative learning and intergroup relations. A. Banks & C. Banks (eds.) *Handbook of Research on Multicultural Education.* New York, NY: Macmillan.

Steinberg, L., Brown, B. B., & Dornbusch, S. M. (1996). *Beyond the classroom: Why school reform has failed and what parents need to do.* New York, NY: Simon & Schuster.

Thomas, M. & Bainbridge, W. (2001). *All children can learn: Facts and fallacies.* ERS Spectrum, Winter.

Vise, D. (2005). *The Google Story.* New York, NY: The Bantam Dell Publishing Group (Random House).

Wenglinsky, H. (2005). *Using technology wisely: The keys to success in schools.* New York, NY: Teachers College Press.

Zillman, D. (ed.) (1992). *Media, children, and the family: Social scientific, psychody-namic, and clinical perspectives.* Hillsdale, NJ: Erlbaum.

8

A Project-Based Approach

Projects, Thematic Units, Collaboration, and Struggling Students

> At their best, projects can serve a number of purposes particularly well. They engage students over a significant period of time and spur them to reflect on their work. They also foster cooperativeness and allow each student to make a positive contribution.
>
> —Howard Gardner

A project is an organized investigation of a topic or theme. Whether it's a search, a construction, or a task, projects are usually directed toward a specific purpose. Like thematic units, projects encourage students to discover their strengths and go a long way to modeling the type of work done in the world outside of school (Roberts & Kellough, 2004). Here we will point out how projects and thematic units are often interdisciplinary and structured around big ideas.

This chapter also

- Introduces project-based learning.
- Explores project components and possibilities.
- Connects projects to the themes of mathematics and science.
- Explains how to design a thematic unit or project.
- Presents interesting units and projects.
- Provides examples of helping struggling students with projects.

Project-based work can be done by individuals, learning groups, or the whole class. We prefer pairs of students—or small groups of three or four who can start, conduct, and finish the work together. Along with research into math and science topics, projects provide students with many opportunities to use a blend of basic skills and higher level reasoning. Whether it's topic or theme driven, project-based learning is a good example of an approach that is designed to help teachers meet the needs of everyone in their class. It's nearly as hard to fail at project work as it is to fail at visiting a science museum. As it is in the world outside of school, eighty percent of the job is showing up. Of course, how well you do with the remaining twenty percent determines how far you advance and how long you stay at it.

Teachers have found that projects are a good way to move beyond a system where students spend too much time learning the same thing at the same time. When teachers take a project-based approach, they usually set the organizational structure, provide guidance, and help students relate their project work to life outside of school. Although there is a lot of student decision making, it's a fairly structured approach for amplifying systematic instruction (Ohana, 2004).

Project work is fairly common for students at the elementary and middle school levels. Teachers find it a good way to respond to the individual and social needs of all learners. Kindergarten and lower grade educators know that project work enriches dramatic play, paintings, and drawings by connecting them to life outside school. Projects offer upper elementary and middle school students many chances to do firsthand research in math and science. From third grade up, Internet research, in-depth study, and collaborative sharing are frequent visitors to the differentiated classroom. Since students are a diverse lot, you can't teach them all math and science in the same way. Recognizing and understanding the learning challenges of students who struggle with math and science is an important part of project-based instruction. As they conduct their projects, even the most disinterested learners can be motivated. Along the way, everyone has opportunities to interact with their partner or small group as they learn to apply the skills and knowledge they are acquiring (Bondy & Ross, 2005).

A project is generally informal and may clarify, extend, or apply math and science skills and ideas. Projects often arise during instructional units, but may be initiated by the students' interest in a topic. Most projects involve independent efforts; however, projects are perfect opportunities for collaborative work (Hill, 2004). For example, when integrating math, science, and technology, a middle school teacher selected a science experiment that incorporated mathematics skills. Student groups estimated how far a straw would travel on a string powered by a blown-up balloon when released. The taut string was balanced on both ends and runs through the straw. A balloon was taped to the straw. Students had to predict, measure the distance with a ruler, and compare with other groups.

Project-based learning ties in learning goals with an authentic project. It gives struggling students an opportunity to demonstrate understanding in multiple ways. A project taps into students' motivation and gives them a sense that learning is interesting and valuable. Project-based learning is multidisciplinary. Real issues involve multiple content areas and connect to the math and science standards (Chard, 2000). A project-based learning method is a comprehensive approach for using multiple intelligences where students solve problems, create a product, and add to their knowledge using all eight of the intelligences (Gardner, 1991). As students participate in projects and practice an interdisciplinary assortment of skills from language arts, math, science, social studies, fine arts, and technology, they become part of the excitement and fun of doing real-world math and science.

Collaborative projects (that make use of available technology) are proven ways of helping at-risk learners learn to work in association with others (Akerlof & Kranton, 2002). However, it does take well-prepared teachers to get the job done. Project-based learning can enhance basic subjects and relate classroom activities to students' normal lives. It can also enrich students' social, communication, and academic skills. Some of the abilities associated with this approach are high up on most lists of desired educational outcomes: teamwork skills, resourcefulness, critical thinking, intellectual curiosity, the ability to communicate, and familiarity with technological tools. The teacher's job is to help provide some realistic choices, give suggestions about the time frame, and provide information about the criteria for evaluation.

Project-based learning often involves fieldwork, collaborative inquiry, presentations, and teacher–parent conferences. Good judgment, technology, and meaningful literacy can go hand-in-hand with a project approach. Teachers have also found that working together on projects makes it possible to help individual students deal with math and science difficulties.

CRITERIA FOR TEACHING INQUIRY-BASED PROJECTS TO STRUGGLING LEARNERS

R. Marx, P. Blumfield, and others have developed some criteria to help teachers decide if a project is important and meaningful. We found the following suggestions helpful:

1. Teachers should help students develop an interesting question so that the project has a focus. Interesting questions should be worthwhile and pose real-life problems that struggling students find meaningful and feel ownership of.
2. Reluctant learners should be engaged in planning and designing an investigation. Investigation is the real work of science, which includes

planning and designing the problem task and conducting research to collect and analyze information so that all students can form conclusions based on inferences about the question.

3. Students should be advised in the collecting and creation of data or (artifacts). Artifacts can consist of rock samples, documents from corporations, or multimedia materials obtained from Internet searches.
4. Students should collaborate. When struggling students work together to plan and complete projects they benefit from the collective intelligence of all group members and learn to value the ideas of others.
5. Teachers should involve students with technological tools. Technological tools make investigations more authentic. As students learn to use these tools to measure, gather, and process information. Inquiry becomes more serious.

The spirit of inquiry can be strengthened when mathematics, science, and literacy are embedded in project-based lessons. It is important to broadly define the content that struggling students need to know in order to become informed, confident, and competent (Marx et al., 1997).

Project-based learning connects learning goals to meaningful projects. It gives students an opportunity to demonstrate understanding in multiple ways. By tapping into motivation underachieving students are given a sense that learning is interesting and valuable (Chard, 2000). Project-based learning is multidisciplinary, It involves important issues from multiple content areas (Ohana, 2004). This integrated learning is a comprehensive approach for seeing connections between mathematics and science. As struggling students participate in thematic units and projects, they will practice an interdisciplinary assortment of skills from reading, math, social studies, fine arts, science, and technology. Project-based learning can enhance basic subjects and relate classroom activities to life outside of school. It can also enrich students' social, communication, and academic skills.

PROJECT COMPONENTS AND POSSIBILITIES

Just about everything in a project can be revised and changed as you go along. Teachers have to start somewhere. They could start with a tentative title or wait until the direction is clear. Procedures vary, but some teachers take this approach:

- Give a brief description of the problem or questions to be considered.
- Provide a project listing of the materials and experiences needed for an investigation.
- Present a hypothesis that explains what the group thinks will happen.

- Outline the steps that will be taken to investigate the hypothesis or problem.
- Develop an organized listing of data in graphs or charts.
- Explain the conclusion based on the investigation results.
- Design ways of sharing the results—report, display, or presentation (Chard, 1994).

During the first phase of the project, the students and the teacher work together to make a list of potential problems or questions to investigate. Parents might be informed so that they can talk with their children about the topic, what they have experienced, and suggest other adults for the students to interview. When possible, face-to-face communication is best. But the Internet and email allows students to get insights from people and experts all over the globe. The experiences collected in this initial phase can be represented in drawings, writing, constructions, or dramatizations. Class and small groups discuss experiences and ideas.

In the lower grades, primary sources—like field trips or classroom visitors—may play the key role in the study of a topic. Upper grade students usually do fieldwork, but use secondary sources more. At all grade levels, the teacher's focus is on providing firsthand experiences and helping students use technology to tap into other resources. Five or six adults with experiences with the subject at hand may be invited to the class (at the same time) to be interviewed by small groups. (Oral history lessons and interviews with elders work well.) The teacher, in consultation with the students, decides what experiences will give them new understandings and help meet curriculum goals. The teacher must also accommodate individual interests and help the students anticipate some of the challenges that they might face.

Whether it's a few days, weeks, or longer, when the time seems right for the project to be completed, the teacher can suggest possible ways for the project to be shared. The culminating event for a project should be part of a process where students summarize their work in a way that creatively represents what they have achieved. Sometimes photos, drawings, writing, or other products can be stored in a portfolio for peers in other groups, teachers, and parents to see. At other times, displays can be set up in the classrooms or in the hallways. Songs, dances, paintings, constructions, skits, games, writing, mathematical diagrams, displays, and demonstrations of math and science experiments are all valid culminating possibilities.

Themes of Mathematics and Science

Themes are the big ideas of math and science. Themes are large ideas that integrate the concepts of various disciplines. There are several criteria developed by Martinello and Cook to help teachers decide if a theme is important and meaningful:

1. Is the big idea true over space and time?
2. Does it broaden students' understanding of the world?
3. Is the big idea interdisciplinary and does it connect to other knowledge?
4. Does the theme relate to students' genuine interests?
5. Does it lead to student inquiry?
6. Does the topic include a collection of resources and technology?
7. Does it require planning?
8. Are the investigations designed to be collaborative?

THEMES OF ELEMENTARY AND MIDDLE SCHOOL MATH AND SCIENCE

History may not repeat itself, but it sure does rhyme.

—Mark Twain

One of the goals of the National Council of Teachers of Mathematics and the National Education Science Standards has long been to help students understand the unifying concepts, processes, and themes that reappear over and over again throughout history (NCTM, 2000; National Academy Press, 1996):

1. Systems and Interactions—a collection of things that can have some influence on one another and appear to constitute a unified whole can be thought of as a system. Some examples of systems: the number system, the solar system, weather systems, oxygen system, monetary system, garbage system, telephone system, electric system, sound system, the communication system, the list goes on. Think of everything within some boundary as being a system.
2. Evidence, Models, and Explanations—a model of something is a simplified version that can help others understand it better.
3. Constancy, Change, and Measurement—constancy refers to ways in which systems do not change (a state of equilibrium). Change is important for understanding what will happen, as well as predicting what will happen.
4. Evolution and Equilibrium—the idea of evolution is that the present arises from the forms of the past. All natural things and systems change through time.
5. Energy, Form, and Function—energy is a central concept of the physical sciences that pervades mathematical, biological, and geological sci-

ences because it underlies any system of interactions. In physical terms, it can be defined as the capacity to do work or the ability to make things move; in chemical terms, it provides the basis for reactions between compounds; and in biological terms, it provides living systems with the ability to maintain their systems, to grow, and to reproduce.

6. Reading—reading a broad range of texts, and literature is part of math, science, and language learning. Reading gives students new perspectives on their experiences and allows them to discover how literature can make their lives richer and more meaningful.

7. Writing and reporting—as students ask questions, pose problems, and generate ideas concerning language, math, and science, they accumulate, analyze, and evaluate data from many sources to communicate information and report their discoveries.

8. Researching—as students engage in the research on issues and interests by asking questions, posing problems, and generating ideas concerning math, science, and technology, they accumulate, analyze, and evaluate data from many sources to communicate information.

Teachers are encouraged to incorporate these or alternative thematic strands into their curricula. Themes provide a structure to guide teachers in developing instructional tools. Themes should be used to integrate content throughout all areas of the curriculum. Math, science, and technology are expanding so rapidly that a thematic approach, a way of uniting, connecting or transferring knowledge from one field to the next, is essential. If these connections are successful, then, it is hoped these intellectual habits will carry will carry over and enrich other fields.

Thematic Units and Projects

A thematic unit or project starts with an important concept or realistic problem within the students' environment and expands to include elements from more than one discipline. A unit or project can center around a relatively narrow theme like trains, or a broader theme, such as transportation. For upper grade students, it could be a narrow theme like Jupiter's moon Europa, or a broader theme such as the moons circling planets in our solar system (Sunal et al., 2000). Before you decide on how to build a thematic unit or project, it is important to consider the students' developmental abilities and their ability to work in a group. The key to success is making sure that students are really interested in the topic.

Themes are an effective way to connect the important ideas of mathematics and science to our lives and the lives of others. Moving well beyond a collection of facts and isolated concepts, themes integrate concepts by building on a variety of facts to link the big ideas that cut across disciplines (Meinbach, Fredericks, & Rothlein, 2000). Thematic units or projects are lessons that bring this right into the day-to-day life of the classroom. Good choices will encourage reluctant learners to integrate their new knowledge willingly and effectively into their lives outside the classroom.

With so many possibilities, teachers have to evaluate the appropriateness and potential of a theme or project. Students can help by letting the teacher know what it is that they find exciting. But it is the teacher who has to make sure that the topic isn't too narrow or so broad that it can only be covered superficially. The next step is designing a lesson or thematic unit or project that will reveal common patterns, similarities, and differences among subjects. A well-designed unit or project can also stimulate teamwork as interrelated group activities to draw students deeper into the topic being studied.

WORKING WITH DIFFERENTIATED INSTRUCTION

Differentiated instruction works well in helping students design thematic units and projects. The teacher responds to the learners needs and differentiates math and science content according to the students' interests, their ability levels, and individual learning profiles. The instructor tries to provide engaging activities that will excite even the most reluctant learner. Here are some suggestions for working with disinterested students:

- Use concrete objects such as pictures, sketches, or signs to get across ideas.
- Demonstrate and model the activity while giving simple clear directions.
- Modify activities as much as possible to avoid frustration among students.
- Give positive reinforcements immediately after each small success (Bender, 2002).

Getting Started

As you design team-based thematic units or projects around lessons that cross subject matter boundaries, it is important to have clear instructional purposes in mind. It might be helpful to ask a few basic questions:

- What important ideas do I want students to learn?
- Why are these important?
- What are the skills that I want to develop?
- What learning activities will help develop these skills and concepts?
- Does the classroom climate encourage teamwork?
- How will I assess both the individual and the team?

Teachers who are enthusiastic about a particular theme instill in their students some of these same attitudes. For a thematic unit or project to be fully successful, teachers must identify what it is that they want their students to know when they are finished. In addition, it is important to involve the students in choosing themes and projects. You might start with a topic that the students have read about, explored on the Internet, or watched on television. Whatever the topic, you will find that student motivation, interest, and the forming of ideas are all increased when students work in teams.

Thematic Integrations

Putting exploration, discovery, and connection back into math and science occurs anytime a struggling learner finds new relationships or meanings in a given situation. An in-depth study of almost any subject can lead to important interconnected reading, writing, and math and science ideas: history, art, music, the environment, medicine, sports, artifacts, cars, anything. Students construct their understanding through questioning and active involvement with the learning processes.

As reading, writing, math, and science skills rapidly expand, a thematic unit or project approach serves as a powerful way of uniting or transferring knowledge from one field to the next. If these connections are successful, then, the ideas should carry over and enrich other fields and disciplines. Connecting talking, reading, writing, science, and mathematical thinking will not only help struggling students develop a meaningful structure for understanding math and science but also help them see the relationship to other subjects and their daily lives.

How to Design a Thematic Unit or Project

A thematic unit is more than a collection of lesson plans. It should be viewed as an exciting team project. The basic goals are set ahead of time through a joint teacher/student effort. The steps to a designing a team-based thematic unit or project include the following:

1. Select a theme or project. The theme or project should be challenging and related to real-world concerns. By building on the students' existing knowledge and abilities, an interdisciplinary unit needs to be rich enough to hold students' interest for at least a week.
2. Decide on a desired outcome. Unit or project outcomes need to be decided in advance. These may relate to comprehending concepts, or successfully working together in teams.
3. Map and brainstorm ideas. This stage of idea collection and organization can include using graphic organizers to outline the

major activities for each subject area or brainstorming possible procedures.

4. Make a time line. As the key decision maker, the teacher determines the length of time for each activity and learning experience.
5. List concepts and skills. It is helpful to outline the concepts and skills that will be part of the process. Make a list of the various disciplines that will be employed and the interdisciplinary areas of concern.
6. Collect resources. Organize the materials everybody needs.
7. Assemble learning centers and bulletin boards. These can serve as vehicles for reaching unit and project outcomes.
8. Plan an introductory lesson. The introductory lesson informs students of the unit or project theme and attempts to engage struggling students' interest in the topic under study.
9. Describe other lessons and activities. Most of the lesson and activity ideas are shown in the graphic organizer, but it is helpful to have several detailed plans clearly spelled out for students who have difficulties before beginning.
10. Formulate a cumulative activity. At this point, students should be able to synthesize what they have gained from the various disciplinary tools applied to the problem.
11. Design an assessment plan. Use performance assessment, portfolios, conferences, anecdotes, and exams. At least an informal evaluation is needed to make it better the next time around.
12. Create daily lesson plans. These need to include specific descriptions of lesson objectives, rationale, concepts, materials, and procedures; change as needed (Wood, 2001).

When thematic units and projects are participatory, rich in content, and related to students' interests, they can inspire enthusiasm in both the teacher and the class.

Organization of Thematic Units or Projects

This section contains three units or projects for the elementary and middle school classroom, with special emphasis on team-based learning. Activities focus on everyday examples and problem-solving experiences in an attempt to give struggling students a real-world sense. Units or projects will provide students with the following abilities:

- Students will become active learners and members of learning teams.
- Students will develop critical thinking and problem-solving skills.
- Students will explore questions and concepts in areas of math and science.

The interdisciplinary units and projects presented here are designed to give elementary and middle school students a chance to thoroughly explore a math and science concept. It is hoped students will enjoy the project activities when they are given a chance to engage in math, science, and language discovery. Teamwork is encouraged in the groups chosen by the teacher or selected by the students.

Each activity focuses students' attention on an interesting event or method. Materials and step-by-step directions for the unit and project activity are provided. Occasionally, some information or method is added within the procedures to help clarify the students' experience. An evaluation section is included in most activities. A "background information" section provides needed information or notes to help the teacher. The goal is to provide teachers with background experiences that will aid in building a repertoire of strategies, activities, and skills for teaching math and science content to all students.

Unit or Project 1: The Study of Rocks

Background Information: There are many questions about how life first evolved. One way we can trace the history of the earth is to teach about the processes that explain the origin of rocks and their changes.

Inquiry Process Skills: Hypothesizing, observing, predicting, estimating, measuring, communicating, collecting data

Math and Science Standards: Inquiry, earth science, problem solving, reasoning, communicating.

Themes: Evidence, models, explanations, systems, writing and reporting.

Activity 1. Finding Out about Rocks

Reading and writing skills are emphasized in this introduction to a unit or project on rocks. For this activity, students bring a rock to class. They get to know their rock by describing it to someone else. They touch their rock. They then pass their rock into the teacher. The teacher collects the rocks in a box. Then the teacher tells the students the rocks will be passed back. The students must get in a circle, put their hands behind their back, pass the rocks to the person next to them. They can't look at the rock in their hand. If they think the rock is theirs, they can take a peek. If successful, they take their rock and sit down. This continues until everyone has found their rock. Next, students do guided imagery or the visualization activity. After the visualization students share what happened in their visualization. Students also write a poem about their rock.

Activity 2. Rock Guided Imagery Experience

Guided imagery is much like a story. The teacher guides students through an imaginary journey, encouraging them to create images or mental pictures and ideas. This activity should be done in a quiet, relaxed atmosphere. Teachers may wish to dim the lights or have students rest at their desks while they read the visualization. After reading, have students follow up with some kind of creative activity: discussing their experience in their team, writing in their science log, or creating an artistic expression of some kind. This is a good way to start a thematic unit on rocks. Students write and share ideas about their rock.

Activity 3. Guided Fantasy: A Rock

Close your eyes and imagine that you are walking in a lush green forest along a trail. As you are walking, you notice a rock along the trail. Pick up the rock. Now make yourself very, very tiny, so tiny that you become smaller than the rock. Imagine yourself crawling around on the rock. Use your hands and feet to hold onto the rock as you scale up its surface. Feel the rock. Is it rough or smooth? Can you climb it easily? Put your face down on the rock. What do you feel? Smell the rock. What does it smell like? Look around. What does the rock look like? What colors do you see? Is there anything unusual about your rock? Lie on your back on the rock and look at the sky. How do you feel? Talk to the rock. Ask it how it got there, ask how it feels to be a rock. What kind of problems does it have? Is there anything else you want to ask the rock or talk to the rock about? Take a few minutes to talk to the rock and listen to its answers. When you're done talking, thank the rock for allowing you to climb and rest on it. Then, carefully climb down off the rock. When you reach the ground, gradually make yourself larger until you are yourself again. When you are ready, come back to the classroom, open your eyes, and share your experience (Hassard, 1990).

Instruct students to make a list of as many observations as they can. Then, direct them to write a Japanese poem following these directions:

Line 1—Identify the object.
Line 2—Write an observation of the object.
Line 3—Share your feeling about the object.
Line 4—Write another observation about the object.
Line 5—End with a synonym for the name of the object.

Unit or Project 2: Popcorn Project

Inquiry Process Skills: Hypothesizing, observing, predicting, estimating, measuring, communicating, collecting data.

Math and Science Standards: Inquiry, earth science, problem solving, estimating, reasoning, communicating.

Themes: Evidence, models, explanations, systems, reading, writing, and reporting.

Materials: Butcher paper, air popper, popcorn, rulers.

Background Information:

What makes popcorn pop? Popcorn—a favorite snack of millions, small hard kernels of dried corn that explode into a fluffy tasty treat. What makes that happen? Listen to the noise in the popcorn popper. You will hear the tiny grains of corn popping open. They are turning inside out. The corn looks different now. It is big and fluffy and white.

What puts the "pop" in popcorn? A little bit of water is the magic ingredient that puts the "pop" into popcorn. In order to pop properly, a kernel should contain about 13.5 percent water. When the popcorn is heated to 100 degrees C (212 degrees F) the water changes to steam. Trapped inside the kernel of corn, the steam pushes outward trying to escape as the temperature rises even higher. At about 200 degrees C, there is so much pressure that even the tough kernel can no longer hold the steam inside. The corn explodes with the familiar pop. It puffs up thirty to thirty-five times its original size. If you weigh popcorn before it pops, you will find it weighs more than after it explodes, even though popping increases its size about 300 percent or more. Can you figure out why?

What makes the popcorn pop? Heat is what makes popcorn pop. Fire makes the corn hot. The inside swells up. It gets bigger. Soon the inside is too big for the outside kernel cover. So the corn seed pops open.

Facts about popcorn:
- Long ago, colonists served popped corn with cream for breakfast.
- Columbus saw Native Americans wearing popcorn as jewelry.
- Popped corn 5000 years old was found in a bat cave.
- Popcorn was brought to the first Thanksgiving dinner.

Activity 1. Connecting Math and Science Skills

Put out large pieces of butcher paper and give each group an air popper and some popcorn.

1. Estimate how far kernels will go.
2. Pop (with top off), observe the trajectory of the kernels as they pop, have students draw the arcs of the kernels.
3. Discuss the physics behind this phenomenon.
4. Measure the kernels' distances.
5. Eat.

Heat makes other things get bigger or longer too. Watch telephone wires in summer. On very hot days the wires get longer and sag. Why do you think the wires get shorter in the wintertime? Can you think of other things that change because of hot or cold?

Activity 2. Readers' Theater: Song of the Popcorn

This interdisciplinary activity connects readers' theater (a language arts activity) with math and science. The math and science part: put out large pieces of butcher paper and give each group an air popper and some popcorn.

1. Have children estimate how far kernels will go.
2. Pop (with top off), have children observe the trajectory of the kernels as they pop. You may wish to have students draw the arcs of the kernels.
3. Discuss the physics behind this phenomenon.
4. Measure the kernels' distances.
5. Eat.

Next, it's time for students to become actively involved in a team reading of a children's story. For older students, you may direct them to present this poem and reader's theater to a primary classroom following the directions listed.

Directions for Reader's Theater:

Kneel down. When your turn to read comes, hop up and read your part. When not reading, kneel back down. (You could use chairs—stand when reading, sit when listening.) Groups can write these stories from anything that they are reading or they can use scripts already prepared. Groups practice with their team first and do their reading in front of the whole class. (If you have five children in a team and eight roles, some students get to read two.)

> The Song of the Popcorn (first grade level story)
> Everyone: Pop, pop, pop!
> 1st child: Says the popcorn in the pan!
> Everyone: Pop, pop, pop!
> 2nd child: You may catch me if you can!
> Everyone: Pop, pop, pop!
> 3rd child: Says each kernel hard and yellow!
> Everyone: Pop, pop, pop!
> 4th child: I'm a dancing little fellow!
> Everyone: Pop, pop, pop!
> 5th child: How I scamper through the heat!
> Everyone: Pop, pop, pop!
> 6th child: You will find me good to eat!

Everyone: Pop, pop, pop!
7th child: I can whirl and skip and hop!
Everyone: Pop, pop, pop, pop!
          Pop, pop, pop!

Organizing an interdisciplinary lesson around a theme can excite and motivate all students to actively carry out projects and tasks in their groups (Wineburg & Grossman, 2000). These elementary and middle school students have studied about the Mayan and Aztec Indians. They have had many experiences working on this unit. As a culminating activity, students enjoy the fun of the math, science, and the readers' theater activity mentioned above. They can eat the popcorn when they're done.

Unit or Project Activity 3: Experimenting with Paper Airplanes

Inquiry Process Skills: Predicting, estimating, experimenting (forming hypotheses, identifying variables, collecting data, analyzing, and explaining outcomes).

Math and Science Standards: Inquiry, physical science, problem solving, reasoning, communicating.

Themes: Evidence, models, explanations, systems, energy.

Description: Teachers can turn classroom distractions into a project of design and discovery. In this activity, students will discover that there's more than just folding and tossing paper involved. As they work on perfecting design plans, they will learn to hypothesize, experiment, and draw conclusions. Students will work in small groups to design a paper airplane of any size using any or all of the materials provided. Their challenge: to design a plane that will fly farther and straighter than the planes built by the other groups.

Students should develop understandings of how the learning processes of forming a hypothesis, identifying, and analyzing data are closely related to the math and science curriculum. Problem solving is emphasized. (Adapted from Blackburn & Lammers, 1996)

Materials:
- Six or seven grades of paper: typing, onion skin, computer paper, construction paper, paper towels, cardboard, milk cartons.
- Paper clips in various sizes, staples, tape.
- Directions for designing paper airplanes.

Objectives:
1. Students will design a plan for their airplane.
2. Students will formulate a hypothesis describing their design and their projection of a successful flight pattern.

3. Students will experiment with the materials and modify or alter their design.
4. Students will identify the variables that influenced the outcome of their investigation and record their efforts.
5. Students will carry out the investigation and generate data.
6. Students will communicate their data through written procedures.
7. Students will actively participate in the plane throwing contest.

Procedures:
1. Give each group a copy of the paper airplane directions and at least three sheets of paper.
2. Introduce the class to some factors that can affect the performance of paper airplanes.
   Folding: Symmetry and sharp folds are crucial in designing the plane.
   Adding weight: A paper airplane needs weight at the front tip (nose). In many cases, the folded paper provides the weight, but if the nose isn't heavy enough, the plane will rise up in front, then fall straight down. Paper clips, staples, tape, or additional folds can add weight. If a plane is too heavy, it'll dive to the ground. To give it more lift, cut and fold flaps on the backs of the wings. If the flaps are folded at ninety-degree angles, the plane will fly differently than if they're only slightly turned up.
3. Encourage students to experiment as they adjust the variables. They'll learn a lot about trial and error as well as making and testing hypotheses.
4. Next, groups will test their designs and try out their model experiment. Allow lots of time for practice.
5. Before the contest begins, the class may wish to design posters (stating their purpose and the skills involved) and invite other classes to watch their science and math airplane contest.
6. As a class, conduct the airplane contest. Airplanes will be judged on how far they flew and how long they stay in the air (use a stop watch). If students create designs that loop in flight, students may also want to judge the number of circles. The best place to hold the contest is in the school auditorium (no wind, plenty of space). Allow each group to fly their model two or three times, then take the best score.
7. Groups should present their model explaining their hypotheses and how it was assembled.

Evaluation: Students will have the opportunity to ask questions and share designs and launching tips with their classmates. Students will write their reflections and feelings about the project (frustration, satisfaction) in their notebook or portfolio.

SHARING THE PROJECTS WITH PODCASTS

For upper elementary and middle school students, podcasts are one of the several approaches that we used to encourage the sharing of project findings. Podcasting is the posting of an audio recording on the Internet so that it can be heard on a computer anywhere—or downloaded into a mobile device like an iPod. A podcast can run anywhere from five to fifteen minutes. Potentially, anyone in the world with a computer or mobile listening device can tune in. Students often find it more motivating than doing a paper and turning it in to the teacher for a grade.

Podcasting is following the footsteps of email, blogs, and online classes as a teaching tool. Struggling students or absentees can listen to the teacher's explanation or classroom discussions several times. Teachers can even share teaching ideas with this medium. All you need to get going is a computer with an Internet connection and a microphone that can be bought at Toys "R" Us or RadioShack. These results can even be syndicated over Apple's iTunes music store. (For more information see: *Podcasting: Do it yourself guide* by Todd Cochrane. For an online step-by-step tutorial: www.feedforall.com or podcastingstarterkit.com.)

CONNECTING STRUGGLING STUDENTS WITH INTERESTING UNITS AND PROJECTS

Combining teamwork with thematic units and projects has been shown to be effective with students at the elementary and middle school levels (Roberts & Kellough, 2000). Clearly, learning teams are a good way to approach student immersion in a print and number rich environment. When students talk to each other, they can help others in their group who are having trouble, learn to apply written language, and solve number problems. Of course, there are times when lessons, like sustained silent reading, require silence and working alone. As a teacher, you will sometimes find the process of implementing differentiated instruction challenging and time-consuming; you will also find that it can be deeply rewarding.

Things usually work out for the better when teachers find natural avenues for content integration (Chapman & King, 2005). As students and teachers go about their daily work, they can look for naturally occurring links and the powerful ideas that cut across disciplines. If you like, the focus of instruction can be on communication and meaning, with specific subskills falling into place along the way. It will be up to the teacher to provide the opportunity for students to be socially engaged, active learners who are determined to find the answers to the questions they've raised. The idea is to collaboratively go beyond subject matter boundaries to a new awareness of the underlying themes that hold the content together. Finally, you want to make sure that students are encouraged to see how they can apply what they have been learning.

WAYS TO HELP STRUGGLING STUDENTS
WITH UNITS AND PROJECTS

Some examples of how to help students who are having problems connecting themes to projects or units are listed below:

1. Encourage student partners to spend time thinking about what they want to research before they commit to a project.
2. Have students examine their topic of interest. Why is it important to them? Encourage them to think of a theme that relates to their topic or subject. For example, if the students are interested in a unit or project on movement, have them discuss about moving from one place to another. Think about what moves (people, objects, plants, weather, and so on), make a list of what moves and how things move.
3. Have students select a project and theme.
4. Next, have them come up with a good question to explore and form a hypothesis.
5. Encourage students to do some research on the topic, speak to experts.
6. Have students investigate their questions.
7. The teacher arranges a culminating event to bring the project to a close.
8. In the last phase of the project, students review their work and share their results; perhaps a display is necessary.

As students and teachers go about their daily work, they can look for naturally occurring links and powerful ideas that cut across disciplines. It is up to the teacher to provide the opportunity for every student to be socially engaged as an active learner who is determined to find the answers to the questions raised. The idea is to go beyond subject matter to understand the underlying themes that hold the content together.

Early in the twentieth century Einstein wrote about the thematic unity of math, science, and big ideas: "Beyond observations and theory lay the music of the spheres that reveal a preestablished harmony exhibiting stunning symmetries . . . The laws of nature are waiting to be plucked out of the cosmos by someone with a sympathetic ear." Much the same could be said about students trying to understand math and science—and teachers coming to better understand the characteristics of effective instruction.

PROJECTS, THEMES, AND THE SOCIAL NATURE OF LEARNING

As children grow and mature, they naturally construct knowledge through personal experience and social interaction with others. In the classroom, how the teacher has students work together to achieve a common learning goal is directly related to the academic results. The goal for teachers should be to understand when and how to use a wide range of approaches and goal structures. By focusing on a big idea (theme) for projects, teachers can ensure that students use skills and techniques from multiple disciplines, while respecting each subject's content, processes, and ways of knowing. This kind of team-based learning can be even more meaningful for students who have a knowledge base and age-appropriate competency in math and science.

Students now have to go beyond basic subject matter concepts to understand the underlying themes that hold the content together. This is one of the reasons that in this chapter we suggested some themes for math and science that are likely to help students make connections between subjects. One of the potential benefits of a thematic project-based approach is that it can be highly motivating for students who have difficulties with the content. Since heterogeneous grouping is now the norm for elementary and middle school students, this approach is also a good way to develop teamwork skills and get everybody actively engaged in math and science (Mercer & Mercer, 2004). The goal is to make sure that a diverse group of students can all produce work of a high quality and feel confident and successful.

Professional development, adequate planning, preparation time, and systemwide support all help improve science and math instruction. But the reality is that teachers usually can't make all of these elements come together at just the right time. Still, with or without a lot of support, they can successfully implement collaborative project-based learning (Oehlberg, 2005). Once teachers have some experience with projects and thematic units, they will welcome the possibilities for differentiating instruction. The result is bound to have a positive impact on the academic achievement of struggling students. Better yet, as teachers become more knowledgeable and more enthusiastic about engaging students with teamwork and differentiated themes, they will be able to act on their highest visions as they draw the instructional maps for their classrooms.

SUMMARY AND CONCLUSION

Teachers who enthusiastically adapt and use the topic or theme-based project approach are more likely to motivate reluctant learners to experience the beauty and power of math and science understandings (Mercer & Mercer, 2004). As they interactively explore the big ideas that cut across disciplines, students will have the chance to model positive attitudes toward math and science. The results of interesting small group work is bound to be infectious. Experienced teachers know that interdisciplinary understandings are usually easier to grasp after students have a base of understanding in the subjects being connected. As teachers search for better ways to engage struggling students, they look for naturally occurring links between the powerful ideas and organizing concepts that cut across disciplines. Many current programs build on interdisciplinary themes, so the ideas, examples, and activities included here can be incorporated into a wide range of math and science programs.

The benefits of combining collaborative inquiry with thematic units and projects are undeniable. But there are times when any teacher will find the process of implementing project-based learning with students who are disinterested challenging and time-consuming. It can also be deeply rewarding. This is especially true when teachers find natural avenues for content integration and set up the classroom environment so that students can cooperatively apply what they have been learning. This is not an all or nothing proposition. You may want to start on a small scale and expand your scope as you experience success.

To provide educational opportunities for struggling students requires an understanding of the barriers that get in their way and having the pedagogical knowledge to open up the paths to accomplishment. Whether a project deals with a topic, a theme, or both, there is general agreement that project-based learning is a strong motivator for reluctant learners. It is also seen as an effective way for such students to demonstrate the kinds of understandings that have been achieved in the course of the regular math and science instruction (Krajcik, Czerniak, & Berger 2003). Approaches like thematic units and projects "engender a feeling of deep involvement or flow, substituting intrinsic for extrinsic motivation" (Csikszentmihalyi, 1990). And deep involvement has been shown to be one of the key motivators for reluctant learners (Katz & Chard, 2000).

Unless ways are found to interest all students in math and science, some of them will back off learning and we will back our society into a corner. As teachers help underachieving students build on alternative but equally valid ways of learning math and science they will learn that differentiated instruction works. The teacher not only has to get the students to work together, but has to provide them with a structured situation where they have to use social skills to get the job done. As a consequence, projects can help to build the social aptitude and the academic ability of each student. Also a project-based approach accommodates differences and helps each student learn about math and science to their full capacity (Jackson & Davis, 2000).

Redefining math and science education in the twenty-first century requires nothing less than changing the landscape from which people derive their ideas about the nature of teaching and learning these subjects. The standards, the research, and professional development all help teachers move along the path toward a more instructionally differentiated classroom. So does understanding that curriculum reform doesn't have to be geared to the academically oriented. This doesn't mean neglecting the top students because engaging students in collaborative group projects is good for everybody. Hopefully, a rising tide of quality instruction will raise all boats.

As teachers become more knowledgeable and enthusiastic about promising approaches, they will be more able to act on their highest visions and map the future of math and science instruction in their classrooms.

The visions we offer our children shape the future.

—Carl Sagan

SUGGESTIONS FOR TEACHERS

1. Have students work with a partner to choose a theme and topic to study.
2. Students should follow the steps to create a project:
   Review their current knowledge of the topic.
   Ask questions.
   Discuss ideas for a project.
   Select a topic.
3. Once students have selected a topic have them write an introduction, make a list of materials they will need, relate the standards they will use, and form an hypothesis.
4. Have students write out their project including background information, step-by-step directions for carrying out the project, and questions for discussion.
5. Encourage students to provide an assessment plan to evaluate their project—include extensions and references.

(It would be especially good for teachers new to the process to follow some of the same procedures before trying it out with students.)

REFERENCES AND RESOURCES

Akerlof, G. & Kanton, R. (2002). Identity and schooling: some lessons for the economics of education. *Journal of Economic Literature*, 40 (4), 1167.

Bender, W. (2002). *Differentiated instruction for students with learning disabilities*. 6th ed. Thousand Oaks, CA: Corwin Press.

Blackburn, K. & Lammers, J. (1996). *Kids paper airplane book*. New York, NY: Workman.

Bondy, E. & Ross, D. (2005). *Preparing for inclusive teaching: Meeting the challenges of teacher education reform*. Albany, NY: SUNY Press.

Chapman, C. & King, R. (2005). *Differentiated instructional strategies for writing in the content areas*. 4th ed. Thousand Oaks, CA: Corwin Press.

Chard, S. (1994). *The project approach*. New York, NY: Scholastic Inc.

Chard, S. (2000). *Engaging students' minds: The project approach*. 2nd ed. Norwood, NJ: Ablex Publishing.

Cochrane, T. (2005). *Podcasting: Do it yourself guide*. Indianapolis, IN: Wiley Publishing.

Cook, G. E. (1999). *Interdisciplinary inquiry in teaching and learning*. Upper Saddle River, NJ: Prentice Hall.

Csikszentmihalyi, M. (1990). *Flow*. New York, NY: Basic Books.

Gardner, H. (1991). *Frames of mind: The theory of multiple intelligences*. New York, NY: Basic Books.

Hassard, J. (1990). *Science experiences: Cooperative learning and the teaching of science*. Menlo Park, CA: Addison Wesley.

Hill, D. (2004). Research, reflection, practice: The mathematics pathway for all children. *Teaching Children Mathematics, 11*(4), 127–133.

Jackson, A. & Davis, G. (2000). *Turning points 2000: Educating adolescents in the 21st century*. New York, NY: Teachers' College Press.

Katz, L. & Chard, S. (2000). *Engaging students' minds: The project approach*. 2nd ed. Norwood, NJ: Ablex Publishing.

Krajcik, J., Czerniak, C., & Berger, C. (2003). 2nd ed. *Teaching science in elementary and middle school classrooms: A project approach*. Boston, MA: McGraw-Hill.

Martinello, M. & Cook, G. (1994). *Interdisciplinary inquiry in teaching and learning*. New York, NY: Macmillan.

Marx, R., Blumenfield, P., Krajcik, J., & Soloway, E. (1997). Enacting project-based science. *Elementary Science Journal, 97*(4), 341–358.

Meinbach, A., Fredericks, A., & Rothlein, L. (2000). *The complete guide to thematic units: Creating the integrated curriculum*. Norwood, MA: Christopher-Gordon.

Mercer, C. & Mercer, A. (2004). *Teaching students with learning problems*. 7th ed. Upper Saddle River, NJ: Prentice Hall.

National Academy Press. (1996). *National science education standards*. Washington, DC: National Academy Press.

National Council of Teachers of Mathematics (NCTM). (2000). *Principles and standards for school mathematics*. Reston, VA: NCTM.

Ohana, C. Editor's Note. *Science and Children, 41*(7), 6.

Oehlberg, B. (2005). *Reaching and teaching stressed and anxious learners in grades 4–8*. Thousand Oaks, CA: Corwin Press.

Roberts, P. & Kellough, R. (2004). *A guide for developing interdisciplinary thematic units*. 2nd ed. Upper Saddle River, NJ: Merrill/Prentice Hall.

Sagan, C. (1994). *Pale blue dot*. New York, NY: Random House.

Singleton, A., Tucker, B., & Weaver, T. (2005). *Teaching math to all children*. 2nd ed. Upper Saddle River, NJ: Prentice Hall.

Stachel, J. (1999). Einstein's miraculous year: Five papers that changed the face of physics. *American Journal of Physics, 67*(5), May.

Sunal, C. S., Powell, D., Rovegno, I., & Smith, C. (2000). *Integrating academic units in the elementary school curriculum.* Fort Worth, TX: Harcourt Brace College Publishers.

Wineberg, S. & Grossman, P. (2000). *Interdisciplinary curriculum: Challenges to implementation.* New York, NY: Teachers College Press, Columbia University.

Wood, K. E. (2001). *Interdisciplinary instruction: A practical guide for elementary and middle school teachers.* Upper Saddle River, NJ: Prentice Hall.